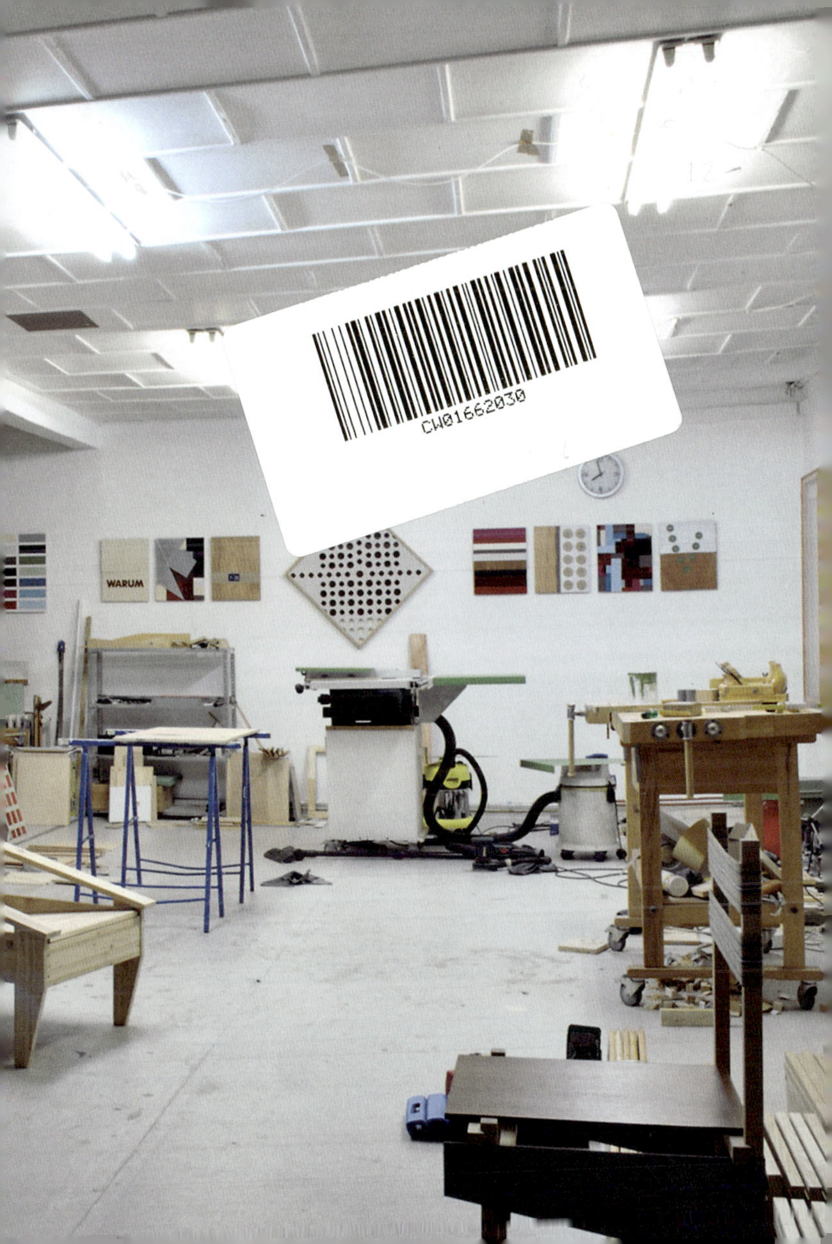
WARUM

PARTNERS

be Berlin

airbnb

FIAT

Berlin Partner

Etsy

Dussmann
das KulturKaufhaus
Ein Unternehmen der Dussmann Gruppe

Published in 2012 by Alphabet Press GbR, Berlin
thedesignguide.org

Fonts: FF More, FF Good (FontShop, Berlin)

Printing: Das Druckteam Berlin
Binding: Stein+Lehmann Die Buchbinder, Berlin

Worldwide distribution:
Gestalten, Berlin
www.gestalten.com
sales@gestalten.com

Cover photo **Oliver Helbig**
oliverhelbig.com

Inside cover **The studio of furniture designer Sven Temper**
tempermoebel.com

ISBN 978-3-89955-478-6

THE BERLIN DESIGN GUIDE

BERLIN BY DESIGN

A PRACTICAL GUIDE TO A CITY THAT HAS LONG FUNCTIONED AS A REFUGE FOR THOSE WHO REFUSE TO FIT THE MOULD.

Bringing together the results of months of research, writing, questioning, talking and interviewing, the Berlin Design Guide is an assembly of many pieces of information that, when viewed together, shed light on the questions – and hopefully some answers – that are often forgone by conventional travel guides.

INTRODUCTION

What shapes a creative community? What are the forces bolstering that of Berlin? What drives those who undertake creative endeavours here? While this is not the first time we have asked ourselves these questions, one thing distinguishes Berlin from all other creative cities we are familiar with. Here, a single theme pervades: the desire to do things differently. Berlin's creators, designers, architects and artists look back upon a tradition that – shaped by the city's social and cultural history – has always worked to reinvent and reimagine the status quo. Naturally, this means things aren't always perfectly resolved; it's more important to challenge conventions than to produce a polished result. This guide uncovers and explains many of the forces, events, people and places that have formed the creative city you find today. It is designed as a primer to sharpen your senses and understanding for this city, but, as anywhere, many exciting encounters will be up to serendipity. Happy exploring!

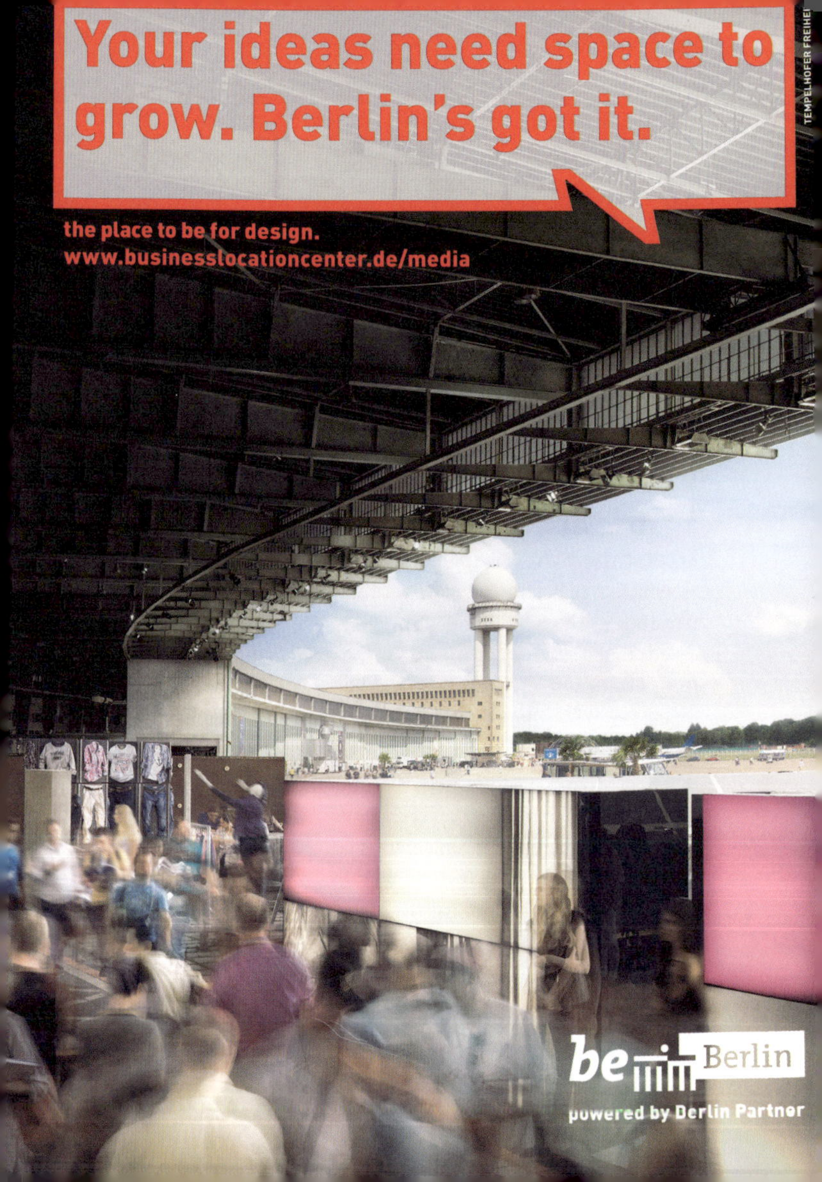
Your ideas need space to grow. Berlin's got it.
the place to be for design.
www.businesslocationcenter.de/media
be Berlin
powered by Berlin Partner

be inspired

be multi-faceted, *be* berlin

Berlin is a creative magnet and also home to a variety of talented professionals. More than anywhere else, young creatives are drawn to Berlin, where they are inspired to realize their ideas. The Berlin cultural scene offers an abundance of unusual locations and niches, as well as a rich landscape with cultural offerings and museums. Berlin has established itself as an international center for design. The capital's marketing campaign *be* Berlin, which was launched in 2008, continues to spotlight Berlin's multifaceted nature as a cultural metropolis. It has accomplished this - as has this book - by identifying aspects of the city and introducing creative locations that visitors may not notice at first sight. To further sharpen the focus on Berlin's diverse design landscape, a competition takes place in 2013, inviting designers to create their own interpretation of Berlin souvenirs. The best and most bench-breaking ideas become part of the new Berlin collection — "Berlin4U." Precisely these kinds of artistic and creative business ideas are what make this capital so exciting!

Yours sincerely, Berlin Partner GmbH
berlinpartner.de

DONE. FOR FUN.

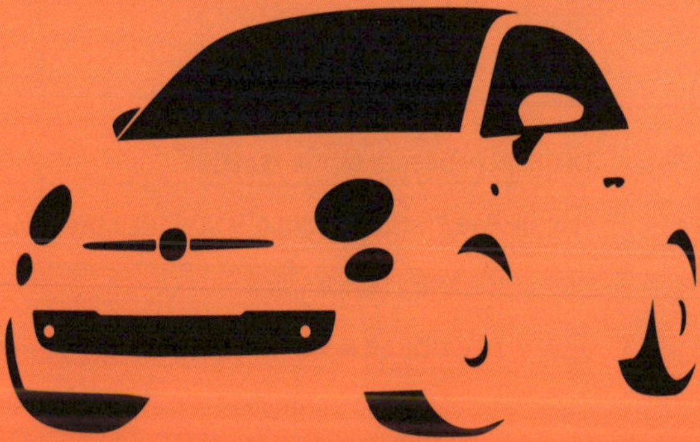

fiat500.de

THE BERLIN DESIGN GUIDE TEAM

Publishers | **KRISTINA LEIPOLD & VIVIANE STAPPMANNS**

Editor | **VIVIANE STAPPMANNS**

Design | **LILY TIDHAR & SHONA STARK** (wolfgangshlomoandmax.com)

Contributors | **NINA ALTSCHILLER** (Jewellery), **DAN BORDEN** (Built Environment), **STUART BRAUN** (Eat/Drink/Sleep), **TARA DOMINGUEZ** (Eat/Drink/Sleep), **NICHE ART & ARCHITECTURE TOURS** (Art, Built Environment), **LEONIE PFENNIG** (Art), **CELINA PLAG** (Co-Working), **NINA TRIPPEL** (Fashion)

Sub-editing | **TARA DOMINGUEZ**

Additional Research & Editing | **MEGAN GANNON**

Proofreading | **BECKY CROOK, BARB SEXTON**

Print Production | **CAROLA KILIAN**

THE FACTS

BERLIN IN CONTEXT

All clichés you've heard about this city are most probably true. It is vibrant due to its metropolitan density and cultural diversity, as 26% of Berliners come from a migrant background[1] (though many have a German passport). The city is quite poor and gritty due to modest economic activity and relatively high unemployment. It's particularly green and characterised by lots of vacant space. Sometimes, a few numbers say more than a thousand words ...

Artists in Berlin

33,000

Germany's second most creative city, Hamburg, is home to just over 13,000 artists[2].

University-level degrees in design and art[3]

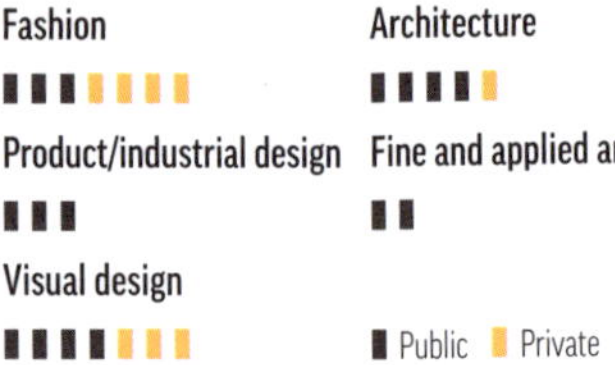

Parks and green public spaces

14.3%

of total metropolitan area. By comparison, Munich offers citizens 8.5 % of its total area as public parks and greenery.[4]

Creatives in Berlin

About one in ten working Berliners is part of the creative industries.[5]

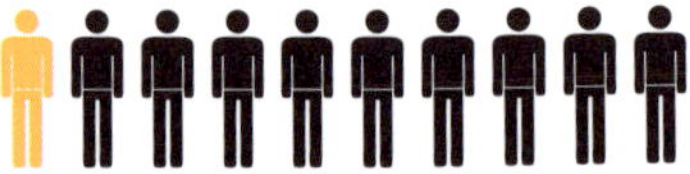

[1]Source: in-berlin-brandenburg.com/Berliner/auslaender.html
[2]Source: HWWI/ Berenberg Cultural City Ranking 2012
[3]courses also include related fields such as Urban Design or Games Design

Metropolitan snapshot

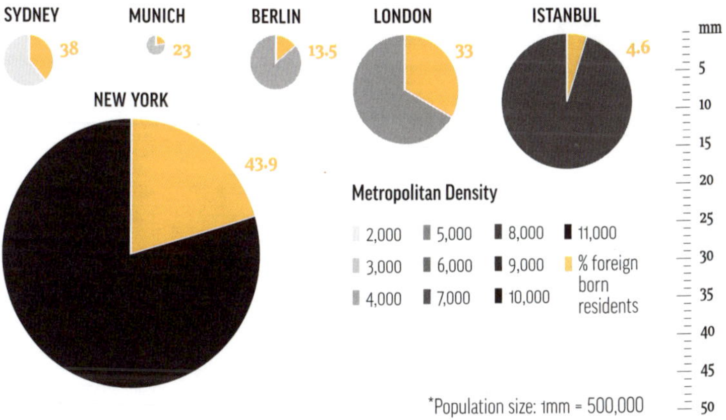

Sources: **Population density** New York City = en.wikipedia.org/wiki/New_York_City. All other cities = citymayors.com (2007 data) **Population size** = citymayors.com | **Foreign residents** Berlin & Munich, Süddeutsche Zeitung, 'Stadt der Vorzeigemigranten', 27.12.2010.), Sydney = Australian Bureau of Statistics, censusdata.abs.gov.au, 2006, London = en.wikipedia.org/wiki/London, Istanbul = http://en.wikipedia.org/wiki/Istanbul) show/55813

Cost of living

On average, a 100sqm apartment in Berlin costs less than a similar place all other major German cities. [6]

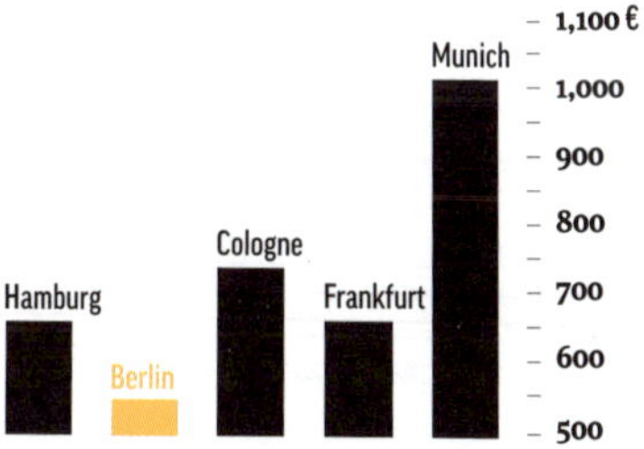

Unemployment

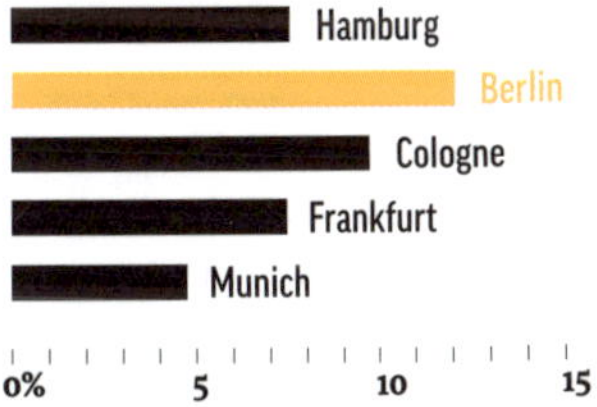

Above source: 'Arbeitsmarkt Großstadtvergleich', Unemployed in German Major Cities, June 2012, stuttgart.de/item/show/55813

[4]Source: Taz, 2.8.2012, w/references to data by Senatsverwaltung Berlin.

[5]Source: German Intitute of Economic Research, Weekly Report, 9/2009

[6]Net rental cost (not including bills) Source: Spiegel Online, 17 Dec. 2010, w/reference to a report by market researchers F+B Immobilien.

URBAN MINDSCAPE

"Was this West or East?" is a phrase you'll be asked, or at least overhear, a thousand times if you live in Berlin. Today, the Wall is largely obliterated, its former path marked by a number of memorials and a cobblestone line. Yet, as any urban environment, Berlin has many boundaries, often as significant as they are invisible. This overview provides a quick introduction to the issues and conditions that determine Berlin's psychological geography.

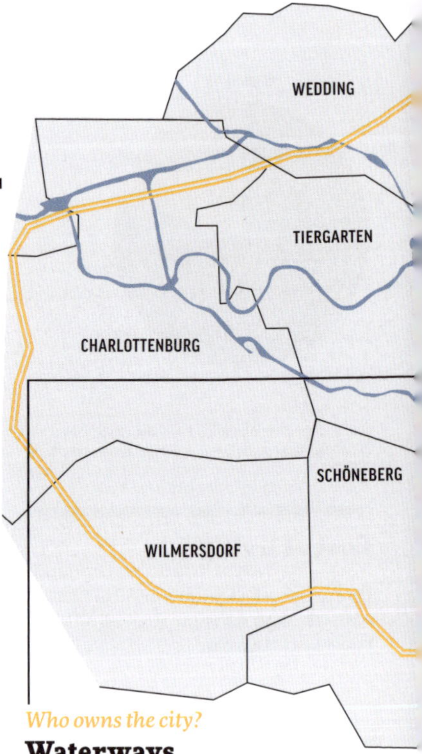

Former East Berlin

Former West Berlin

Former East/West border

Ringbahn

Who owns the city?

Waterways

As Berlin boasts more vacant urban space than most European metropoles, the discussion of urban ownership is alive and kicking. This is especially apparent on the banks of the Spree, where grass-roots initiatives contrast with corporate development.

East & West

Wedding & Prenzlauer Berg

These two former working class districts were once divided by the Wall. In the two decades since reunification, Prenzlauer Berg has developed into a well-to-do area popular with families. Meanwhile, Wedding has remained one of Berlin's poorest neighbourhoods.

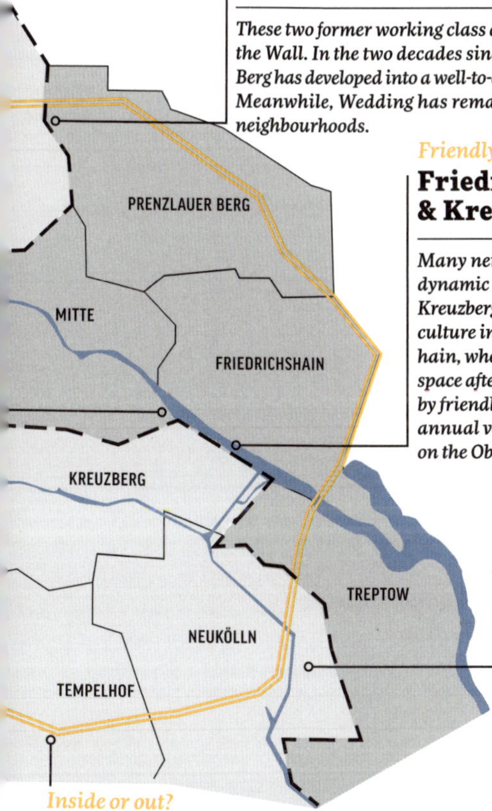

Friendly fire

Friedrichshain & Kreuzberg

Many neighbouring districts maintain dynamic relationships with one another. Kreuzberg, the original seat of alternative culture in West Germany, and Friedrichshain, where punks and squatters found space after the fall of the Wall, are divided by friendly rivalry, as is illustrated by an annual vegetable-throwing/water battle on the Oberbaum Bridge.

Gentrification at work

Neukölln

There's no other topic that keeps Berlin urbanists and locals as firmly engaged (and divided) as gentrification. This is particularly evident in Neukölln. Especially near its border to Kreuzberg, the district is rife with cafés and newly renovated apartment buildings. The speed at which this phenomenon spreads further toward the S-Bahn ring boundary seems mind-boggling to many residents, and differences from one street to the next can appear remarkable.

Inside or out?

The S-Bahn Ring

Although – or maybe because – Berlin doesn't have a definitive city centre, for the locals it's the circular S-Bahn track that describes what's 'inner city' and what isn't.

CREATIVITY AT WORK

It's simple. Since a city is made by its people, the most stimulating places are found where the interesting people are. To pinpoint where that is, we've mapped out the studios of 163 creative producers in product design, graphics and fashion and asked them a few questions.

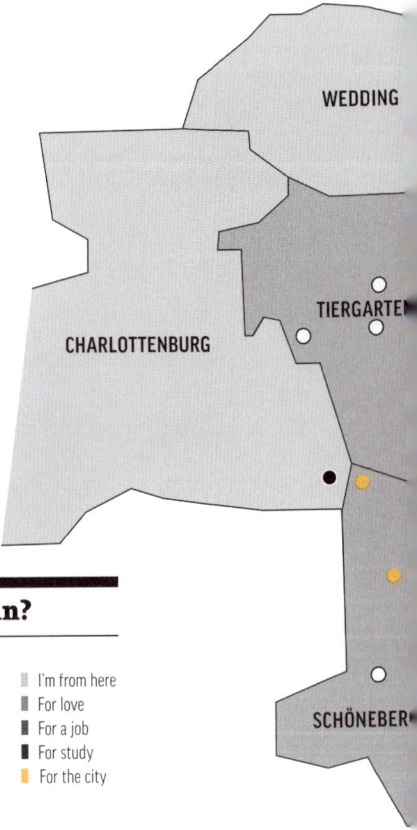

Why did you move to Berlin?

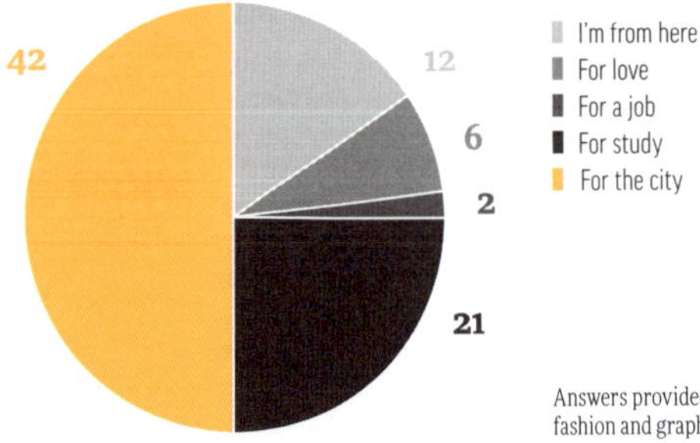

Answers provided by 85 individual product, fashion and graphic designers.

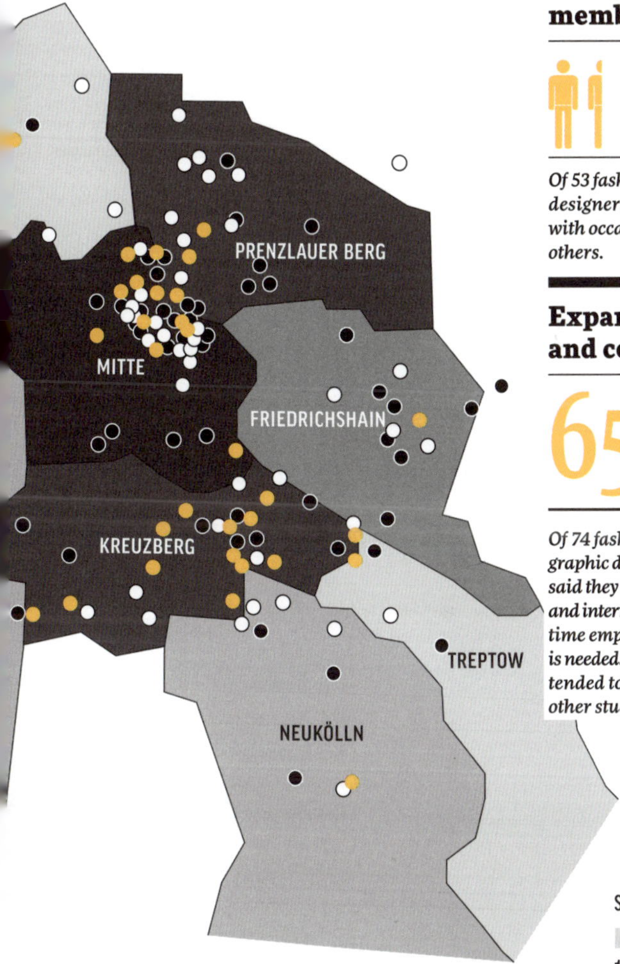

Average studio members

Of 53 fashion and product designers, 38 work alone, with occasional help from others.

Expand and contract

65%

Of 74 fashion, product and graphic design studios, most said they rely on freelancers and interns, rather than full-time employees, when help is needed. Graphic designers tended to collaborate with other studios.

Visual
Product
Fashion

Studios per suburb

1 ——> 40+

AREA MAPS

MITTE

BUILT ENVIRONMENT

1. Aedes Architecture Forum & Aedes Network Campus (ANCB)
2. Pfefferberg
3. Platoon Kunsthalle
4. L40
5. Brunnenstraße 9
6. Schokoladen
7. Auguststraße 51
8. Auguststraße 26A
9. Hackesche Höfe

ART

1. Galerie KOW
2. Galerie Zink
3. Volksbühne
4. Croy Nielsen
5. BQ
6. Christian Nagel Galerie
7. Circleculture Gallery
8. Galerie Eigen + Art
9. ME Collectors Room
10. KW Institute for Contemporary Art - Kunst-Werke Berlin
11. Eigen + Art Lab

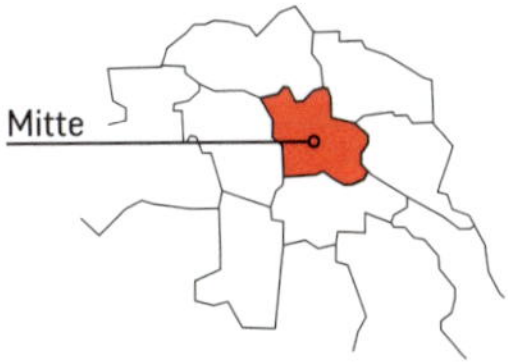

12. Sammlung Hoffmann
13. C/O Berlin
14. Sprüth Magers
15. Kleine Humboldt Galerie
16. LEAP
17. Hamburger Bahnhof
18. Galerie Neu
19. Boros Collection
20. Alte Nationalgalerie (Old National Gallery)
21. Neues Museum (New Museum)
22. Contemporary Fine Arts
23. Schinkel Pavillon

FASHION

1. Civilist
2. Adrett
3. Antonia Goy
4. Thone Negrón Salon
5. Sabrina Dehoff
6. A.D. Deertz
7. Superficial
8. Soto
9. Happy Shop
10. Firmament
11. Q by Umasan
12. Kaviar Gauche
13. Anuschka Hoevener
14. Potipoti Shop Berlin
15. Wolfen
16. Konk
17. C'est Tout
18. International Wardrobe
19. Firma
20. Starstyling
21. Das Neue Schwarz
22. Lala Berlin Store
23. Don't Shoot the Messengers - DSTM
24. Butterflysoulfire
25. Baerck
26. Schwarzhogerzeil
27. Hecking
28. Le Coup Shoes
29. YUU
30. Atelier Awash
31. Rike Feurstein

MITTE CONTINUED

FASHION CONTINUED

32. Wald
33. Adddress
34. Apartment
35. Ulf Haines
36. Esther Perbandt
37. A7
38. Jet
39. Wood Wood
40. Trippen
41. Nightboutique
42. Darklands
43. Garments Vintage
44. XVII
45. Zeha

OBJECTS & VISUAL DESIGN

1. Ruth Temur Schmuck
2. Schmuckfrage
3. s.wert Design
4. Jan Kath Flagshipstore
5. into art & furniture
6. Supergrau
7. Appel Design Gallery

8. Moebel Horzon
9. R.S.V.P. Papier in Mitte
10. Pro QM
11. Do You Read Me?!
12. OONA Galerie
13. JR Ledermanufaktur
14. Gestalten Space
15. OK Versand
16. Whiteout & Glare
17. Daniel Heer Showroom
18. ic! Berlin Shop
19. Mykita
20. Buchstaben Museum (Museum of Letters)
21. Pleased to Meet – Februardesign
22. Direktorenhaus
23. Dussmann das KulturKaufhaus

EAT/DRINK/SLEEP

1. Katz Orange
2. The Barn Roastery
3. Soho House
4. Hartweizen
5. Café St. Oberholz
6. Themroc
7. Lokal
8. Mamecha
9. The Barn
10. Clärchens Ballhaus
11. Café Bravo
12. Mogg & Melzer Delicatessen
13. Pauly Saal
14. Pony Bar
15. Casa Camper Hotel
16. Alt Berlin
17. Buscaglione
18. King Size Bar
19. Grill Royal
20. Bebe Rebozo
21. Miniloft Apartment Hotel
22. Bar Tausend
23. Cookies
24. Cookies Cream
25. Drayton Bar
26. Goldneun
27. Chipps
28. Yam Yam

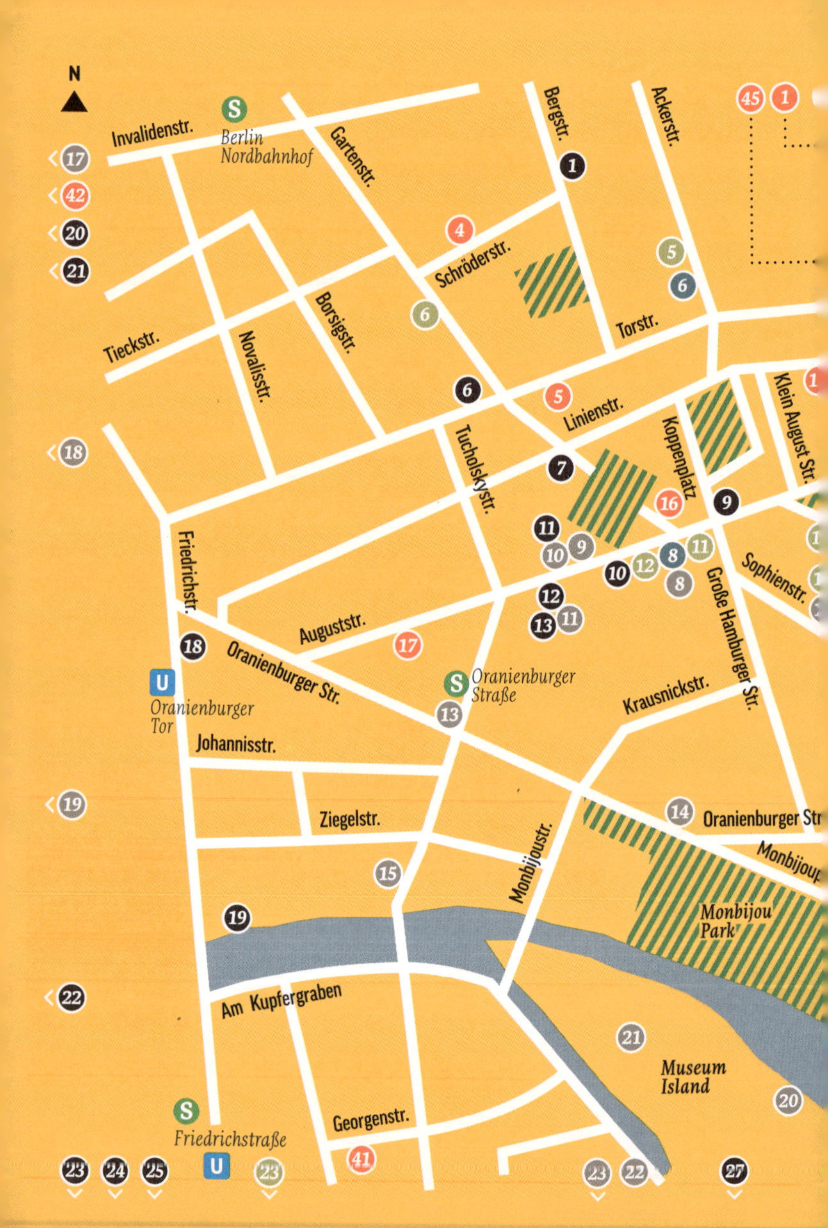

N
Invalidenstr.
S
Berlin Nordbahnhof
Gartenstr.
Bergstr.
Ackerstr.
Schröderstr.
Borsigstr.
Tieckstr.
Novalisstr.
Torstr.
Linienstr.
Tucholskystr.
Koppenplatz
Klein August Str.
Friedrichstr.
Auguststr.
Sophienstr.
Oranienburger Str.
Große Hamburger Str.
U
Oranienburger Tor
S
Oranienburger Straße
Krausnickstr.
Johannisstr.
Ziegelstr.
Oranienburger Str
Monbijoustr.
Monbijoup
Monbijou Park
Am Kupfergraben
Museum Island
Georgenstr.
S
Friedrichstraße
U

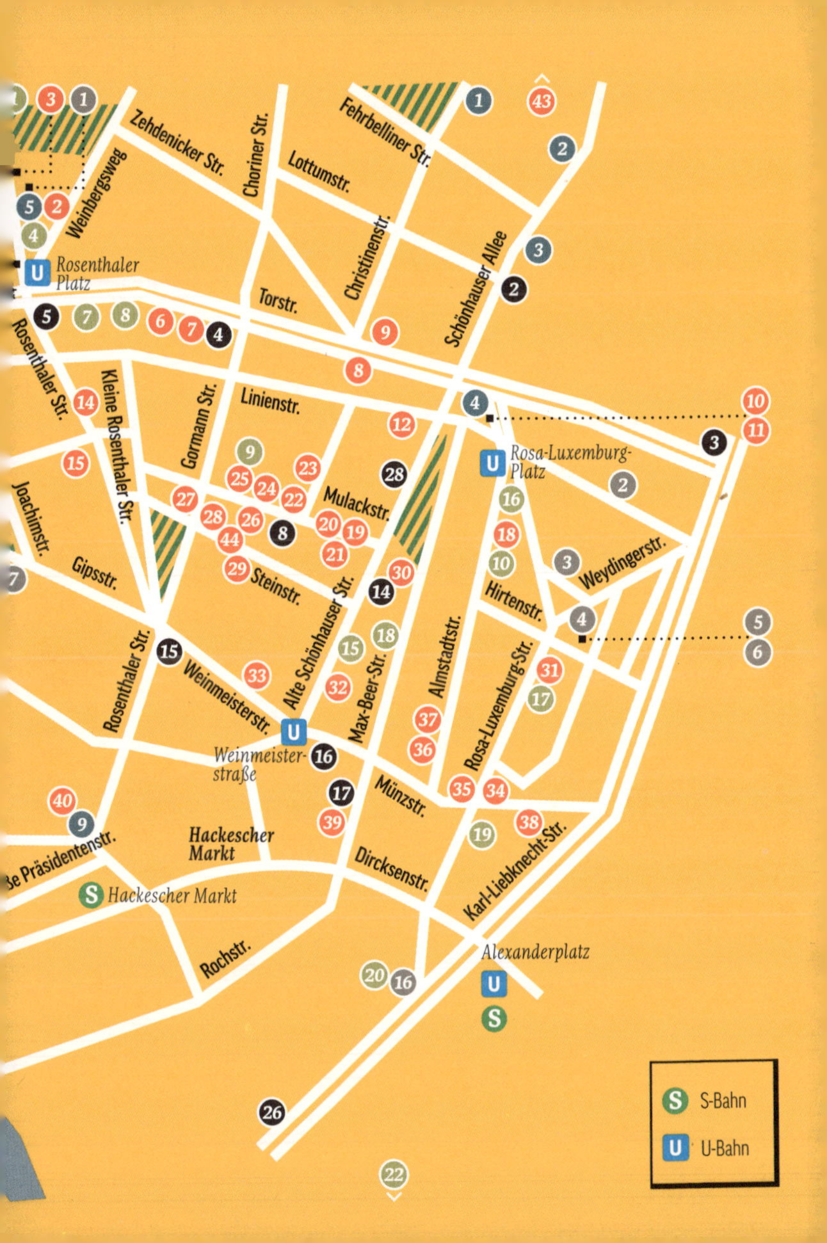

Zehdenicker Str.
Choriner Str.
Fehrbelliner Str.
Lottumstr.
Weinbergsweg
Christinenstr.
Schönhauser Allee
Rosenthaler Platz
Torstr.
Rosenthaler Str.
Kleine Rosenthaler Str.
Gormann Str.
Linienstr.
Rosa-Luxemburg-Platz
Joachimstr.
Mulackstr.
Gipsstr.
Steinstr.
Alte Schönhauser Str.
Weydingerstr.
Hirtenstr.
Almstadtstr.
Rosa-Luxemburg-Str.
Max-Beer-Str.
Weinmeisterstr.
Weinmeisterstraße
Münzstr.
Hackescher Markt
ße Präsidentenstr.
Dircksenstr.
Karl-Liebknecht-Str.
Rochstr.
Alexanderplatz
S-Bahn
U-Bahn

KREUZBERG, FRIEDRICHSHAIN & NEUKÖLLN

BUILT ENVIRONMENT

1. Schokofabrik
2. Prinzessinnengarten
3. Aqua Carré
4. Deutsches Architektur Zentrum (DAZ)
5. Badeschiff
6. Arena
7. Templehofer Freiheit (Former Tempelhof Airport)
8. Architektur Galerie Berlin
9. Karl-Marx-Allee
10. Radialsystem V

ART

1. Künstlerhaus Bethanien
2. Kwadrat
3. SOX
4. Grimmuseum
5. Johann König/ St. Agnes
6. Duve Berlin
7. MD72
8. Sammlung Haubrok (Haubrokshows)

FASHION

1. Voo Store
2. Slowmo
3. PastPresent Store
4. Rita in Palma
5. Knopf Paul

OBJECTS & VISUAL DESIGN

1. Staub Shop & Studio
2. Museum der Dinge (Museum of Things)
3. Die imaginäre Manufaktur (DIM)
4. Schmuck Fritz
5. Noon
6. Schoener waers, wenns schoener waer
7. Minimum
8. Coop Gold
9. Etsy Labs
10. Motto Berlin
11. Motto at Markthalle IX
12. Planet Modulor
13. Uhrenkrüger
14. Schubladen

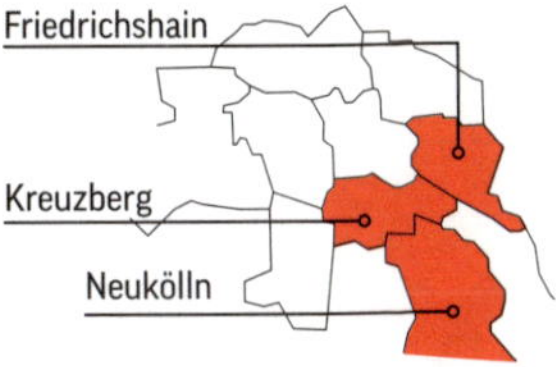

15. Computerspielemuseum (Computer Games Museum)

EAT/DRINK/SLEEP

1. Chez Gino
2. The Wye
3. Long March Canteen
4. 3Schwestern Restaurant
5. Hamam Turkish Baths
6. SO36
7. CK pour Voo
8. Trinkteufel
9. Max und Moritz
10. Betahaus
11. IMA Design Village
12. Kimchi Princess
13. Das Hotel
14. Ankerklause
15. Café Jacques
16. La Raclette
17. Mini Bar
18. Bei Schlawinchen
19. Turkish market at Maybachufer
20. Katie's Blue Cat
21. Five Elephant
22. Wostel Coworking
23. Hüttenpalast
24. Club der Visionäre
25. Freischwimmer
26. Chapter One
27. Molinari & Ko
28. Kater Holzig
29. YAAM
30. Michelberger Hotel
31. RAW
32. Freies Neukölln
33. Weserland Co-working
34. Späti International
35. Ä Bar
36. Tier
37. Lavanderia Vecchia
38. Agora Collective
39. Bar Babette
40. Kino International
41. Berghain
42. Möbel Olfe

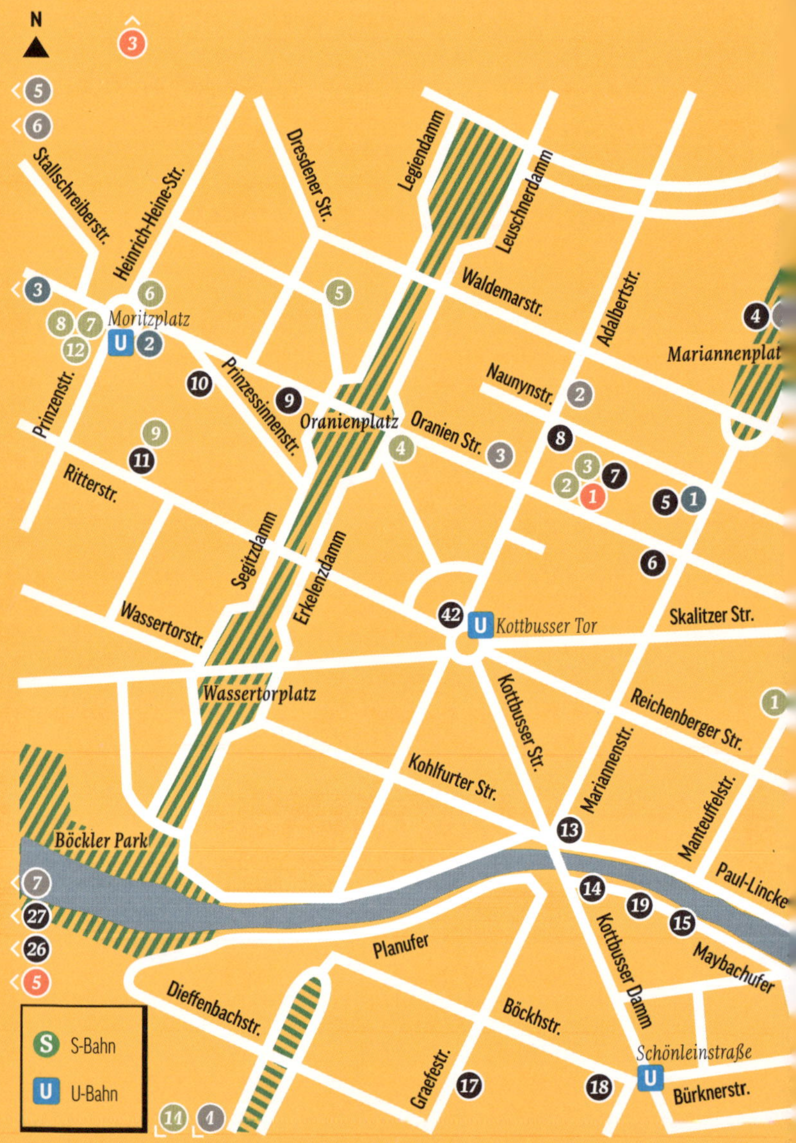
N
Stallschreiberstr.
Heinrich-Heine-Str.
Dresdener Str.
Legiendamm
Leuschnerdamm
Waldemarstr.
Adalbertstr.
Mariannenplat
Moritzplatz
Prinzenstr.
Prinzessinnenstr.
Oranienplatz
Oranien Str.
Naunynstr.
Ritterstr.
Segitzdamm
Erkelenzdamm
Wassertorstr.
Kottbusser Tor
Skalitzer Str.
Wassertorplatz
Kottbusser Str.
Reichenberger Str.
Kohlfurter Str.
Mariannenstr.
Manteuffelstr.
Böckler Park
Paul-Lincke
Kottbusser Damm
Maybachufer
Planufer
Dieffenbachstr.
Böckhstr.
Graefestr.
Schönleinstraße
Bürknerstr.
S-Bahn
U-Bahn

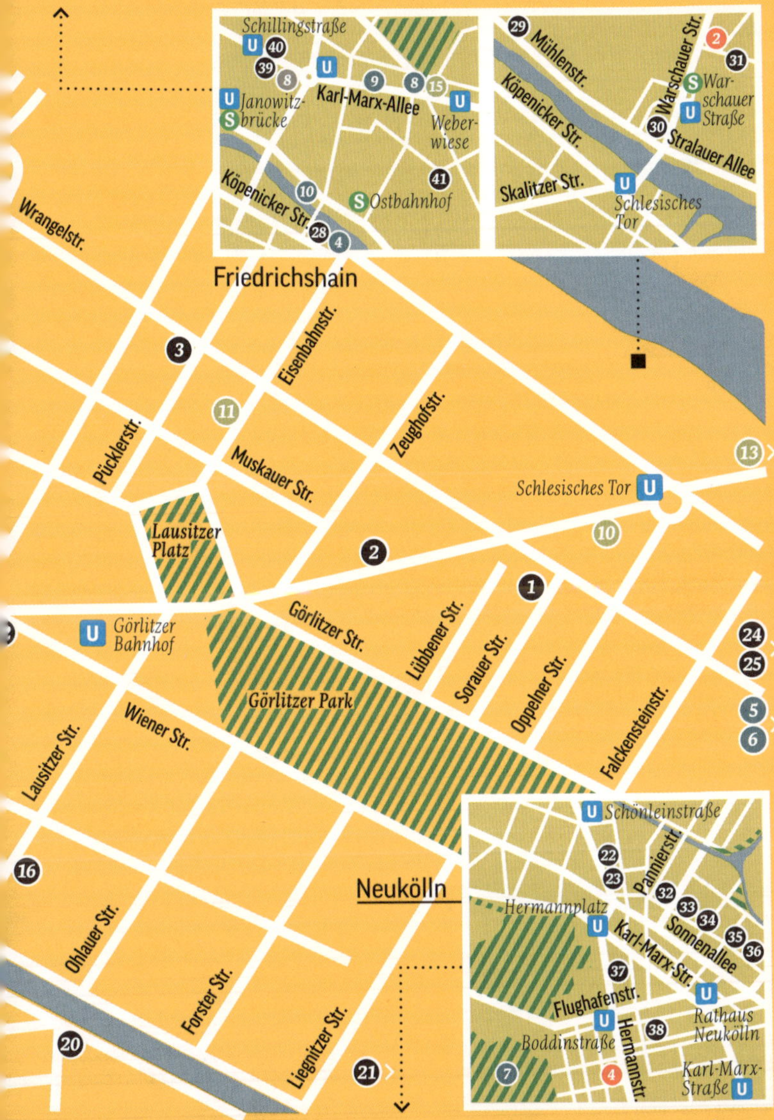

Schillingstraße
40
39
8
Karl-Marx-Allee
9
8
15
Weberwiese
Janowitzbrücke
Köpenicker Str.
10
Ostbahnhof
41
28
4
29
Mühlenstr.
Köpenicker Str.
Warschauer Str.
2
31
Warschauer Straße
30
Stralauer Allee
Skalitzer Str.
Schlesisches Tor
Friedrichshain
Wrangelstr.
3
Eisenbahnstr.
11
Pücklerstr.
Muskauer Str.
Zeughofstr.
13
Schlesisches Tor
10
Lausitzer Platz
2
1
Görlitzer Bahnhof
Görlitzer Str.
Lübbener Str.
Sorauer Str.
Oppelner Str.
24
25
Görlitzer Park
5
6
Wiener Str.
Falckensteinstr.
Lausitzer Str.
Schönleinstraße
Pannierstr.
22
23
16
Neukölln
Hermannplatz
32
33
34
Karl-Marx-Str.
Sonnenallee
35
36
Ohlauer Str.
37
Flughafenstr.
Rathaus Neukölln
Forster Str.
Hermannstr.
38
Boddinstraße
20
Liegnitzer Str.
21
7
4
Karl-Marx-Straße

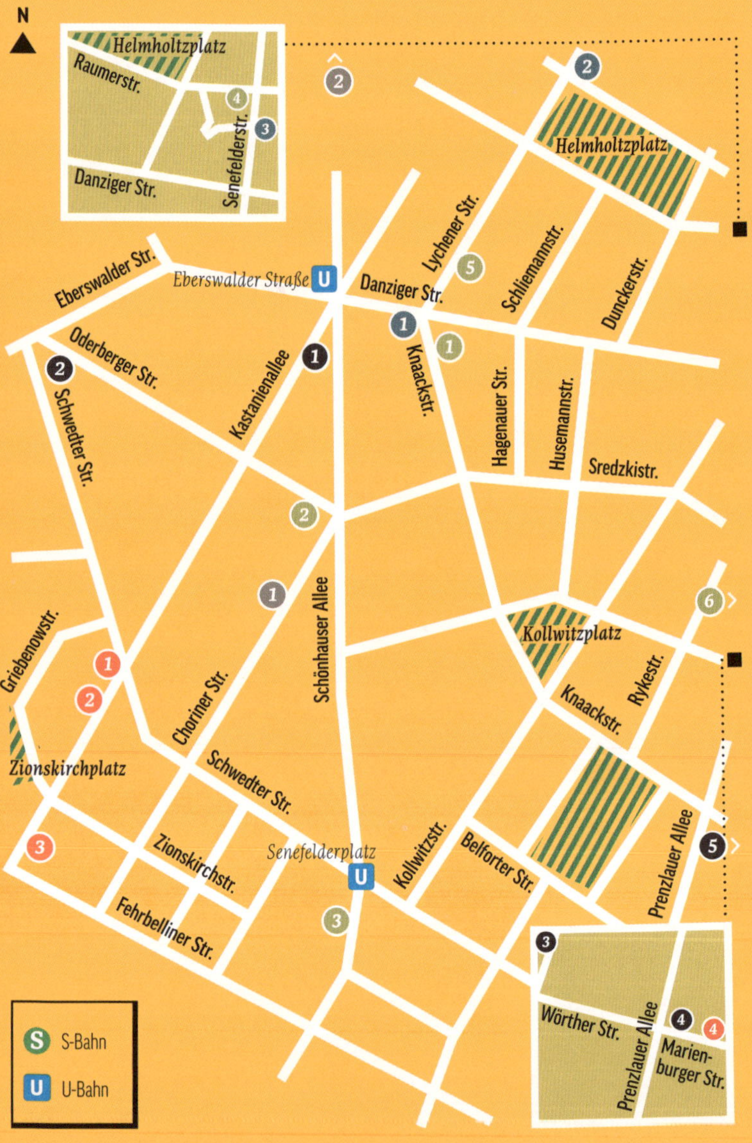
N
Helmholtzplatz
Raumerstr.
Senefelderstr.
Danziger Str.
Eberswalder Str.
Eberswalder Straße
Danziger Str.
Lychener Str.
Schliemannstr.
Dunckerstr.
Oderberger Str.
Kastanienallee
Knaackstr.
Hagenauer Str.
Husemannstr.
Sredzkistr.
Schwedter Str.
Kollwitzplatz
Griebenowstr.
Schönhauser Allee
Choriner Str.
Rykestr.
Knaackstr.
Zionskirchplatz
Schwedter Str.
Prenzlauer Allee
Zionskirchstr.
Senefelderplatz
Kollwitzstr.
Belforter Str.
Fehrbelliner Str.
Wörther Str.
Prenzlauer Allee
Marien-
burger Str.
S-Bahn
U-Bahn

PRENZLAUER BERG

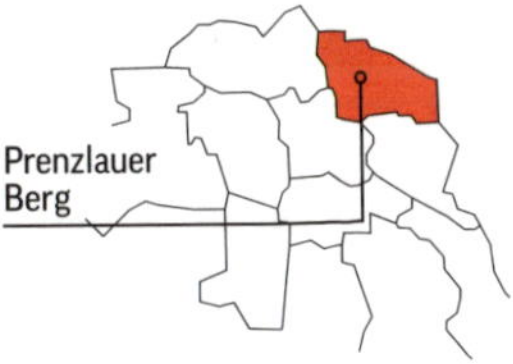

BUILT ENVIRONMENT

1. Kulturbrauerei
2. Lychener Straße 43
3. MACHmit! Museum für Kinder

ART

1. Volksboutique Small Business
2. REH Kunst

FASHION

1. cHkA/Styleserver
2. Temporary Showroom
3. C.Neeon
4. Wertvoll

OBJECTS & VISUAL DESIGN

1. G96 – New Values
2. BLESS home
3. Blumenfisch (VIA Werkstätten)
4. Pomeranza Design Ranch
5. Erfinderladen
6. Kunstschule

EAT/DRINK/SLEEP

1. Remise Berlin
2. Bonanza Coffee Heroes
3. No Fire, No Glory
4. Café CK
5. Godshot Coffee

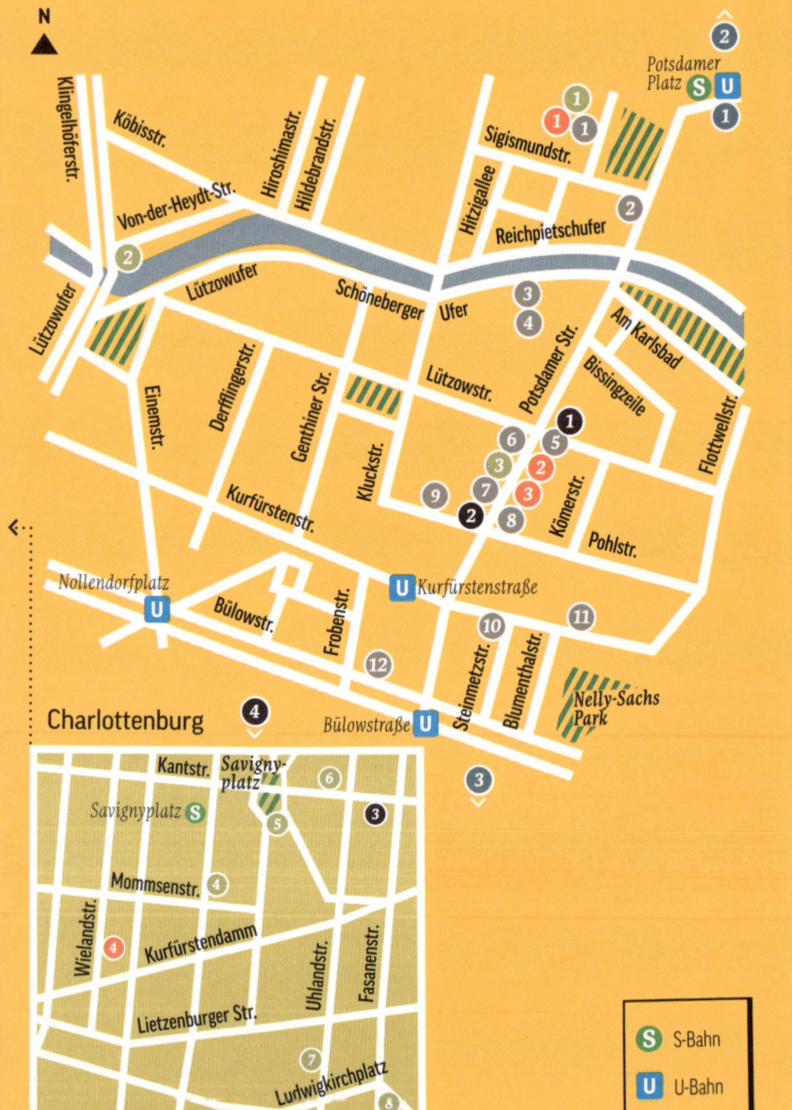

N
Potsdamer Platz
Klingelhöferstr.
Köbisstr.
Hiroshimastr.
Hildebrandstr.
Sigismundstr.
Von-der-Heydt-Str.
Hitzigallee
Reichpietschufer
Lützowufer
Lützowufer
Schöneberger Ufer
Am Karlsbad
Potsdamer Str.
Bissingzeile
Einemstr.
Derfflingerstr.
Genthiner Str.
Lützowstr.
Flottwellstr.
Kluckstr.
Kurfürstenstr.
Körnerstr.
Pohlstr.
Nollendorfplatz
Kurfürstenstraße
Bülowstr.
Frobenstr.
Steinmetzstr.
Blumenthalstr.
Nelly-Sachs Park
Charlottenburg
Bülowstraße
Kantstr.
Savignyplatz
Savignyplatz
Mommsenstr.
Wielandstr.
Kurfürstendamm
Uhlandstr.
Fasanenstr.
Lietzenburger Str.
Ludwigkirchplatz
S-Bahn
U-Bahn

TIERGARTEN, SCHÖNEBERG & CHARLOTTENBURG

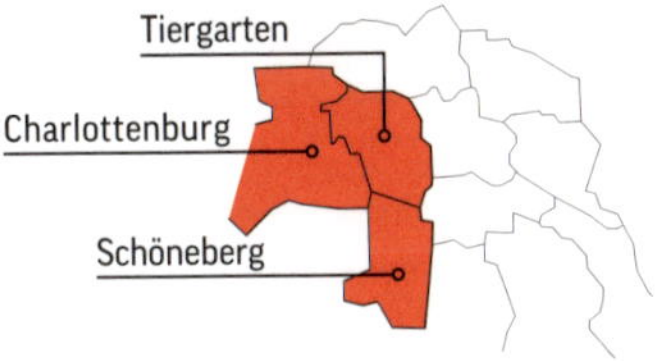

BUILT ENVIRONMENT

1. Potsdamer Platz
2. Reichstag
3. Sozialpalast

ART

1. Kunstbibliothek (Art Library)
2. Neue Nationalgalerie (New National Gallery)
3. Esther Schipper
4. Wien Lukatsch
5. Blain|Southern
6. Arndt
7. Die Tür
8. Klosterfelde
9. Galerie Tanja Wagner
10. Tanya Leighton Gallery
11. Sommer & Kohl
12. Kunstsaele

FASHION

1. Kostümbibliothek (Costume Library)
2. Murkudis
3. Fiona Bennett Salon
4. The Corner

OBJECTS & VISUAL DESIGN

1. Kunstgewerbemuseum (Decorative Arts Museum)
2. Bauhaus Archive
3. Reading Room & Shop
4. Hans-Peter Jochum Galerie
5. Bücherbogen am Savignyplatz
6. Stilwerk
7. Karena Schüssler Galerie
8. Die Werkstatt Galerie

EAT/DRINK/SLEEP

1. Kumpelnest 3000
2. Victoria Bar
3. Paris Bar
4. Winterfeldmarkt (Winterfeld Market)

HOW TO USE THIS BOOK

In compiling this book, we approached our task as scientists conducting field work. We asked, probed, observed and analysed. As a consequence, we identified themes and common threads and put them together in various chapters. All of our findings are presented in one of five ways. The **Tours** help visitors discover a geographic area or a particular theme by foot, bike or sometimes even public transport. Often, we observed that a number of places had something in common and so we shared these findings as **Field Notes**. Because it's best to learn about a city from its locals, we asked professionals from all fields of creativity to share with us the locations they feel are important to know about in the **My City** profiles. Meanwhile, some architects and designers let us peek **Behind the Scenes** of their studios and work spaces. Last but not least, the **Address Books** at the end of each chapter provide basic information about more stores, galleries or hotels. Finally, a word about opening hours. We have included them where possible, but recommend that you check websites before you visit, since they can change frequently and aren't always strictly obeyed.

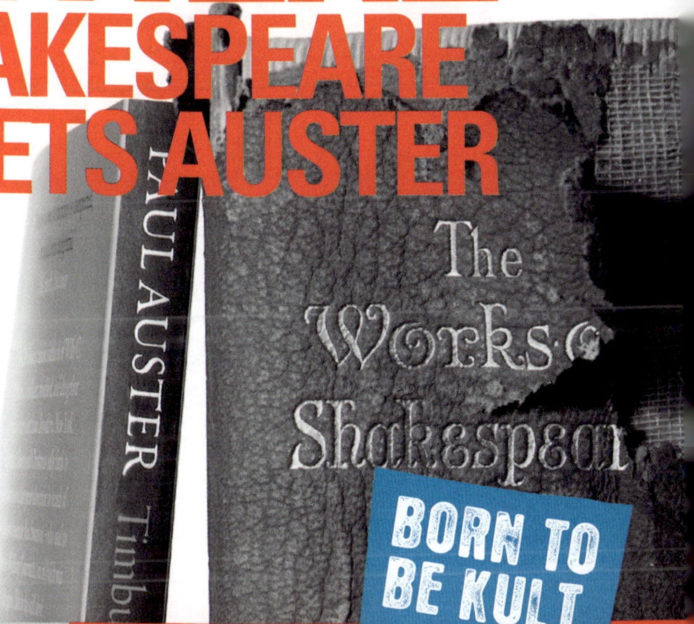
PAUL AUSTER Timbu
The
Works o
Shakespear

BUILT ENVIRONMENT

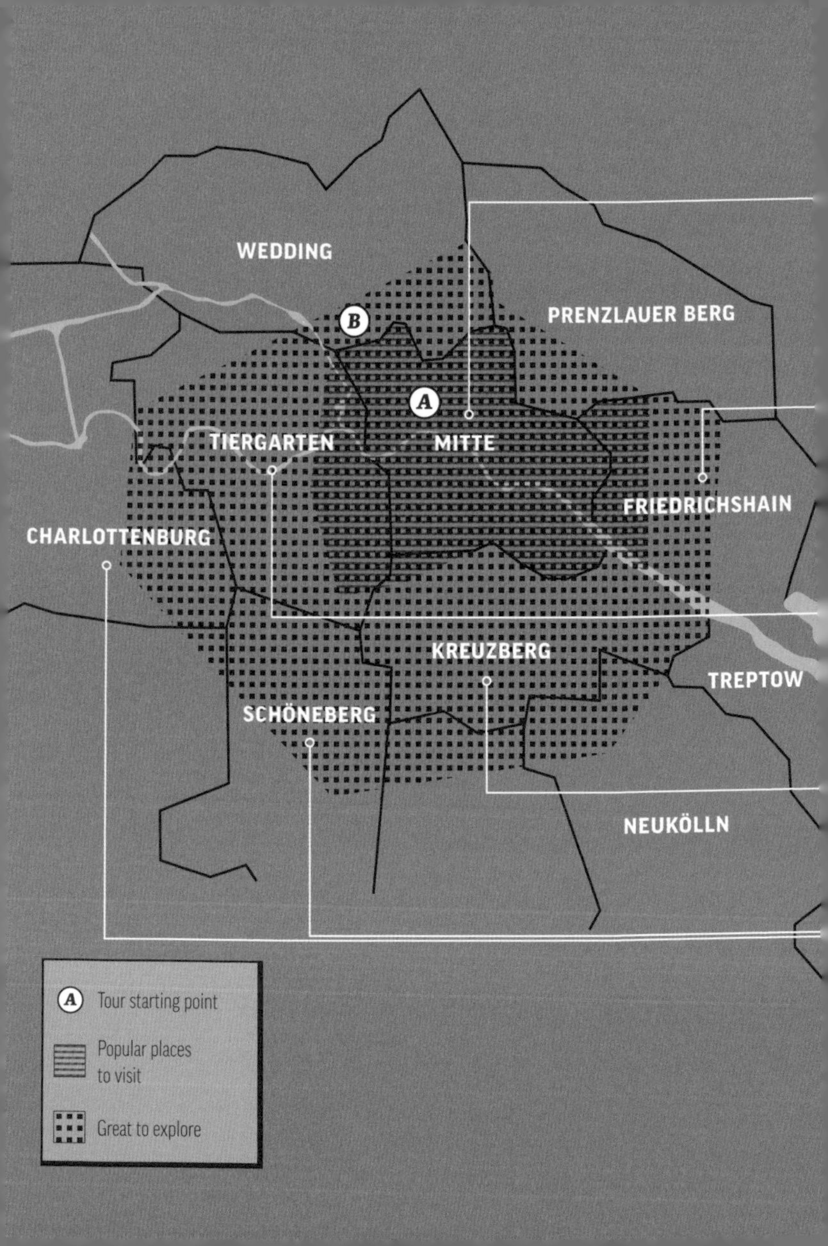
WEDDING
PRENZLAUER BERG
B
A
TIERGARTEN
MITTE
FRIEDRICHSHAIN
CHARLOTTENBURG
KREUZBERG
TREPTOW
SCHÖNEBERG
NEUKÖLLN
A Tour starting point
Popular places to visit
Great to explore

THE DISPLAY CASE

Mitte is the city's most diverse district when it comes to architecture thanks to its historic buildings and newer additions, such as the renovated Reichstag, Neues Museum and Potsdamer Platz, as well as countless embassies and government buildings created by an international architectural avant-garde.

THE EAST

Friedrichshain's Karl-Marx-Allee, the socialist-designed boulevard and Europe's longest monument, should be the starting point for anyone looking to explore GDR architecture. A bit further, **Lichtenberg's** *Plattenbau* estates provide an authentic insight into domestic life in former East Berlin.

THE UNDERDOG

Tiergarten's architectural assets are often overlooked, especially the Hansaviertel. Nowhere else in the world can one appreciate the legacy of modernism's great masters in such a diverse inhabited setting.

THE ACTIVIST

A number of sites along **Kreuzberg's** banks of the Spree river, with their various developments and semi-legal occupants, serve as global showcases for contemporary, participatory urbanism.

THE OLD WORLD

Charlottenburg and **Schöneberg** don't feature the density of architectural or historical showpieces you might find in other districts, but their grand, bourgeois residential *Gründerzeit* architecture tells many stories about life in Berlin during the Golden Years.

THE SPACE RACE

THE PARTICULARITIES OF BERLIN'S URBAN CONDITION

Berlin's turbulent history and the destruction and reconfiguration it engendered have deeply shaped the city's form and character, creating a unique built environment that doubles as an open space for all kinds of creative practice.

Many guidebooks capture the buildings in this city. They place them in their historical context, discuss how their stories are manifested in their appearance, explain their purpose. This guide is not one of them. Rather than focusing on the architectural marvels and alluring post-Wall constructions that grace the covers of other books on Berlin architecture, we regard architecture and the built environment as the seismograph that reads the vibrations of the creative city. Which developments in architecture and the built environment describe and illustrate the character of the city?

> ***"Which developments in architecture and the built environment describe and illustrate the character of the city?"***

What is truly fascinating about Berlin's architectural and design discourse is a recurring theme, a continual inspiration for any number of creative ventures in the city: all that space. Berlin boasts hundreds of buildings and locations seemingly waiting for inspired architects and artists to stretch the limitations of possibility or create temporary utopias that drive the city's artistic and cultural projects and development. In the following three chapters, this book highlights the main themes that underpin Berlin's dynamic activity and discourse concerning the built environment, architecture and the creative community at large. First, we highlight how contemporary architects and urban activists engage with the city's vacant spaces by way of architectural or temporary insertions. Second, we feature a selection of re-purposed industrial sites that provide room for the city's cultural offerings, before concluding with an illustration of how the lifestyle experiments taking place in the city belong to a long tradition of engaging with – and questioning – new ways of dwelling.

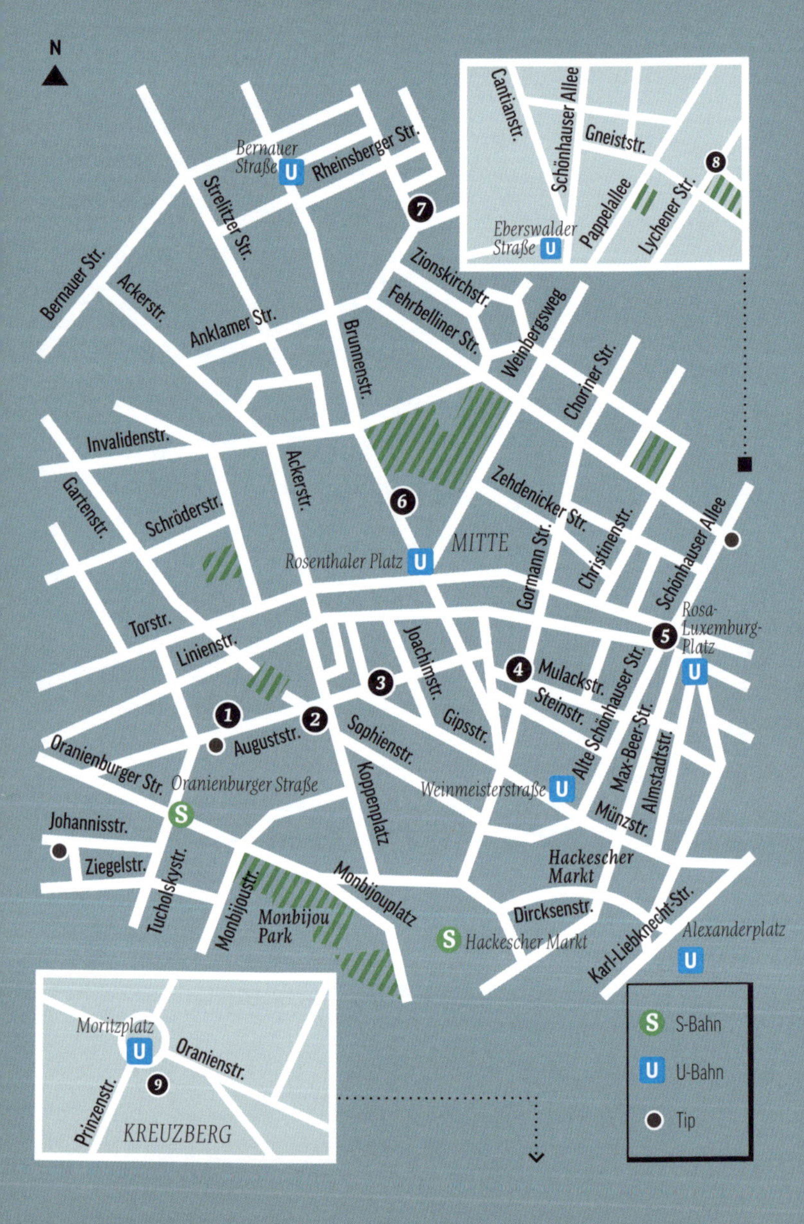
N
Bernauer Straße
Rheinsberger Str.
Strelitzer Str.
Bernauer Str.
Ackerstr.
Anklamer Str.
Zionskirchstr.
Fehrbelliner Str.
Brunnenstr.
Weinbergsweg
Choriner Str.
Invalidenstr.
Gartenstr.
Schröderstr.
Ackerstr.
Zehdenicker Str.
MITTE
Rosenthaler Platz
Gormann Str.
Christinenstr.
Schönhauser Allee
Torstr.
Linienstr.
Joachimstr.
Rosa-Luxemburg-Platz
Mulackstr.
Steinstr.
Gipsstr.
Alte Schönhauser Str.
Auguststr.
Sophienstr.
Max-Beer-Str.
Almstadtstr.
Oranienburger Str.
Oranienburger Straße
Koppenplatz
Weinmeisterstraße
Münzstr.
Johannisstr.
Ziegelstr.
Tucholskystr.
Monbijoustr.
Monbijou Park
Monbijouplatz
Hackescher Markt
Dircksenstr.
Hackescher Markt
Karl-Liebknecht-Str.
Alexanderplatz
Cantianstr.
Schönhauser Allee
Gneiststr.
Pappelallee
Lychener Str.
Eberswalder Straße
Moritzplatz
Oranienstr.
Prinzenstr.
KREUZBERG
S-Bahn
U-Bahn
Tip

Ⓐ TOUR

MIND THE GAP

After the fall of the Wall, large scale building activity boomed. Today, it's a raft of smaller scale, often residential projects where the engagement of local architects with Berlin's unique urban condition can best be witnessed.

Once one of the densest cities in Europe, Berlin was sealed with a carpet of five-storey tenement buildings before WWII bombings left the city a jagged urban canyon. Over the years, these gaps have been filled as part of a number of urban planning strategies. The results range from 1960s and 70s housing blocks to the nondescript buildings that characterised the 1990s phase of 'Critical Reconstruction', when city planners demanded that any insertion into the existing streetscape should correspond to its 19th century predecessors in proportion, eave height and façade. However, in the last decade, the city's architects have enriched and extended Berlin's urban patchwork, employing much more creative approaches.

Right Gallery and studio building Brunnenstr. 9, Brandlhuber + ERA, Emde, Schneider
Photo Michael Reisch, Köln

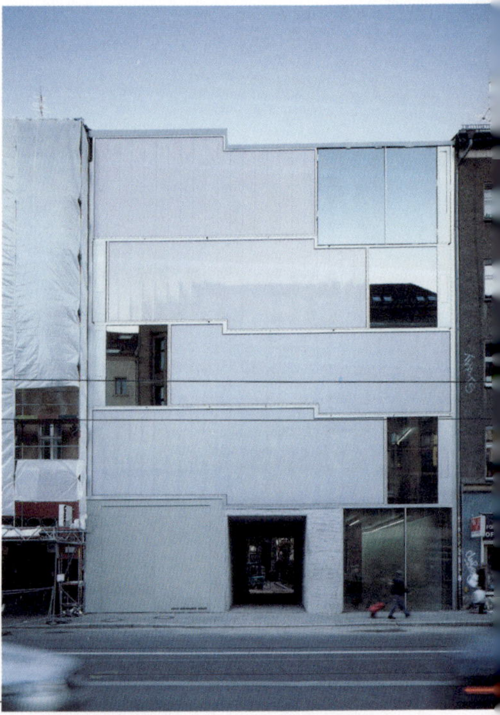

6

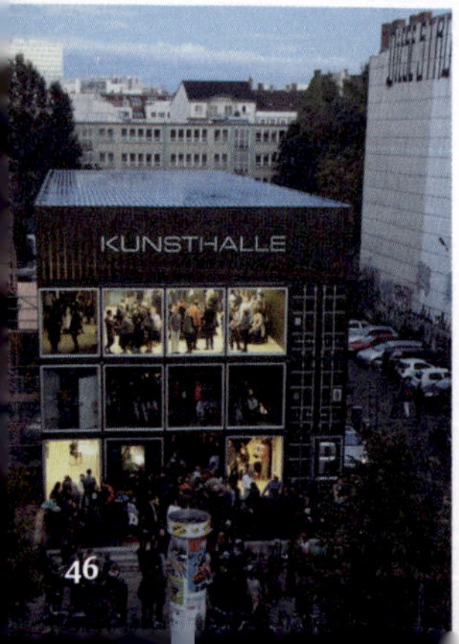

Left Platoon Kunsthalle
Photo Volker Hanneck

Right Ruppiner Straße 52, Zanderroth Architekten
Photo Andrea Kroth

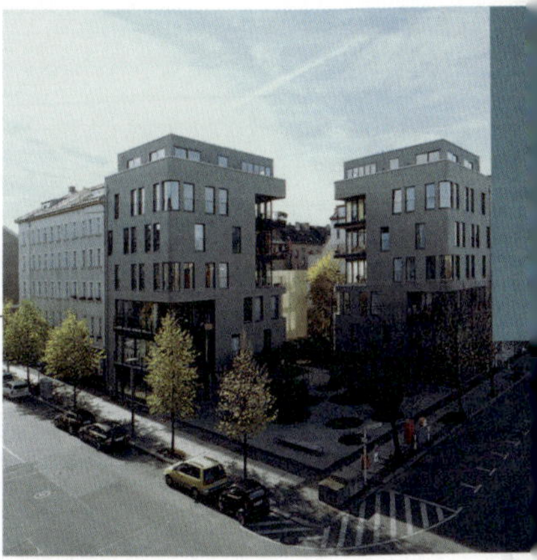

7

3

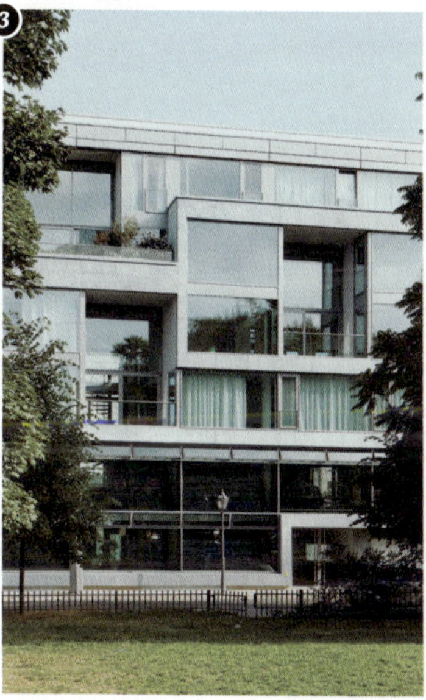

Left Auguststraße 51, Grüntuch Ernst Architekten, 2008
Photo Jan Bitter

4

Right Abcarius + Burns' Urban Living II
Photo Hisao Suzuki

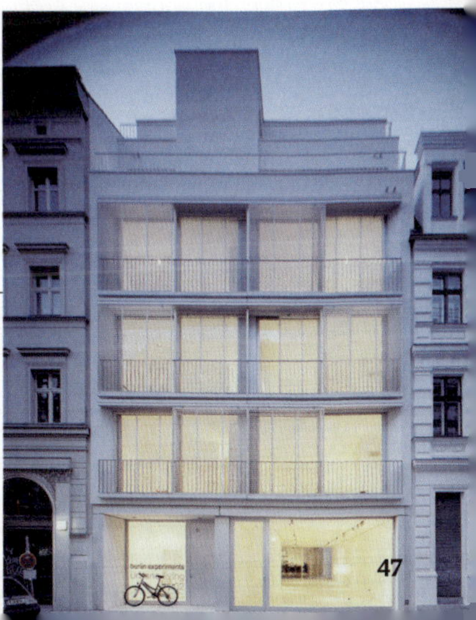

❶ **Café Bravo** *Dan Graham, 1998 | Auguststr. 69, Mitte*

The projects on this tour are united by their innovative approaches to a similar set of existing conditions: to find optimal uses for every inch of their compact sites and to respect their historic neighbours. This building is a perfect illustration of how this can be done despite a major departure from the surrounding structures. Replacing the side wing of the war-damaged margarine factory that became Kunst-Werke in the 1990s (*see page 90*), this small glass pavilion was designed by American artist, writer and curator Dan Graham, whose work blurs the line between sculpture and architecture. Supported by Berlin architecture practice Nalbach + Nalbach, Graham created two intertwined glass cubes that house a small café. The artist's central focus was to merge inside and outside, achieved by the use of two-way mirrors which reflect the exterior or allow an interior view depending on the angle of the light. Café Bravo does more than close a gap between buildings, it also redefines the spatial relations of the courtyard.

Tip... This tour could start at Johannisstr. 3, a few steps further west, past S-Bahn station Oranienburger Straße. Completed in early 2012, this residential building is the first Berlin work of celebrated architect **Jürgen Mayer H.** (*see page 66*) and relates to many buildings on this tour by refusing to overtly reference the existing historic streetscape as required of all newly built structures in the 1990s.

Tip... This pavilion reflects many of the elements that characterise dozens of other **Dan Graham**-designed structures around the world. To create a space that is somewhat disorienting, his pavilions usually use materials such as glass and mirrors, fish eye lenses or small pools of water.

❷ **Auguststraße 26a** *Jörg Ebers, 2005* *ebers-architekten.de*

Architect Jörg Ebers completed his hybrid domestic and retail building in 2005, although the 7.80m gap between two residential buildings was previously declared too small for construction. Housing a ground floor retail space, a first floor apartment and the two-storey residence of the architect and his family, the design utilises every inch of space by treating each room as a piece of furniture – for example, by regarding a windowsill as part of the room and using it as seating. In his design, Ebers found innovative means of addressing the requirement of fitting his building into the existing urban fabric, though he refused to replicate the historic stucco façades of his neighbours. Mosaic tiles from various shades of green glass create a connection with the rendered façades of adjacent buildings, producing an effect of depth and texture without being tacky.

❸ **Auguststraße 51** *Grüntuch Ernst, 2008*

gruentuchernst.de

Home to a group of owner builders who are part of the Berlin-specific 'Baugruppe' phenomenon (*see page 65*), this ensemble of buildings encompasses a front house and a smaller building in the courtyard. Seven individual parties commissioned husband-and-wife team Almut Grüntuch-Ernst and Armand Ernst to design the complex, which has won numerous awards and also houses the firm's offices. The most interesting aspect of this design is perhaps the façade. Uncharacteristically for Berlin, where until recently architects were required to replicate the largely sealed façades with small window openings typical of historic buildings, the exterior of this building boasts a large glass front which allows observers to distinguish the individual apartment units. These encompass two-storey loggias that open up to the park across the road.

Tip ... **Grüntuch Ernst Architekten** are also behind the refurbishment of a former Jewish Girls' School, now an art and dining hotspot (*see page 241*) not far from here, which opened to great fanfare in 2012.

❹ **Urban Living II** *Abcarius + Burns, 2004*

Mulackstr. 12, Mitte | abcariusburns.de

This residential building was built on a vacant lot between two elaborately designed 19th century buildings. In the design process, Berlin-based architects Jean-Marc Abcarius and Christopher Burns challenged the strict division between private and public life that is evident in the building's historic neighbourhood. As a consequence, the façade consists largely of steel lamellae that can be pushed aside. A highlight of the design is the courtyard, where the reduced aesthetic produces a zen-like atmosphere.

Tip ... The building's ground floor is home to one of Berlin's best fashion stores, **Baerck** (*see page 132*)

Optional ... For those interested in yet another manifestation of the multitude of temporary uses for vacant plots in Berlin, make your way up Schönhauser Allee. Built from 34 shipping containers, **Platoon Kunsthalle** is an exhibition and performance space for contemporary art. It moved here in mid-2012, its second location after first popping up on Rosenthaler Str.

Schönhauser Allee 9, Mitte | kunsthalle.com

❺ L40 *Roger Bundschuh, Cosima von Bonin, 2010*

Linienstr. 40, Mitte | l-40.de, bundschuh.net

On a triangular block facing the busy Rosa-Luxemburg-Platz intersection sits the monolithic, sculptural result of a unique collaboration between an artist and an architect. L40, so-named after its location on Linienstr. 40, is the antidote to the 1990s dictum of 'Critical Reconstruction'. This exposed black concrete sculpture self-confidently defies its surroundings, overtly disregarding eaves height and historic façade structure. However, the building is not as imposing as it may seem, weaving into the urban fabric by way of many small gestures. Its interiors are lofty, light and always surprising in volume and shape.

❻ Brunnenstraße 9 *Brandlhuber + ERA, Emde, Schneider, 2009 | brandlhuber.com*

This unusual building has been one of the most hotly discussed structures in town since its completion in 2009. It consists of a raw concrete core and a temporary polycarbonate skin. The building is home to Galerie KOW, the headquarters of art magazine 032c and the office and apartment of architect Arno Brandlhuber. When the architect bought the site, he took over a basement full of water from a previous developer. The building he created adhered strictly to the existing conditions while creating a connection to the surrounding environment (for instance, by matching its floor height to that of the neighbouring properties). The result was an extremely cost-effective structure, an outstanding example of restrained innovation. A highlight is the exterior, courtyard-facing stairwell, which lends a sculptural element to a utilitarian object.

❼ Ruppiner Straße 52 *Zanderroth Architekten, 2007*

zanderroth.de

The twin properties immediately adjacent to the former Wall strip on Ruppinerstr. are distinguished by an uncommon feature; despite being private land, the architects have created a generous public space between the two buildings. It is a rare gesture in a city where many residents fear that almost all vacant property is for sale to the highest bidder. The building presents an alternative to the city's still popular practice of building to a site's perimeter – here, access to light and space take centre stage.

❽ Lychener Straße 43 *Nägeli & Zander, 2001*

zanderroth.de

This parcel of land near Helmholtzplatz was initially thought to be irreclaimable due to its small proportions. In fact, there had never been a building on the 35m deep and just over 10m wide block. Architects Walter Nägeli and Sascha Zander decided to divide their 12-unit domestic building into two mirroring parts with central access. In doing so, the architects allowed for more light to reach the individual living units, with floor to ceiling windows facing street and courtyard. Like some of the other developments on this tour, this project questions the necessity of building to the perimeter of a block in an already dense urban environment. This design also addresses the strict division between public and private by creating a semi-public space.

❾ **Prinzessinnengarten** *Nomadisch Grün, 2009 | Prinzenstr. 35-38, Kreuzberg prinzessinnengarten.net*

The Prinzessinengarten, located in Kreuzberg far off the trajectory of this tour, offers a new perspective on how to deal with free spaces in a much more transient and – in every sense of the word – grass-roots sort of way. Prinzessinengarten represents the uniquely 'Berlin' way of creating something from nothing with very little financial means but with an unusual amount of civic pride, lateral thinking and community spirit. Back in 2009, the 6,000sqm site was a nondescript vacant lot. Inspired by the Cuban phenomenon of urban gardening

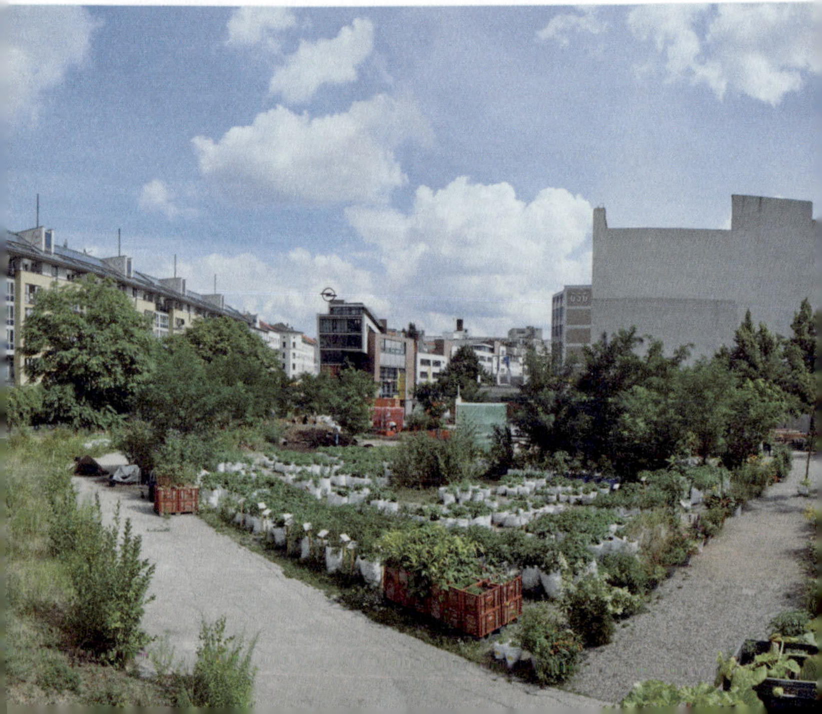

and passionate about bringing the community together, Marco Clausen and Robert Shaw, two locals in their mid-thirties with backgrounds in film, gardening and hospitality, signed a temporary lease on the city-owned site, and gathered a crowd of volunteers to start a mobile vegetable garden where all plants grow in movable containers. Three years on, the project has made waves around the world and has grown into a destination for many Berliners who come to garden, buy vegetables or simply enjoy the many events hosted here during the summer months. At the time of writing, Prinzessinengarten's founders and their dedicated team were campaigning for a lease renewal to continue their quest for rethinking the use of urban space.

Photo Marco Clausen/ Prinzessinnengarten

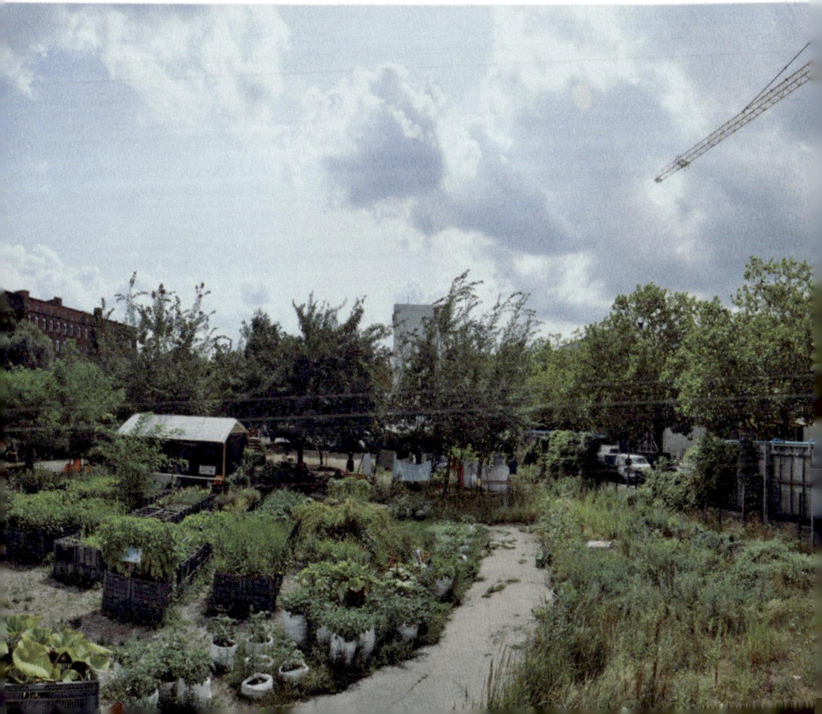

MY CITY WITH

FRIEDRICH VON BORRIES

Urban Thinker

The World Improvement Machine

Friedrich von Borries' ultimate goal is ambitious: he wants to create a world improvement machine. Before they can get there, he and his team are team tackling smaller but no less complex tasks in the area of 'urban intervention', ranging from built projects and exhibitions to research reports, recommendations and publications. A professor of design theory, former curator of Germany's entry for the Venice Architecture Biennale and a genuinely interesting character, Friedrich recommends three architectural locations that, for him, perfectly sum up the spirit, history and character of this city.

friedrichvonborries.de

1 **"The often overlooked Hansaviertel, where I live, is (to me) one of the most interesting locations in Berlin as it is a living, inhabited tribute to modernism.**
Most people probably associate with Berlin the residential *Gründerzeit* architecture of Mitte or Prenzlauer Berg, but Hansaviertel represents the 1950s ideals of clean lines, rationality and healthy living *(see page 62)*. As the original inhabitants leave, more and more people who appreciate art and architecture are moving here."

U ***Hansaviertel*** S ***Bellevue***

2 **"The Internationales Congress Centrum (ICC), built in the 1970s at the height of the space race, has a counterpart in East Berlin; while its cousin – the television tower – looks like a satellite, ICC is a space ship.**
The world's most expensive building at the time, it sits next to the former Avus car race track, which now accommodates a restaurant and a swinger's club between its lanes.

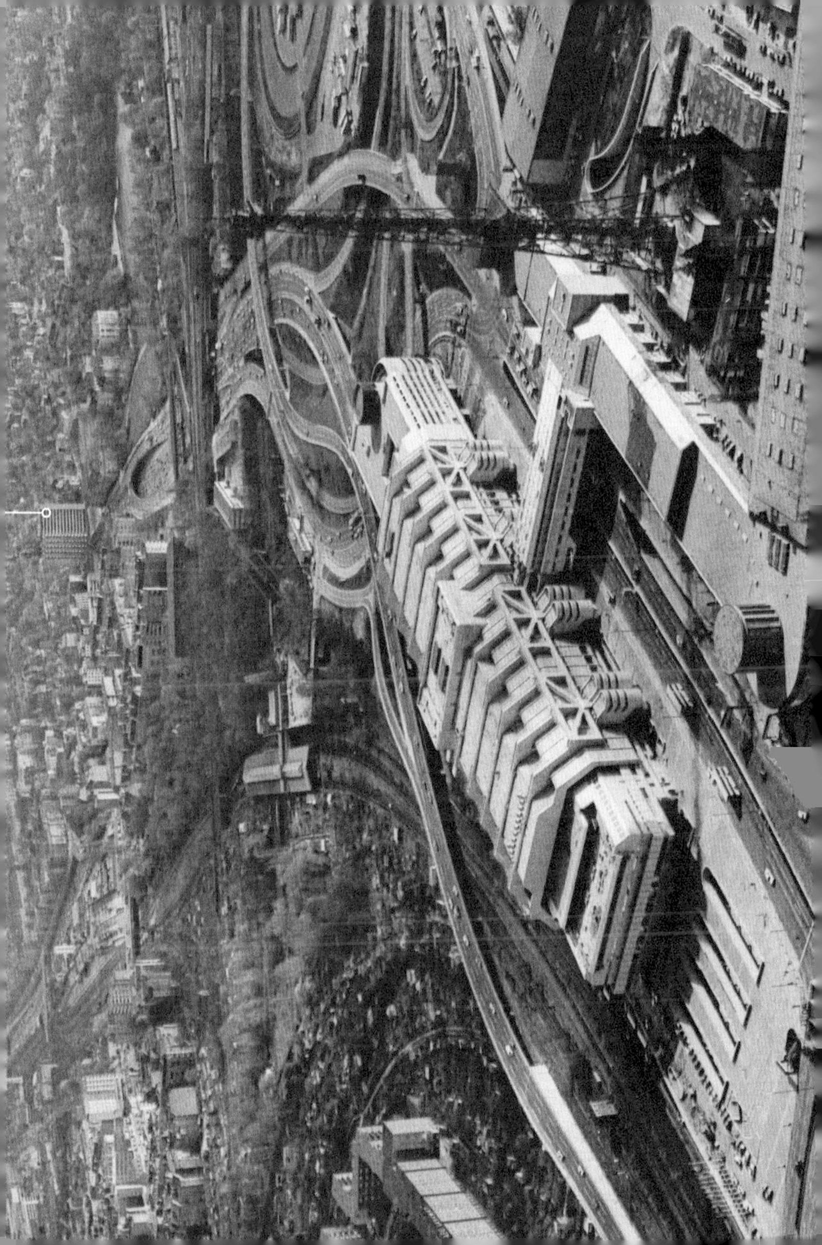

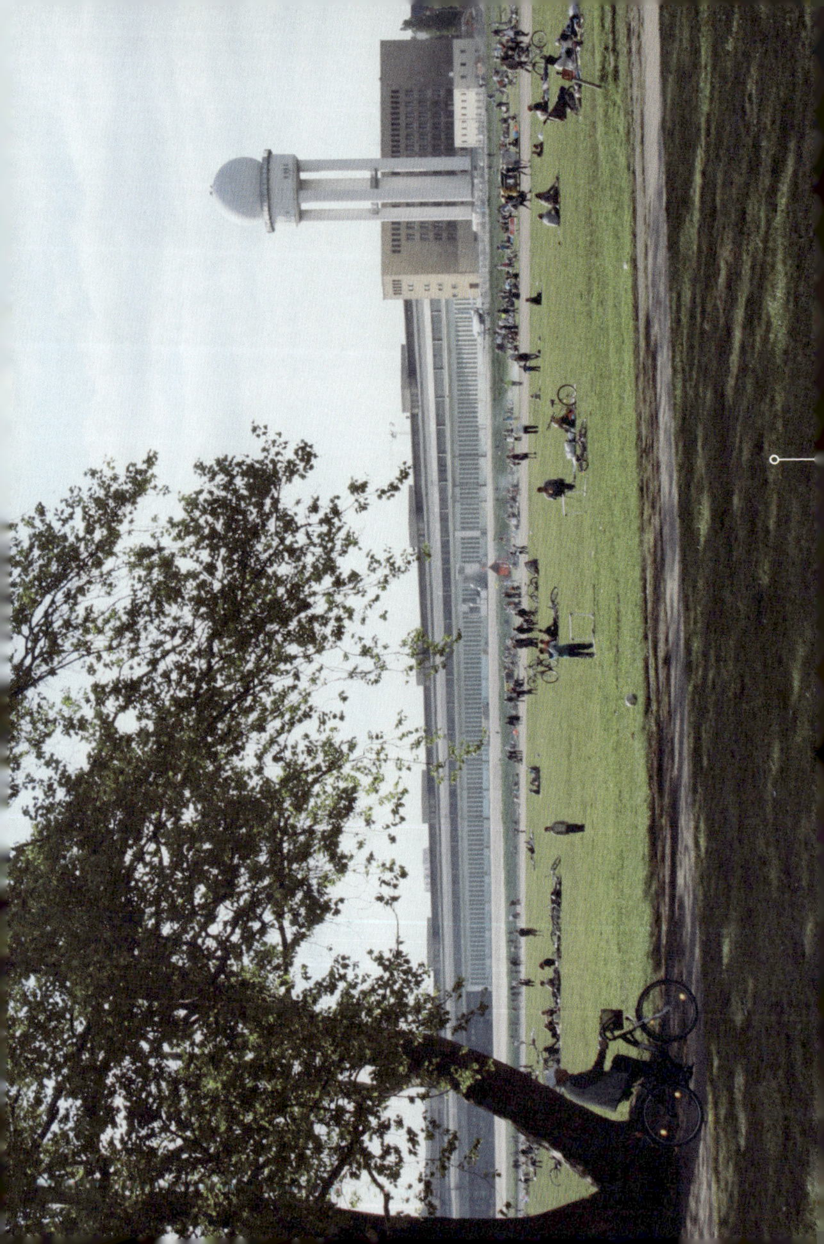

Right behind is a colony of garden allotments where the city's inhabitants find their respite from high-density living. This mixture of futurism and architectural no man's land really represents the more grotesque side of Berlin."

S *Messe Süd or Messe Nord*

ALSO ... For those who are after a more offbeat experience, I'd recommend **Old Texas Town**, a Wild West-style town that was built in an industrial estate in Spandau in the 1950s. It is fascinating that this sheltered compound – complete with a cemetery, watchtowers and saloons – existed inside what was effectively another giant sheltered compound: West Berlin. Old Texas Town was – and continues to be – a place where reality is left at the door and ordinary people can become Sheriff for the evening.

old-texas-town.de

3 **"While my first two recommendations relate to 1950s and 1970s utopias, Flughafen Tempelhof combines the monumental architecture that was popular with the Nazi regime with the contemporary culture of participatory urbanism.**

The former airfield, now referred to as Tempelhofer Freiheit (Tempelhof Freedom) is earmarked to become a landscaped park, though its current state is incredibly popular with the public. In some spots, 'pioneer users' have created vegetable patches and hospitality ventures and offer other experiences. Tempelhofer Freiheit is a very exciting space, both to visit and from a scientific viewpoint, as it addresses the issue of what 'public space' means to the community."

tempelhoferfreiheit.de

Various Entrances, best reached from
U S ***Tempelhof, Hermannstraße or***
U ***Boddinstraße, Platz der Luftbrücke***

Previous page ICC, captured sometime between 1979 and 1980
Photo Messe Berlin

This page Tempelhofer Freiheit
Photo Tempelhof Projekt GmbH

WELCOME TO UTOPIA

An observation of the city's wild and varied history as a laboratory of living.

The history of Berlin's domestic architecture reveals a city perpetually in search of perfect living conditions, though this was rarely motivated by the goal of achieving maximum personal comfort. Enormous, master-planned building programs and grassroots movements all shared the goal of creating living environments that were socially, politically, economically or just physically superior to the status quo. The places and spaces in this excursion serve to illustrate myriad stories of social utopias gone right and wrong, architectural standards revisited and citizen action reinvented.

High density living – The tenements ('rental barracks')

You don't have to go far to encounter the first specimen on this journey. It seems Berlin is endlessly lined with its characteristic six-storey residential buildings. Today, these lofty apartments couldn't be more popular, but this wasn't always the case. Planner James Hobrecht, who developed the first generalised building strategy for the city in 1862, conceived the distinctive three-tiered structure – consisting of a *Vorderhaus* (front house), *Seitenflügel* (side wing) and *Hinterhaus* (back house) – to accommodate as many people as possible. In order to relax the dramatic housing shortage as the population tripled around the start of the 20th century, dwellings of this type were erected quickly and efficiently across town, with more generously spaced examples in the wealthier Western suburbs and smaller, more cramped versions in working class neighbourhoods where buildings were usually extremely overpopulated and became incubators of disease.

Below Tenements near Prenzlauer Berg's Kopenhagener Str. *Photo* from the series 'Leere Stadt' ('Plain City'), more at bildstelle.net © Frank Schirrmeister

Tip... The **Hackesche Höfe** is Europe's largest ensemble of connected buildings and courtyards. Although sometimes uncomfortably busy with tourists, it is still an impressive example of the building type that is characteristic of this city.

Rosenthaler Str. 40-41, Mitte
hackesche-hoefe.com

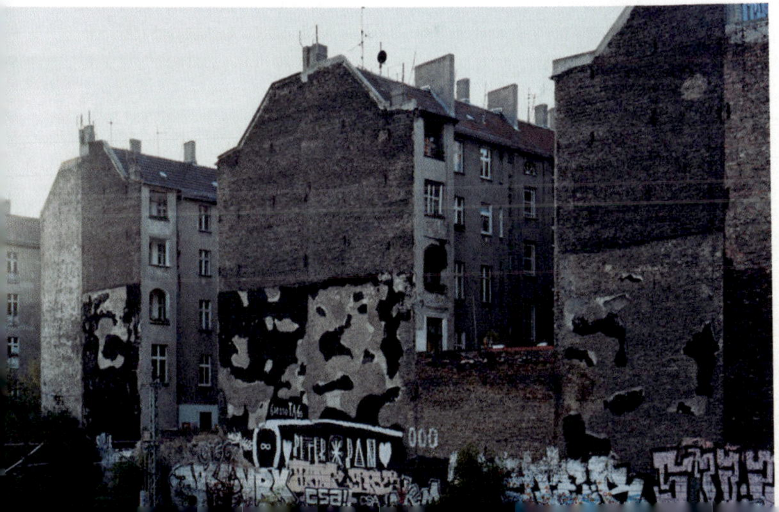

Quality for Everyone – The Housing Estates of Classical Modernism

At the start of the 20th century, tuberculosis was rampant in the poorly aired, unhygienic and overcrowded rental barracks. In the 1920s, an unprecedented alliance formed between the artistic avant-garde and politicians, merging the architectural vanguard of classical modernism with ideas of social utopia to provide members of the working class with a 'healthy home'. One of the earliest, largest and best-regarded examples is the Hufeisensiedlung (horse-shoe estate) in Britz, the south of Neukölln. Intended to house 5,000 people, it was designed by architect Bruno Taut. In 2008, this estate and five others in the city became UNESCO Cultural Heritage sites. Built between 1913 and 1934, all of them exemplify both the architectural as well as the socio-cultural beliefs of the time: rational, clean lines and simple yet modern apartments with access to air, light and sun.

Tip ... True aficionados will want to see all of the six estates, which also include **Gartenstadt Falkenberg**, Treptow (1913), **Schillerpark-siedlung**, Wedding (1924–30), **Wohnstadt Carl Legien**, Prenzlauer Berg (1928–30), **Weisse Stadt**, Reinickendorf (1929–31) and **Groß-siedlung Siemensstadt**, Charlottenburg/Spandau (1929–31) (*see page 174*).

For more information, visit stadtentwicklung.berlin.de

U ***Blaschkoallee*** | *Info station, Fritz-Reuter-Allee 44, Britz | Fri 13–17, Sun 15–19 | hufeisensiedlung-berlin.de*

Below View of Bruno Taut's 'horse-shoe estate' *Photo* © Berlin Partner/FTB-Werbefotografie

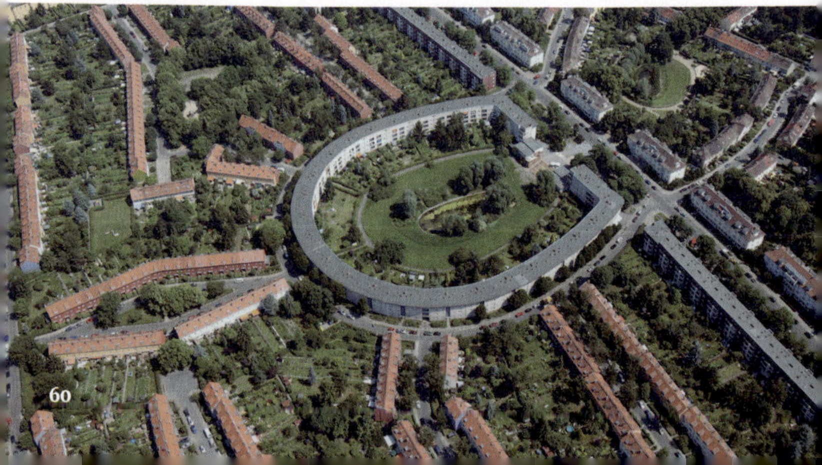

The Workers' Palaces – Karl-Marx-Allee

Spanning 2.3km from Alexanderplatz to Frankfurter Tor, the majority of East Germany's answer to the Champs-Elysées is lined with the so-called 'workers' palaces', nine-storey neoclassical apartment buildings conceived to show the world that even the ordinary citizens of communist East Germany could live at the country's first address. When construction on what was originally named Stalinallee began in 1949, an army of 40,000 volunteers participated in the National Reconstruction Program. Those who accumulated enough half-shifts on the site after their day jobs entered a raffle to win a lease to one of the apartments, the amenities of which included the luxury of central heating, telephones, running water and a balcony view of the parades held on national holidays. The neoclassical 'gingerbread' style of Karl-Marx-Allee's northern end is reminiscent of the Soviet palaces of the time. The southern part of Karl-Marx-Allee – closer to Alexanderplatz – was completed in the 1970s. By then, the GDR ideal had shifted towards the International Style of modernism, appropriated for the socialist context, with modular buildings that were replicated all over East Germany.

U *Alexanderplatz, Schillingstraße, Strausberger Platz, Weberwiese or Frankfurter Tor*

SOCIALIST SHOPPING

— *Karl-Marx-Allee was designed to be East Berlin's leading location not only in terms of living standards but also as a shopping and entertainment destination. Of the initial stores, only the lighting store* ***Wolle*** *remains open, though the once-grand bookstore* ***Karl Marx Buchhandlung*** *also remains intact.*

Tip ...

– Be sure to patronise some of the iconic entertainment venues nearby. Closer to Alexanderplatz, the **Kino International** cinema is one of the city's best movie theatres, while the former cosmetics **Salon Babette** is now a bar and venue for art exhibitions (*see page 111*).

– Once a beloved Sunday afternoon destination, **Café Sibylle** now contains an information centre on the history of the boulevard.

Karl-Marx-Allee 72, Mon to Fri, 10–20, Sat & Sun 12–20

– While pillars strewn along the boulevard provide information, you can go all out with a 2.5 hour audio tour, which can be borrowed at Café Sibylle for a modest fee.

For more information, visit stadt-im-ohr.de

Modernist Utopia – The Hansaviertel

As tensions between East and West intensified during the 1950s, each side took every available opportunity to display the superiority of their ideologies, both in terms of their political power and the benefits afforded to their citizens. While Stalinallee was erected at mind-boggling speed, the West hatched its own plan to construct a concrete (in every sense of the word) symbol of its ideological superiority. As part of the 1957 International Building Exhibition, an entire area in Tiergarten, the Hansaviertel, was cleared of rubble and existing buildings to construct the 'City of Tomorrow', planned by an international architectural avant-garde of 53 architects including Alvar Aalto, Oskar Niemeyer, Arne Jacobsen and Le Corbusier. The resulting 35 buildings embody the ideals of 1950s living: clean, modern, hygienic and with access to nature.

U *Hansaplatz* S *Bellevue or Tiergarten*

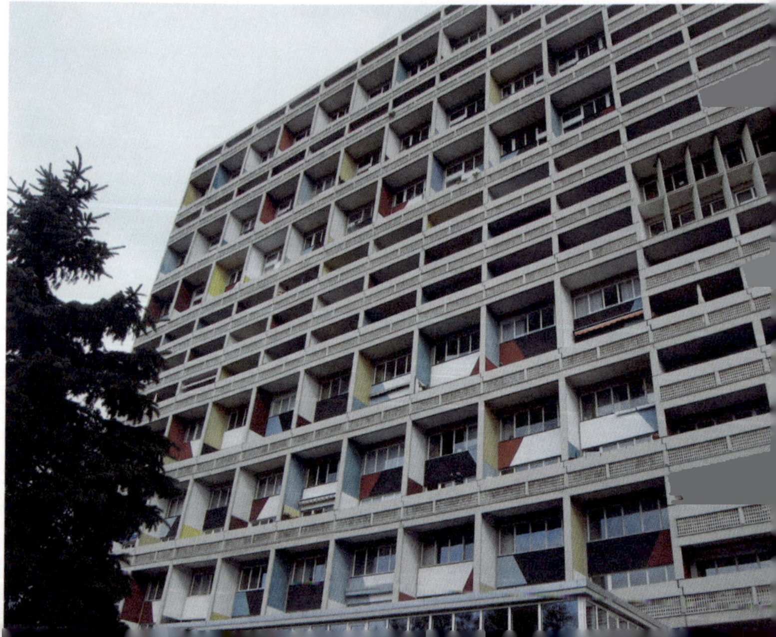

Social Housing of the 1960s and 1970s

Many find it difficult to positively describe the social housing that was built in the 1960s and 1970s. Suffering from an acute housing shortage, West Berlin undertook enormous building projects, many of them reflecting the era's fascination with mobility and technology. The much-disputed Wohnpark Wilmersdorf, colloquially referred to as 'Schlange' (snake) because of its location in Schlangenbader Str., stretches 600m across a four-lane highway. With over 1,000 apartments, it is one of the largest housing complexes in Europe. Other projects from this era form bridges across the city streets, including the so-called 'Sozialpalast' (social palace) in Schöneberg and a large apartment complex near Kottbusser Tor. In the early 1980s another International Building Exhibition took place, conducted in the spirit of finding new, inclusive ways of reconstructing the city and creating living space that was better integrated into the city's urban fabric.

Left Conceived as part of the 1957 building expo, Le Corbusier's 'L'Unité d'habitation', the second rendition of his 'machine for living', was too large for the Hansaviertel site and thus was built near Charlottenburg's Olympiastadion.
Photo Gesa Schenk

Squats

Though Germany's first official squat – a building occupied against the will of its legal owners – was not in Berlin, the capital city became synonymous with this approach to living in the 1970s and 1980s. The phenomenon emerged as the result of a number of factors. The post-war housing shortage in West Berlin was counteracted by demolishing the buildings of entire streets to make room for new developments, a slow process that saw hundreds of buildings left unoccupied, often for years. At the same time, a young, left-oriented crowd was uneasy with the city government's political line and eager to experiment with new forms of living. Although many squats were subsequently legalised, their peak period was accompanied by sometimes violent clashes between police and squatters. In the eastern part of Berlin, many squats were established during the turbulent post-Wall years, especially around Friedrichshain. Some live on in the neighbourhood, although their numbers are dwindling due to recent evictions following years of protests. The squatter movement created an awareness of the political nature of dwelling, made a statement against real estate speculation and campaigned for a more inclusive approach to the politics of housing. It may be these ideologies that helped establish Berliners' eagerness to counter the status quo and come up with new approaches to community-oriented building.

Sweet Occupation ... In 1980, Kreuzberg's **Schokofabrik** (chocolate factory) was a decrepit factory building destined for demolition, until a group of feminists formed an initiative to restore it as a community centre and living space for women. Several decades and thousands of working hours and bureaucratic hurdles later, the women took ownership of the building, which is now a residence as well as a site for cultural and community events and also houses a kindergarten and popular Turkish baths for women.

Mariannenstr. 6, Kreuzberg
schokofabrik.de

Mitte Monopoly ... The similarly named, but not to be confused **Schokoladen** in Mitte shares an equally turbulent history and was only recently put out of jeopardy. Taken over shortly after the fall of the Wall, the residential building and its downstairs cultural and concert venue is a lone survivor. After much campaigning, its residents' initiative took ownership in 2012, ensuring that its colourful existence can continue indefinitely.

Ackerstr. 169, Mitte
schokoladen-mitte.de

Baugruppen

A city dominated by high density living arrangements, undermined by a culture of civic action and populated with adventurous architects, is a natural hotbed for new approaches to communal living and building. Although the model of the *Baugruppe* (building group) was initially conceived in southern Germany, Berlin is its spiritual home. The concept is based on a simple mix of pragmatism and idealism: to avoid commercial real estate firms, groups of prospective apartment owners purchase land or existing buildings to realise their personal concepts of communal living. This approach, though often tedious and lengthy, has spawned hundreds of architecturally and socially outstanding results in which families share communal space and model new forms of inter-generational and inter-cultural domestic life, at times integrating disadvantaged members of society or making portions of their property available for cultural events.

Below An exceptionally large and architecturally significant project, which won a 2011 German Architecture Prize, is situated on Prenzlauer Berg's Zelterstr. It was initiated by no less than 72 individual parties and designed by Zanderroth Architekten.
Photo Simon Menges

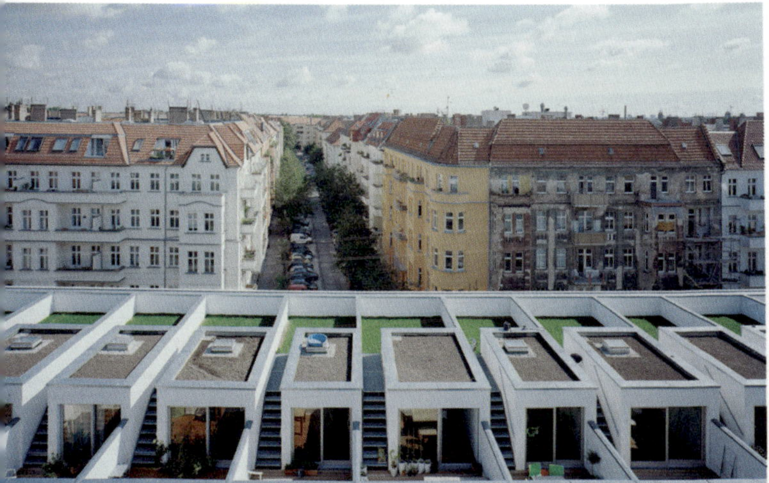

MY CITY WITH

WILKO HOFFMANN
& JESKO JOHNSSON-ZAHN

Architects with the studio of Jürgen Mayer H.

The Layered City

These days, most foreign media reports on Berlin architecture usually include a reference to Jürgen Mayer H. within the first paragraph. The architect has been running his studio from a former apartment in Charlottenburg since arriving from New York in 1996, though Berlin has only recently been graced with one of his designs, a residential building in Mitte. We've gone to those who ensure that Mayer H.'s daring structures are actually built – his long-time staff, architects Wilko Hoffmann and Jesko Johnsson-Zahn. The question: which structures or places best communicate what Berlin is all about?

jmayerh.de

1 **"For many, the so-called Bierpinsel gracing a busy Steglitz intersection is simply an example of 1970s building 'sin'. Designed in the late 1960s and opened in 1976 as the first project of architects Ralf Schüler and Ursulina Schüler-Witte, who later also built the ICC (*see page 54*), the futuristic space-age structure was a central entertainment venue for West Berliners during the Wall years, consisting of a restaurant, a bar and a nightclub.**

For us, this 46m tower holds special significance. It is a reminder of a time when architects and society at large embraced the future with all kinds of utopian ideas and were euphoric about technology and mobility. Even though this thinking no longer dominates public discourse, our office likes to continue generating ideas and applying a little bit of utopian thinking. What if the future were a happy place? For us, the Bierpinsel is a reminder of a time when this seemed possible."

U ***Schlosstraße | Schlossstr. 17, Steglitz***

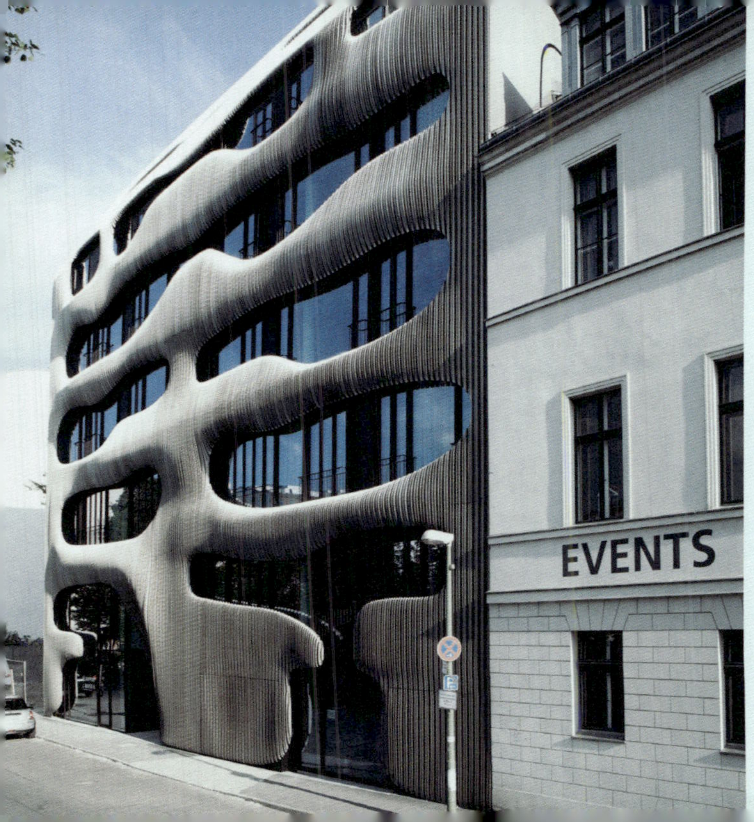

2 **"One aspect that characterises this city is the tension between public and private interests and the discussion of ownership this creates. Many former industrial estates – including some very prominent ones near the river Spree – have been sold to private investors to be left in a state of decay until they are either demolished or converted into corporate or residential buildings.**

In the meantime, some of these areas are used and repurposed by residents. You can witness this at the Eisfabrik, a former ice factory on the banks of the river that has been slowly dilapidating since 1995. It seems to have been subject to a very particular process for years: skateboarders, urban explorers and other curious folk randomly use it until it gets fenced off. This keeps people out until the next curious, brave or ignorant person kicks down the fence and the cycle starts again. Berlin is a city characterised both by no man's land and a culture of civic action."

3 **“Berlin oozes history from every corner. However, as more and more memorial sites are renovated, restored, repurposed or closed, very few sites still afford a raw experience, one that allows built edifices to tell the tumultuous story of this city. However, the only remaining WWII flak tower – initially there were three – at Volkspark Humboldthain in Wedding is one of those rare places.**

It is accessible through the tours of an organisation called Berliner Unterwelten (Berlin Underworlds), who have made it their mission to explore and show the many underground spaces – including a fully equipped surgical bunker and abandoned underground train stations. Berliner Unterwelten’s head office is also located in a former underground bunker.”

U ***Gesundbrunnen | Brunnenstr. 105, Wedding | berliner-unterwelten.de***

ALSO … Yet another place where history is both preserved and well-presented is the under-funded **Stasi Museum**, far off the beaten track in its original, intimidating compound in Lichtenberg.

Haus 22, Ruschestr. 103, Lichtenberg stasimuseum.de

AND MORE … Wedding is worth a visit for its mixed-use developments that include both artists’ studios, small businesses and generous living spaces. Cases in point are **Stattbad Wedding** and the **ExRotaprint** factory (*see page 74*).

Previous page Jürgen Mayer H.’s JOH3 residential building in Mitte
Photo Ludger Paffrath

Below Air lock at Berliner Unterwelten Museum, Berliner Unterwelten e.V.
Photo Frieder Salm

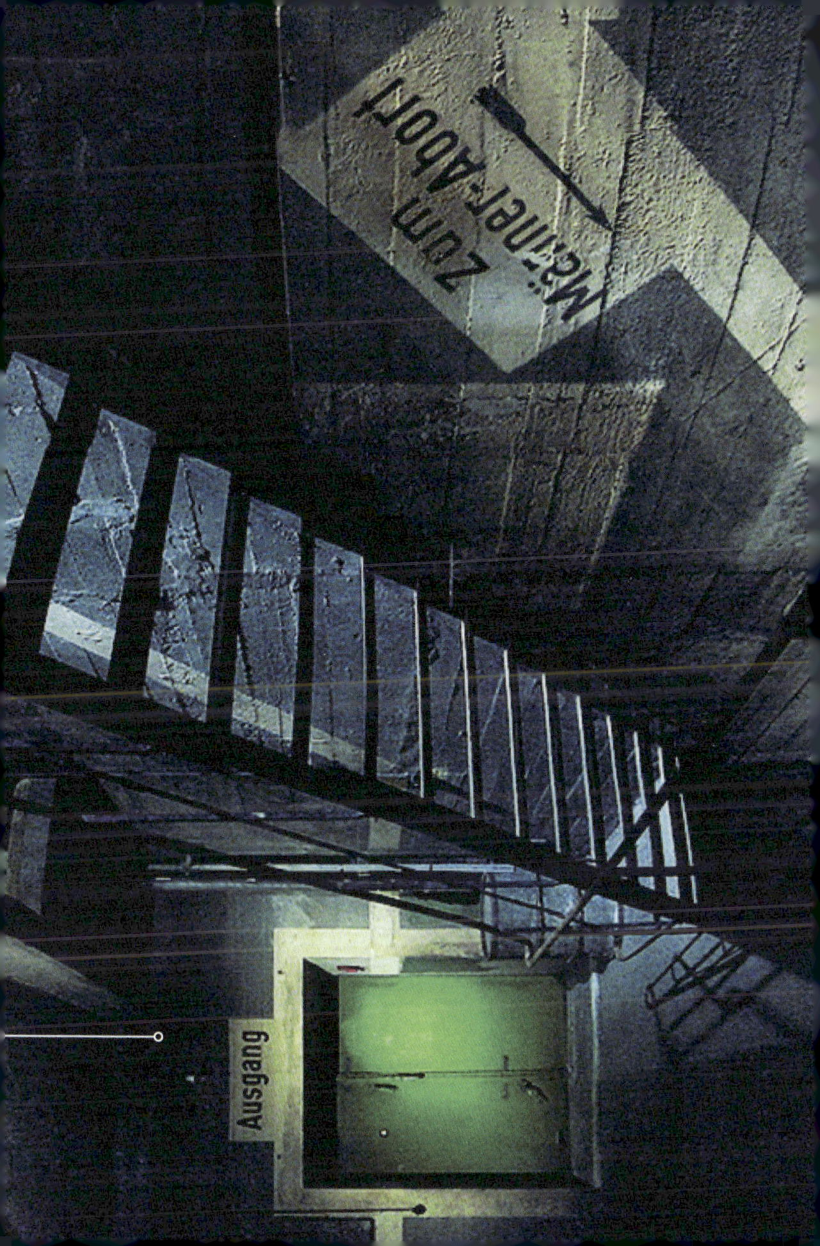
Zum
Männer-Abort
Ausgang

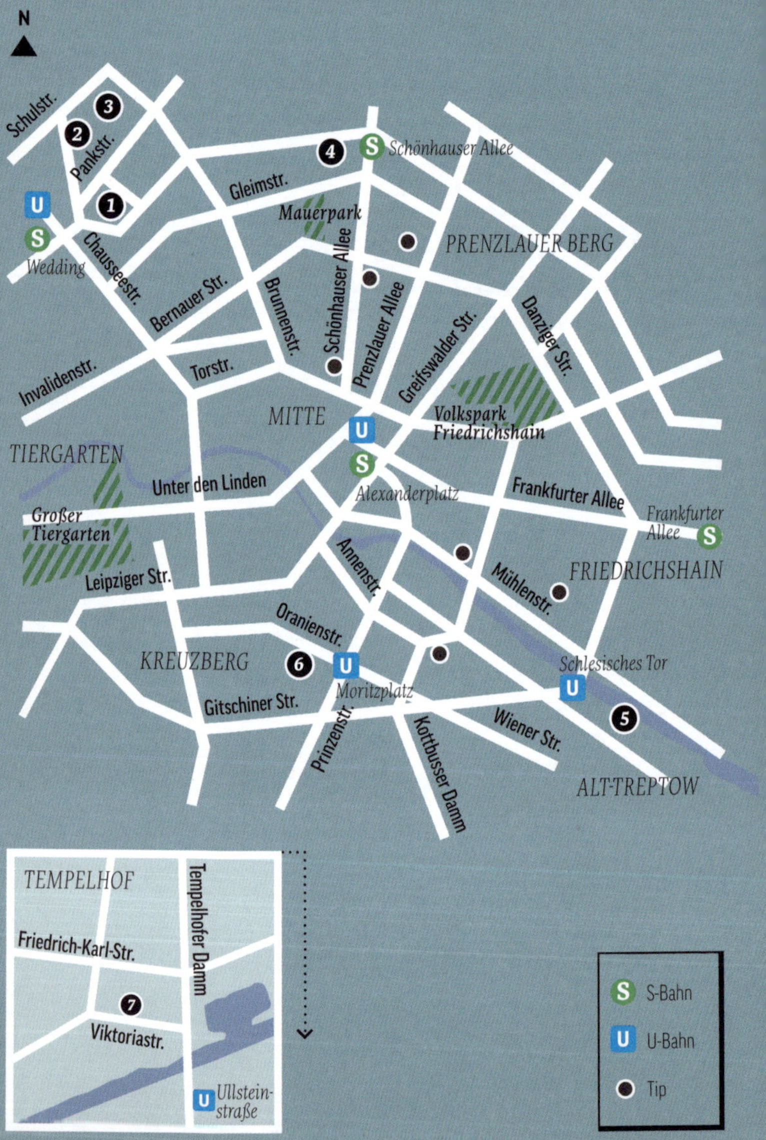
N
Schulstr.
Pankstr.
Wedding
Chausseestr.
Gleimstr.
Schönhauser Allee
Mauerpark
PRENZLAUER BERG
Bernauer Str.
Brunnenstr.
Schönhauser Allee
Prenzlauer Allee
Greifswalder Str.
Danziger Str.
Invalidenstr.
Torstr.
MITTE
Volkspark
Friedrichshain
TIERGARTEN
Unter den Linden
Alexanderplatz
Frankfurter Allee
Frankfurter Allee
Großer Tiergarten
Annenstr.
Mühlenstr.
FRIEDRICHSHAIN
Leipziger Str.
Oranienstr.
KREUZBERG
Schlesisches Tor
Moritzplatz
Gitschiner Str.
Prinzenstr.
Kottbusser Damm
Wiener Str.
ALT-TREPTOW
TEMPELHOF
Tempelhofer Damm
Friedrich-Karl-Str.
Viktoriastr.
Ullstein-straße
S-Bahn
U-Bahn
Tip

RE:PURPOSE

The creative refashioning of old buildings is old news. What major city doesn't boast a derelict warehouse converted to luxury lofts? But Berlin is different. Its myriad former industrial buildings provide the frequently cited, ceaselessly praised and seemingly inexhaustible 'vacant spaces' which form the foundation for Berlin's thriving cultural community.

Why is a converted industrial structure in Berlin different from one in, say, London? The straightforward answer: there's power in numbers. The sheer abundance of abandoned factories and warehouses, dating from a time when the German capital was an industrial boomtown, coupled with a bleak economy, meant that until recently there was limited demand for high-end accommodation. Sure, the city also has its share of landmarks that have been primped into exclusive refuges for the wealthy, but many other buildings were taken on an alternative path to salvation. Thanks to the city's strong traditions of civic activism, many buildings have been rescued and renovated, often with small budgets or by the residents' own hands, to be revived as artistic havens or homes for socially minded collectives.

1

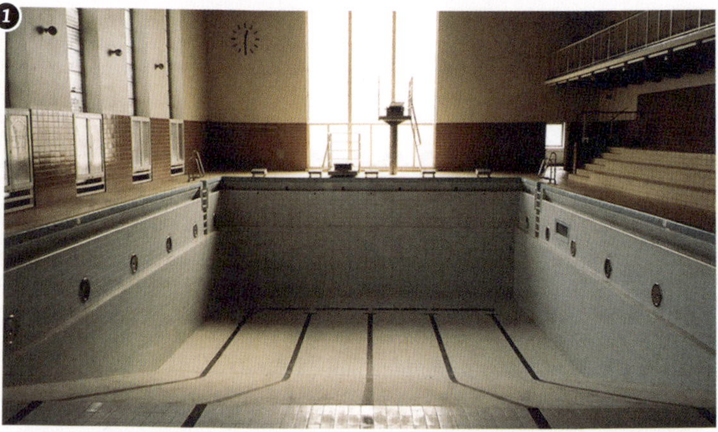

Above The drained swimming pool of Stattbad Wedding is an atmospheric space for events. *Photo* Maxime Ballesteros / STATTBAD

5

Below In winter, the floating Badeschiff pool at Arena transforms into a sauna enclosed in PVC-membrane cocoons. *Photo* Marcel Mettelsiefen

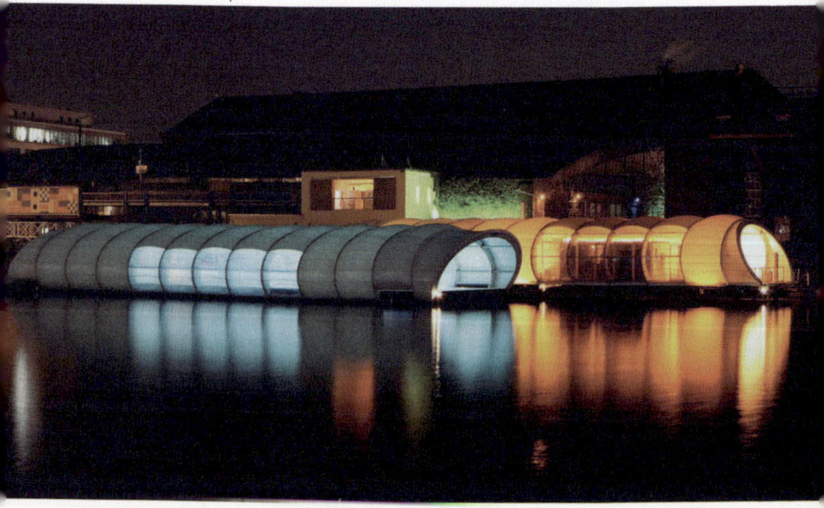

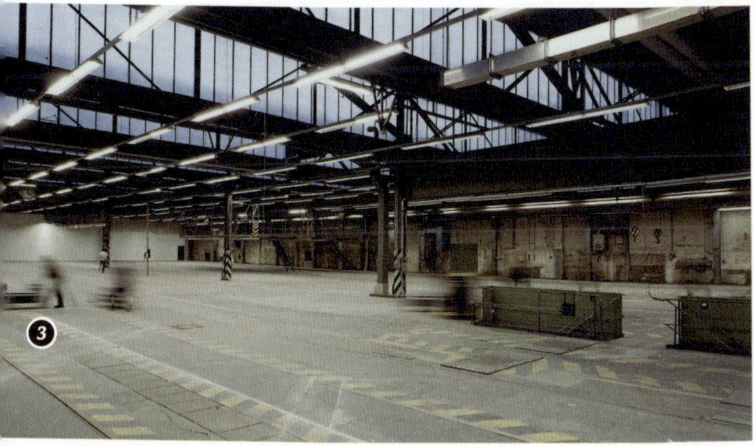

Above UferHallen's open spaces provide flexibility and freedom, ideal in an age when art forms are in flux. *Photo* UferHallen AG

Below Humboldt Umspannwerk
Photo Courtesy Tippin Corporation

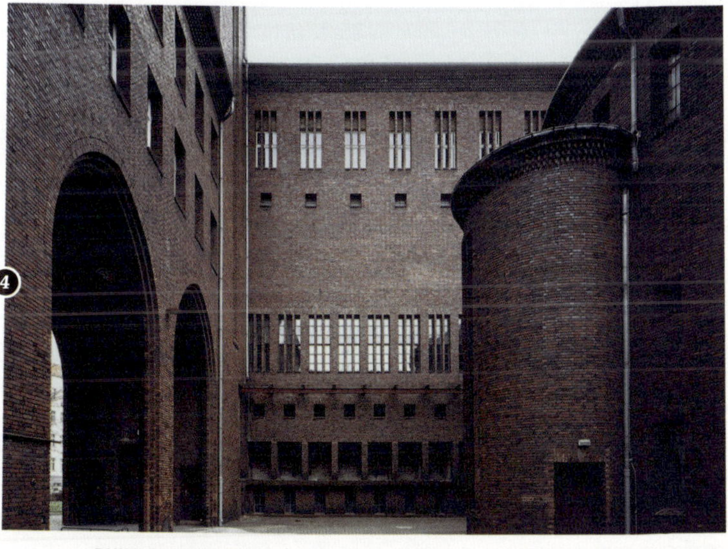

❶ **Stattbad Wedding** *U Wedding S Humboldthain | Gerichtstr. 65, Wedding | stattbad.net*

While it is by no means exhaustive, this rambling tour through the fringe of Berlin's inner city (best accomplished on a bicycle) is as much a showcase of ideas as it is of architecture. It's perhaps unsurprising that a tour of the most noteworthy building revivals starts with three venues in rough-edged Wedding where one, Stattbad Wedding, has become a vibrant focal point for the district's burgeoning art scene. Opened in 1907, the Stadtbad (city bath) Wedding provided rentable tubs and showers to counter the lack of bathrooms in the city's early-20th century tenements. Designed by Ludwig Hoffmann, an architectural star in his time, it was an example of elaborate Prussian architecture, now invisible from the outside due to a modernisation in the 1950s. The Stadtbad closed in 1999, but having been sold to a culture-loving investor, it reopened in 2009 as a free-form cultural center renamed as Stattbad (instead-bath) Wedding. Though renovations were minimal, the drained swimming pool is a great place for lectures, concerts and film screenings, and the tiled showers and change rooms are perfect for hanging art.

Tip ... While the former administrative offices are rented out to artists on a permanent basis, there's a laptop-friendly cafeteria here too.

❷ **ExRotaprint** *U Nauener Platz | Gottschedstr. 4, Wedding | exrotaprint.de*

An artists' collective founded this cooperative community center in Wedding with two goals. The first: subvert the pattern of speculative land-buying in their working-class neighbourhood. Second: preserve the architectural integrity of the campus, a former printing plant. With the help of the non-profit Trias Foundation, they bought the site in 2007.

Industrial spaces were converted to studios, workshops, a cafeteria and classrooms for anything from German language courses to Indonesian cooking. The buildings are a pastiche of Victorian brick blocks and a 1950s addition. The latter was designed by architect Klaus Kirsten in a sleek Bauhaus style. His five-story concrete entry tower was never completed and stands today as the defining symbol of ExRotaprint, a rough, proto-Brutalist gun turret warning land speculators to keep their distance.

Tip ... To experience the flair of this unusual place, visit the canteen, open Mon to Fri 8–16.

❸ UferHallen

U *Pankstraße or* S *Humboldthain*
Uferstr. 8-11, Mitte/Wedding | kunst-aktien.de

Berlin was a booming city on the move when this former horse stable was rebuilt in 1926 to house the city's new fleet of electric street cars. Architect Jean Krämer's brick façade is all about motion, with zippy horizontal bands pointing to a dynamic future. The trams are long gone, but the vast halls are alive again with the movement of dancers, musicians and artists. Reborn as UferHallen in 2007, the 37,000sqm complex includes rehearsal halls, exhibition spaces and sound studios. Along with Uferstudios across the street, it's a hothouse for synergy and dialogue and the lively canteen plays host to a crowd of German and international art stars.

❹ Humboldt Umspannwerk

U *Schönhauser Allee | Kopenhagener Str. 57, Prenzlauer Berg | humboldtberlin.com*

While Berlin's Expressionist artists were pushing the boundaries of paint, in the 1920s architect Hans Heinrich Müller was doing equally daring things with brick. The fact that his Berlin projects were lowly industrial buildings makes their beauty even more astonishing. With names like the Cathedral of Electricity, Müller lent a sense of grandiosity to his constructions. This former electrical transformer plant in Prenzlauer Berg is one of Müller's most elegant projects, inspired by early Gothic monasteries but still thoroughly modern. Neglected during the GDR years, it was renovated in the 1990s to house the Berlin branch of the (sadly departed) Vitra Design Museum. The basilica-like main hall is now used for official dinners and receptions, while former workshops play host to Internet-based firms such as clothing retailer Zalando. The oval-shaped tower in the courtyard houses the original Flash Gordon-style control room.

Tip ... As you make your way from here towards the river, a few more unusual conversions cross your path: the **'Mach Mit!' Children's Museum** in a converted church (Senefelderstr. 5), the enormous **Kulturbrauerei**, a former brewery that is now the cultural heart of Prenzlauer Berg (Schönhauser Allee 36) and of course the **Pfefferberg** cultural complex further down the road (*see Aedes, page 78*).

If you cross the river at Schillingbrücke, stop to inspect the much-loved **Radialsystem V**, a multipurpose performance and art space in a former pumping station that was once a central part of the city's sewage system (Holzmarktstr. 33, Mitte).

5 Arena/Badeschiff U *Schlesisches Tor*

Eichenstr. 4, Alt-Treptow | arena-berlin.de

Ever since the early 1990s, this sprawling complex on the Spree has been a symbol of Berlin's DIY-inspired party scene. Built in 1927 to house Berlin's fleet of public buses, its heart is a 7,000sqm shed whose giant roof trusses make it one of the largest open-span interiors in Europe. Caught in no man's land during the Wall years, the complex was left to decay. In 1995, it was reinvented as Arena, an all-purpose entertainment venue. The shed plays host to a weekly dance club, while nearby former workshops house a theatre, artist studios and flea market. A notable addition to the compound is a river barge converted into a floating swimming pool, the *Badeschiff* (bathing boat).

Tip... The city's most notorious club, **Berghain** (Am Wriezener Bahnhof), also occupies a former industrial building, a disused energy plant on the Friedrichshain side of the river, though its name is a composite of 'Kreuzberg' and 'Friedrichshain'.

❻ AquaCarré U *Moritzplatz | Lobeckstr. 35, Kreuzberg | aqua-carre-berlin.de*

In this once bustling industrial neighbourhood, the only building to survive WWII was Aqua-Butzke, a late 19th century factory for bathroom fixtures. When the company moved its operations to Brandenburg in the mid-1990s, the complex was sold to an investor who was forced to abandon initial plans for luxury loft conversion – apparently, the location was undesirable – so the new owners began renting spaces to artists. With 80 studios and a number of hospitality ventures, the project provides both a technical and social infrastructure. There's power in numbers, and the synergistic energy is spreading. In 2009, the co-working space Betahaus (*see page 251*) opened around the corner, followed by creative retail haven Planet Modulor (*see page 205*) in 2011. In the name of the game of urban renewal, AquaCarré helped reinvent the neighbourhood as a nuts-and-bolts art world backstage to Mitte's slick theatrics.

Tip... Other Kreuzberg destinations in the same vein include the imposing former hospital building on Mariannenplatz, **Künstlerhaus Bethanien**, a veritable artistic haven with artist residencies, printing and sculpture workshops and **3Schwestern**, a great garden restaurant (Mariannenplatz 2).

❼ The UFA Fabrik U *Ullsteinstraße Viktoriastr. 13, Tempelhof | ufafabrik.de*

If you are keen to explore the area of Tempelhof, head down to one of the earliest models of creative re-purposing, which has served as an inspiration to many. In 1979, a band of intrepid leftists occupied the vacant sound studios which formerly housed Berlin's UFA film company (Metropolis, The Blue Angel, etc.) and "peacefully reactivated" them as a communal village and arts center. Today, forty residents call UFA home. The grounds include theatres, a café and even a school with its own small farm.

ARCHITECTURAL ADVENTURES

No publication of this scope could accurately reflect the production, let alone the discussion and debate, surrounding contemporary architecture in this city. Nonetheless, Berlin is home to a number of galleries, institutions and publications dedicated exclusively to the study of contemporary architecture and related fields.

Aedes Architecture Forum and Aedes Network Campus (ANCB)

Founded in 1980 as the first privately run architecture gallery in Europe, Aedes has become a veritable institution for architecture exhibition and debate. Aedes maintains a lively international network, negotiating new positions and tendencies in urban design and spatial perception through exhibitions, installations and accompanying programs. Located in the atmospheric Pfefferberg complex, Aedes spawned a new venture in 2009: a cultural and metropolitan laboratory at the intersection of architecture, design, society and technology. ANCB plays host to groups of students and academics from around the globe.
U *Senefelder Platz* | **Christinenstr. 18-19, Prenzlauer Berg**
aedes-arc.de | ancb.de

Architektur Galerie Berlin

Conceived as a space for the examination of architecture in the context of a gallery, Architektur Galerie Berlin was founded in 1999 by architect Ulrich Müller. Its conceptual exhibitions focus on experimentation in architecture, placing much emphasis on discourse, exchange and up-and-coming talent. The gallery's monthly newsletter lists all current and forthcoming architecture exhibitions in the city.
U *Weberwiese* | **Karl-Marx-Allee 96, Mitte | Tue to Fri 14–19, Sat 12–16**
architekturgalerieberlin.de

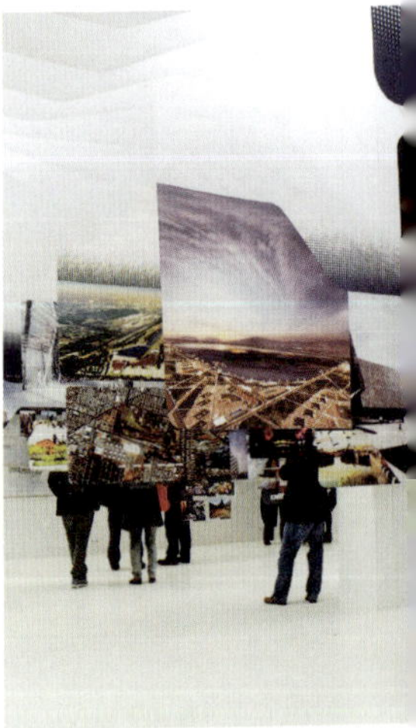

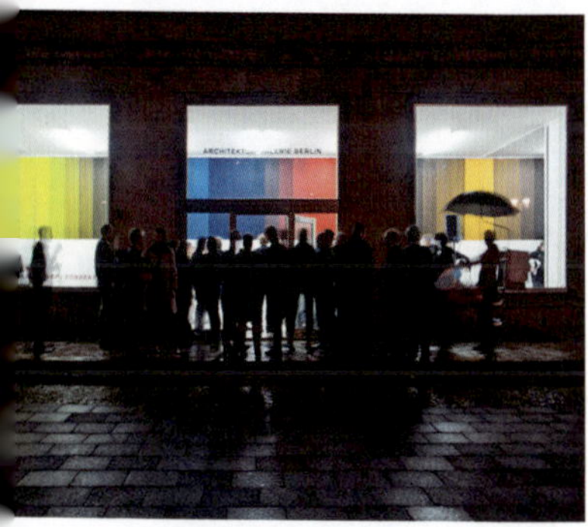

Above Opening of the Behles Jochimsen exhibition
Photo Architektur Galerie Berlin

Deutsches Architektur Zentrum (DAZ)

An initiative of the German Association of Architects (Bund Deutscher Architekten), this space in a former warehouse by the river is a laboratory for ideas, exchange, debate and exhibition. Architects, planners, artists and all others with interest are invited to ponder the essential issues that drive architecture through a curated program of workshops, film nights, book presentations and exhibitions. Visions and utopias are explicitly encouraged. Due to its changing program, it's worth checking the website before visiting.
U ***Heinrich-Heine-Straße*** **| 2nd courtyard Köpenicker Str. 48/49, Mitte | daz.de**

Left An exhibition of the work of Mexican architect and urbanist Iñaki Echeverría at Aedes Berlin

Right The exhibition 'Testify' at DAZ
Photo Till Budde

Haus am Waldsee

Although predominantly an exhibition venue for all forms of contemporary art, this quaint location is worth the excursion. One of its five annual exhibitions usually has a major focus on architecture, and the Haus am Waldsee offers self-guided audio tours through the surrounding area, which is rife with residential modernist architecture by greats such as Ludwig Mies van der Rohe and Walter Gropius. The beautiful sculpture garden includes Werner Aisslinger's celebrated Loft Cube, an experiment in mobile living.
U ***Krumme Lanke*** **| Argentinische Allee 30, Zehlendorf | Tues to Sun 11–18 hausamwaldsee.de**

Berlinische Galerie

Located in what used to be a cultural blind spot, the Berlinische Galerie is a much-respected contemporary art space with a dedicated architecture exhibition program and an enormous collection of local architectural artifacts, drawings and photographs about and from Berlin.
U ***Moritzplatz*** **| Alte Jakobstr. 124-128, Kreuzberg | Daily 10–18 (closed Tue) berlinischegalerie.de**

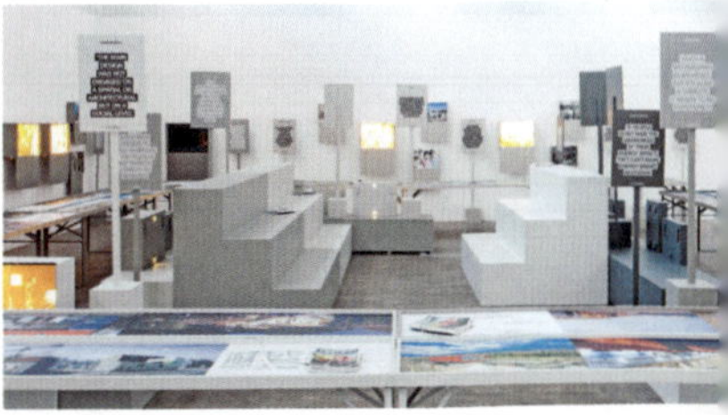

ART

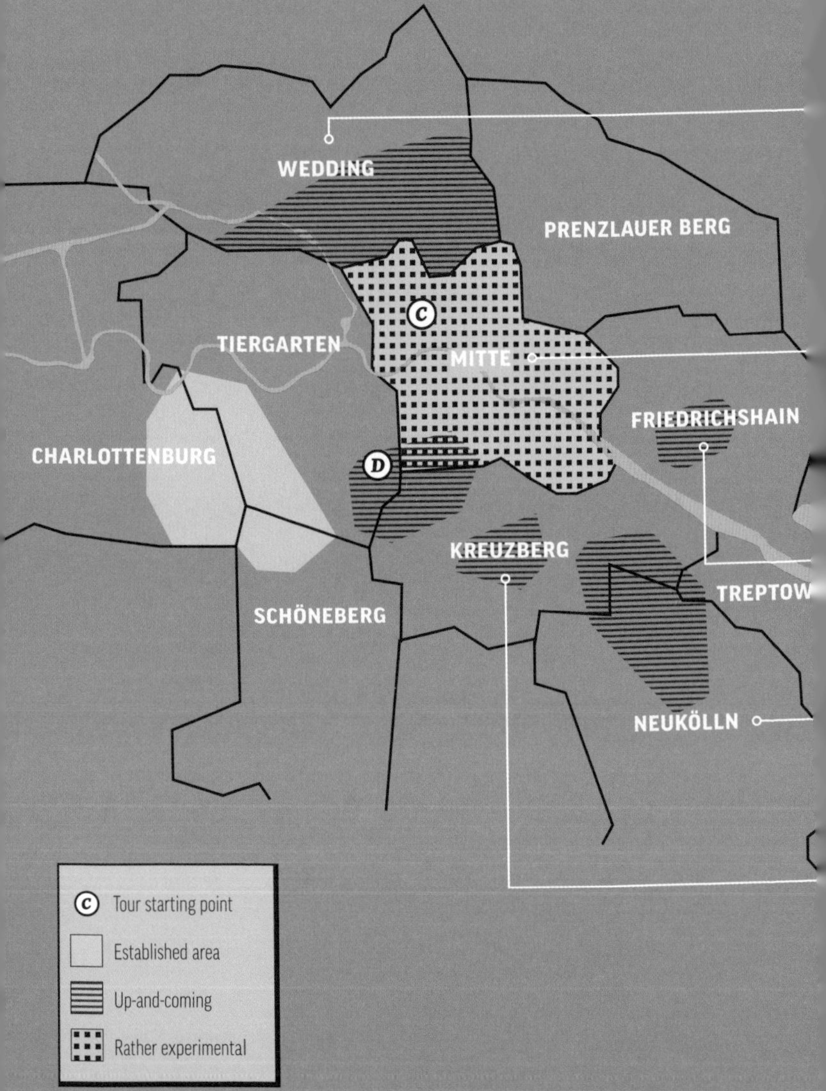
WEDDING
PRENZLAUER BERG
TIERGARTEN
MITTE
FRIEDRICHSHAIN
CHARLOTTENBURG
KREUZBERG
TREPTOW
SCHÖNEBERG
NEUKÖLLN
C
D
Tour starting point
Established area
Up-and-coming
Rather experimental

THE FRONTIERS

While **Wedding is** anything but gentrified, the artistic community is establishing a foothold in this area where over 40 percent of residents are from a foreign background and roughly every fourth is unemployed. Hotspots are few and far between but they are well worth the trip. Meanwhile, **Tiergarten**, near Potsdamer Platz, is where many established Mitte galleries have recently found new homes.

THE HEART

Mitte is undeniably the epicentre of art in Berlin. After two decades as the country's go-to location for art, the avant-garde has moved elsewhere but the raft of commercial galleries and organisations located in the maze of side streets forms a well-established artistic community.

THE LABORATORY

When it comes to art, **Friedrichshain** is an area for creators who like to experiment and don't necessarily put profits at the top of their priority lists.

THE BEEHIVE

Neukölln is a rising art centre. The art world here is transient, with project spaces vanishing before you've finished your vernissage drink, but it's where the Berlin art scene is currently at its liveliest.

THE HOME TURF

Kreuzberg is the place to play, work and live for many artists. The area behind Moritzplatz is currently transforming into a hub of artistic production and presentation.

ADVENTURE CAPITAL

A PORTHOLE INTO THE BERLIN ART COSMOS

The art world gravitates towards Berlin – and it's easy to see why. The city's vibrant, open and engaged creative community has made itself comfortable in just about every possible space, from storefronts to lofts to old factories, forming an art universe that is in constant flux and motion.

Berlin is decidedly the blank slate onto which new ideas project themselves. The cityscape and the various scenes it reflects have been known to incite comparison – the decadence of Belle Epoque Paris with a contemporary twist, New York in the seventies – but in reality, Berlin excels at the act of here and now: constant movement, innovation, reinterpretation and reuse. Artists flock to the city in increasing numbers every year, building bridges with an art world that spans the gamut, from established private galleries to smaller spaces curated by up-and-coming gallerists with an interest in encouraging and developing the next generation of the avant-garde, down to blink-and-they're-gone spaces in off-centre neighbourhoods often run by the artists themselves. A Berlin sojourn, whether lasting mere days or years, has become a rite of passage for nearly all contemporary artists, critics, and curators, each of whom leave their mark on the scene in the form of works or gallery spaces.

> ***"Berlin has become a rite of passage for contemporary artists"***

Taking stock of this multifaceted art scene is an unwieldy, if not impossible task. Some of the former artist-run initiatives now have a high standing and steer the discourse in art, while other organisations focus on keeping tradition alive. These institutions are bolstered by the hundreds of smaller locations which serve as perfect examples of the art scene's flexibility, movability and experimental attitudes towards artistic practice. This chapter covers the width and breadth of the established scene and serves as a compass to provide orientation through the all-too temporary spaces and shows that are constantly coming and going.

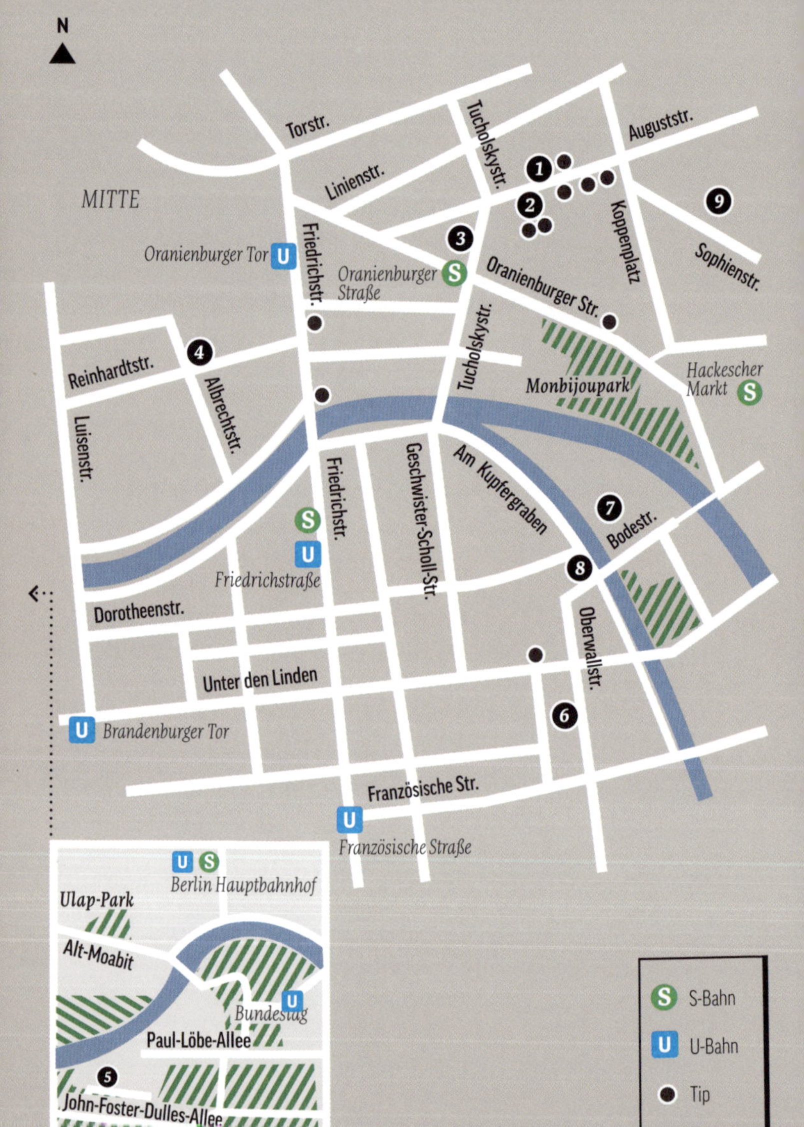
N
MITTE
Torstr.
Tucholskystr.
Auguststr.
Linienstr.
Koppenplatz
Sophienstr.
Oranienburger Tor
Friedrichstr.
Oranienburger Straße
Oranienburger Str.
Tucholskystr.
Reinhardtstr.
Albrechtstr.
Monbijoupark
Hackescher Markt
Luisenstr.
Friedrichstr.
Geschwister-Scholl-Str.
Am Kupfergraben
Bodestr.
Friedrichstraße
Dorotheenstr.
Oberwallstr.
Unter den Linden
Brandenburger Tor
Französische Str.
Französische Straße
Berlin Hauptbahnhof
Ulap-Park
Alt-Moabit
Bundestag
Paul-Löbe-Allee
John-Foster-Dulles-Allee
S-Bahn
U-Bahn
Tip
1
2
3
4
5
6
7
8
9

IN THE HEART OF ART

Museum Island may be Berlin's spectacular cultural centrepiece, but it's the adjacent area that forms the city's dynamic contemporary art centre.

In the 1990s, not long after the fall of the Wall, many of the country's most influential art galleries relocated from West Germany to the maze of streets framed by Alexanderplatz, Friedrichstr. and Torstr. This area of former East Berlin became a playground for the adventurous avant-gardists from all walks of artistic life. Although a number of important galleries have moved on to Kreuzberg or Tiergarten in recent years, the area continues to be a hub of contemporary art that is unrivalled in Europe in terms of its diversity. Two themes characteristic of the city are evident on this tour. Firstly, the refurbishment and reappropriation of existing buildings with a significant history, such as the former Royal Post Office building and Jewish Girls' School or a WWII bunker. Secondly, this tour provides a glimpse into what has become an important aspect of the Berlin art scene: publicly accessible private art collections.

1

Right A site-specific installation by Santiago Sierra at the bunker that houses the Boros Collection. *Photo* © Noshe

4

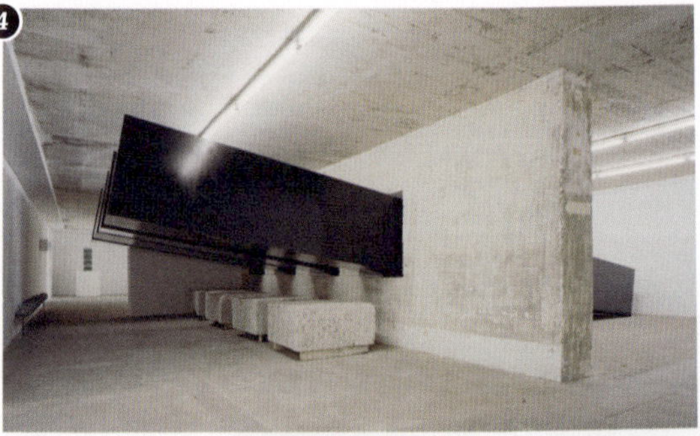

Right Artist Dan Graham designed the glass pavilion that houses Café Bravo at KW Institute for Contemporary Art. *Photo* Fette Sans, 2011

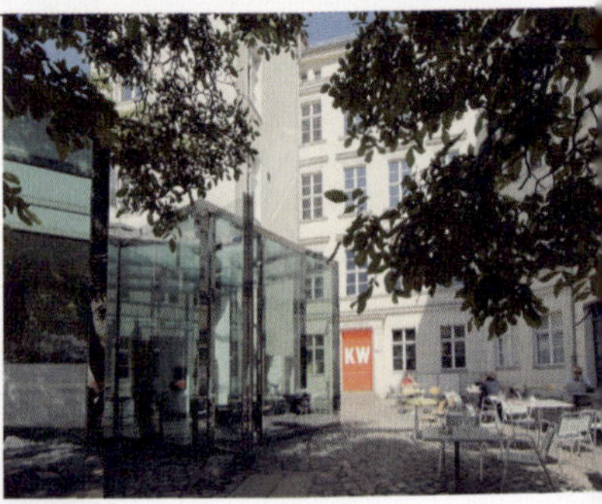

5

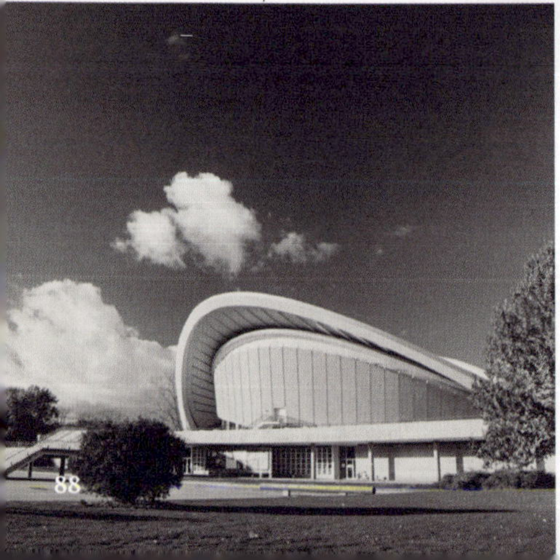

Left Front view of Haus der Kulturen der Welt (House of the Cultures of the World), colloquially referred to as the 'pregnant oyster'. *Photo* Frank Paul © Haus der Kulturen der Welt

Right The stately Royal Prussian Post Office building, current location of C/O Berlin. *Photo* © C/O Berlin

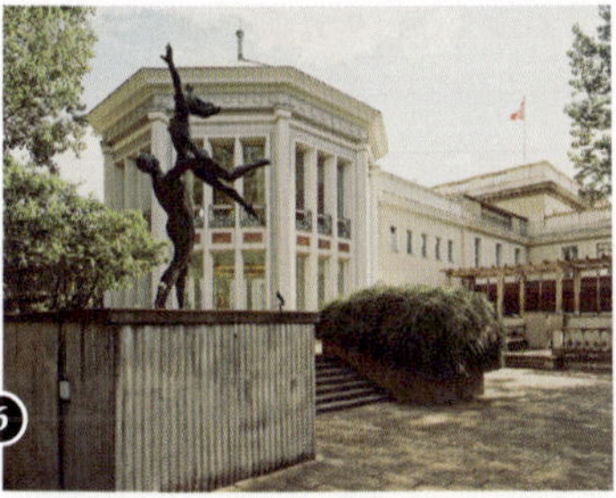

Left Schinkel Pavillon
Photo Thorsten Klapsch

9

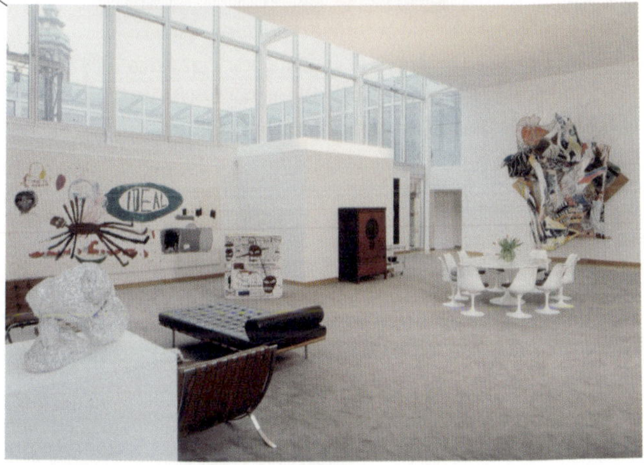

3

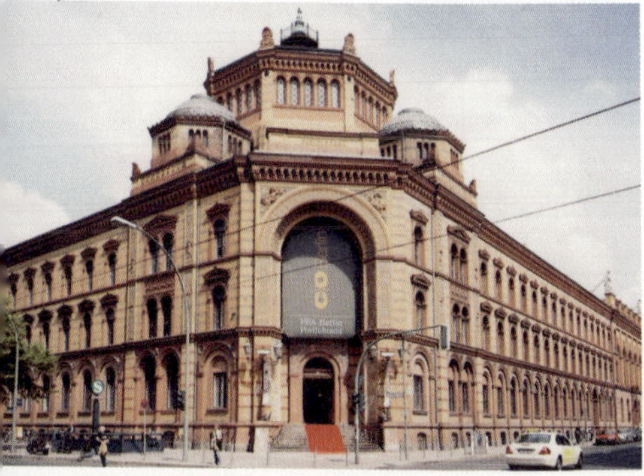

Above View of the 4th floor, Sammlung Hoffmann (Art works: A.R. Penck, Standart Mordell, 1968 Jean-Michel Basquiat, Levétation, 1987/ Jean-Michel Basquiat, Untitled, 1987/ Frank Stella, Of Whales ..., Moby Dick series, chapter 57, 1990).
Photo © Sammlung Hoffmann

❶ KW - Institute for Contemporary Art

Auguststr. 69, Mitte | Tue to Sun 12–19, Thu 12–21
kw-berlin.de

The tour begins in Mitte's side streets, where a number of important and prolific art galleries have settled. KW was a trailblazer for contemporary art in Germany. Not two years after the fall of the Wall, an industrious group of artists and art lovers rented an abandoned margarine factory on Auguststr., called it Kunst Werke, and embarked on what would shortly become one of the most productive, internationally recognised programs of contemporary art exhibitions and artist residencies. Klaus Biesenbach, who was at the centre of its original founding circle, is today Chief Curator at Large of the Museum of Modern Art in New York, as well as director of its affiliated contemporary art incubator PS1 in Queens. Today the KW complex comprises the refurbished factory, the 18th century residential building facing the street, as well a Dan Graham-designed glass pavilion in the courtyard which houses Café Bravo. KW continues to push the envelope, often giving original artistic positions their first public airing. The institution is also the control centre and a major venue for the Berlin Biennale.

Tip ... Optional stops on this street include the **ME Collectors Room** of phy-sician, Wella heir and art collector Thomas Olbricht, which is practically next door (no 68), as well as **Eigen + Art Gallery**, a little further down the road at no. 26.

For those who like to kick off with a drink, stop by **Clärchens Ballhaus** to experience one of the last 1920s dance halls (no 24). One of Germany's most interesting galleries for contemporary jewellery, **Oona**, is also nearby (*see page 187*).

❷ Ehemalige Jüdische Mädchenschule

Auguststr. 11–13, Mitte | Tue to Sat 11–18
maedchenschule.org

Diagonally opposite the KW, this new art hotspot opened in February 2012. The 1930s brick building was purpose-designed by architect Alexander Beer to house the Jewish Girls School, which at that time, was one of the most modern schools in town. Closed in 1942, it was reincarnated as a co-ed school until 1996 and left vacant for a further decade and a half (except for a brief stint in 2006 as the home of the 4th Berlin Biennale). Today, the building houses three restaurants and three galleries. One of the galleries is run by Michael Fuchs, the initiator of the project, while another focuses on contemporary photography, sculpture and painting. The third is an outpost of Eigen + Art, one of the city's most prominent galleries whose owner, Gerd Harry Lybke, is a pioneer of the contemporary art scene and who has helped artists such as Neo Rauch to achieve global fame. Called the Eigen + Art Lab, the gallery features international artists who are still new in Berlin.

Tip ... **Pauly Saal**, one of the three restaurants in this building (*see 241*), is the latest venture co-owned by Stefan Landwehr, who arrived in Berlin in the late 1990s, opened his first club in this street and – through his career as a picture frame maker – has become a prolific contemporary art collector who also co-runs two other hospitality ventures, **Grill Royal** (*see page 235*) and the tiny **King Size Bar** (*see page 225*). More suitable for a quick bite is the comfortable Jewish deli **Mogg & Melzer** (*see page 240*), which has graced Berlin with the perfect pastrami sandwich.

❸ C/O Berlin *Oranienburger Str. 35/36, Mitte*

Daily 11–20 | co-berlin.info

The 'International Forum for Visual Dialogues' was founded in 2000 by three individuals from different disciplines; photographer Stephan Erfurt, designer Marc Naroska and architect Ingo Pott. Since 2006, the splendid Postfuhramt – built as the headquarters for the Royal Prussian Post Office – has been home to the institution now known as C/O Berlin. C/O has gained an international reputation with large photography shows by prominent artists but there is also a focus on the promotion of emerging talent with dedicated programs for promising critics and photographers. At the time of writing, C/O's future was uncertain, as it has fallen victim to the much-discussed gentrification process in the area and will eventually have to vacate the building to make room for an investor's plans.

Tip ... One of Germany's well established art galleries, **Sprüth Magers**, is nearby. As they represent artists like Thomas Demand and Andreas Gursky, it's always worth the visit.

Oranienburger Str. 18
spruethmagers.com

❹ Boros Collection *Reinhardtstr. 20, Mitte*

Fri 14–18, Sat & Sun 10–18 (by appointment only)
sammlung-boros.de

Christian Boros, who forged a career in advertising and started collecting art at a young age, is not afraid of large gestures. His collection is housed in a former WWII bunker with a colourful history, having served as a cooling house for tropical fruit in the GDR years and a location for S&M parties in the 1990s. In 2003, a Japanese investor realised he would be unable to remove this indestructible edifice from its valuable land, and Boros and his wife purchased it to display their contemporary art collection and build a private residence on the roof. Over 300sqm, they display installation pieces, sculptures, light and performance works, many of which were created specifically for the space.

Tip... If you only have time for one museum, make it **Hamburger Bahnhof** museum of contemporary art, not far from here. In 1996, the former railway terminus became one of Europe's foremost museums for contemporary art. The expansive front hall is used as a venue for temporary exhibitions and installations.

Invalidenstr. 50 | Tue to Fri 10–18, Sat & Sun 11–18 hamburgerbahnhof.de

❺ Haus der Kulturen der Welt

John-Foster-Dulles-Allee 10, Tiergarten | Mon to Sun 10–19 (exhibitions Wed to Mon 11–19) | hkw.de

A little off the beaten track inside the vast Tiergarten park you'll find one of Germany's most unique art institutions, another example of a structure that was re-invented and where the site determined – to a large extent – the program. The Haus der Kulturen der Welt (House of the Cultures of the World – HKW), focuses on artistic productions from non-European cultures and societies. Initially a congress hall, the building was a US-financed contribution to the 1957 Interbau Building Exhibition that also spawned the Hansaviertel (*see page 54 & 62*). Conceived as the conflicts between East and West intensified, the open shape of the structure symbolises the values of Western societies, freedom of thought and information. Today, HKW presents artistic productions from around the world, with a special focus on non-European cultures and societies. Visual arts, music, literature, performing arts, film, academic discussions and digital media are all linked in its interdisciplinary program.

Tip ... As you pass by the imposing buildings of Humboldt University, you can opt for a stopover here. **Kleine Humboldt Galerie**, in the atrium behind the main entrance, is an initiative of the university's art history students, who take turns curating contemporary art shows, some of which garner significant attention in the art world.

Unter den Linden 6, Wed to Fri 12–18

❻ Schinkel Pavillon *Oberwallstr. 1, Mitte*

Thu to Sun 12–18 | schinkelpavillon.de

This small pavilion, an example of the neoclassical style popular with the GDR government, is today one of the most celebrated art organisations in Berlin. Built in 1969 and used mainly for entertaining official government guests (who undoubtedly enjoyed the spectacular view of East Berlin's landmarks), the pavilion was vacant for many years. Since 2008, Nina Pohl, a successful artist in her own right, has been staging art exhibitions here. For the impressive list of international artists who have shown here, the glazed octagonal space presented challenges that were in most cases overcome by creating site-specific works. This in turn has lifted its profile, placing it in an interesting niche among the institutional and privately run galleries. In many ways, the pavilion embodies all the reasons why Berlin is such fertile soil for its art community. When buildings such as this one, which unite a colourful history with a perfect location, are discovered by entrepreneurial creatives, their instant reaction is to recover the structure from its decaying state and 'do something'. Programming often develops as a corollary, which leads to innovative uses of space and entirely unique site-specific programs.

❼ Neues Museum *Bodestr. 1, Mitte | Mon to Sun 10–18 | neues-museum.de*

Despite being named the 'new museum', the Egyptian and prehistoric artifacts exhibited here are far from contemporary. However, the interventions that were undertaken by British architect David Chipperfield as part of its refurbishment are more in tune with its moniker. Undoubtedly one of the most spectacular renovations in town, it also stands for an approach that is typical of recent architectural and artistic concepts: the careful restoration of spaces and buildings with a potent mixture of respect for the old and an appreciation of the new. The purpose of the museum, opened in 1859, was to create an experience of the universal history of humankind. Every room corresponded in colour and furnishings to a particular era. Almost entirely destroyed in the war, the museum reopened to much fanfare in 2009. The architect carefully restored missing parts and complemented the classical forms of original architect Friedrich August Stüler, using strict and reduced elements without imitating the original. This is without a doubt one of the most impressive museum buildings in Germany.

❽ Contemporary Fine Arts

Am Kupfergraben 10, Mitte | Tue to Fri, 11–18, Sat 11–16 cfa-berlin.com

Directly opposite Neues Museum sits another David Chipperfield building, this time a contemporary one, housing a private art space and one of the country's most renowned galleries, Contemporary Fine Arts. Occupying the lower two floors of the building, CFA showcases artists such as Georg Baselitz, Cecily Brown, Anselm Reyle and Dash Snow. The owners of the building are collector couple Céline and Heiner Bastian, the latter of whom was Joseph Beuys' secretary as well as curator of an important collection at Hamburger Bahnhof museum until 2007. His private collection is presented on the second floor of the building, which is open to the public.

❾ **Sammlung Hoffmann** *Sophie-Gips-Höfe (Entry C) | Sophienstraße 21, Mitte | Sat 11–16 by appointment only | sammlung-hoffmann.de*

A former sewing machine factory with a somewhat hard to find entrance houses the private art collection of Erika Hoffmann and her late husband Rolf. The couple accumulated wealth as textile manufacturers in the far west of Germany, building a sizeable art collection that started in the 1960s with acquisitions from German artist collective ZERO. It now includes important works by Bruce Nauman, Jean-Michel Basquiat, Frank Stella and Gerhard Richter, to name but a few. In 1997, the couple moved their private home and some of their works to this location and opened it to the public. Not all of their art is constantly on display; once a year, it is rotated to allow for a new perspective.

AXEL HAUBROK

Art Collector

The Open House

In a showroom at Strausberger Platz, Axel and Barbara Haubrok share their private art collection with the public.

Initially, Axel Haubrok was only interested in painting. The first piece that the formerly Düsseldorf-based financial consultant bought was a canvas by self-taught Belgian painter Raoul de Keyser. It became the cornerstone of an enormous collection now partially on display in a dedicated showroom on Karl-Marx-Allee. The Haubroks are known for collecting unwieldy and sometimes difficult pieces, many of which fall into the category of conceptual art, often by young, yet to become established artists. Here are the collector's Berlin recommendations.

U *Strausberger Platz | haubrokshows, Strausberger Platz 19, Mitte | Sat 12 – 18*
sammlung-haubrok.de

1 **"The Paris Bar is one of my favourite places in Berlin. Historically it's a very important meeting spot for the art world, yet it is still very interesting now since you always run into someone."**
The restaurant in Berlin-Charlottenburg has been popular with artists and performers since the 1970s. Testament to this are its walls, adorned with the works of many renowned regulars.

U *Uhlandstraße | Kantstr. 152, Charlottenburg*
parisbar.net

2 **"Berlin's private art collections are an interesting portal into the world of art collectors."**
Ivo Wessel, for instance, who is a software developer by day, has acquired an impressive array of contemporary works, displayed over three levels in his loft in Berlin-Mitte. Open by appointment.

email@ivo-wessel.de

3 "I am a big fan of Udo Kittelmann's work, so I recommend having a very good look at it." Udo Kittelmann has been Director of the Nationalgalerie since 2008. His directorship is not limited to the two big locations for contemporary and modern art – Neue Nationalgalerie and Hamburger Bahnhof – but also includes the Alte Nationgalerie on Museum Island, the Friedrichswerdersche Kirche am Schlossplatz, Museum Berggruen and the Sammlung Scharf-Gerstenberg in Charlottenburg.

smb.museum

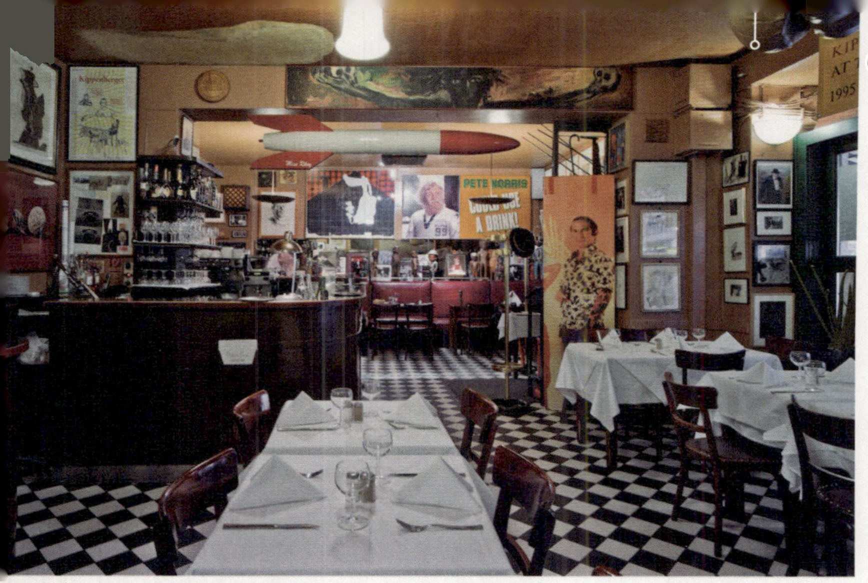

Above The legendary Paris Bar, where painter Martin Kippenberger paid his tab by lending one of his works – depicting the restaurant's interior – which famously sold for about EUR 2.5 million at auction in 2009.
Photo © Arno Baur

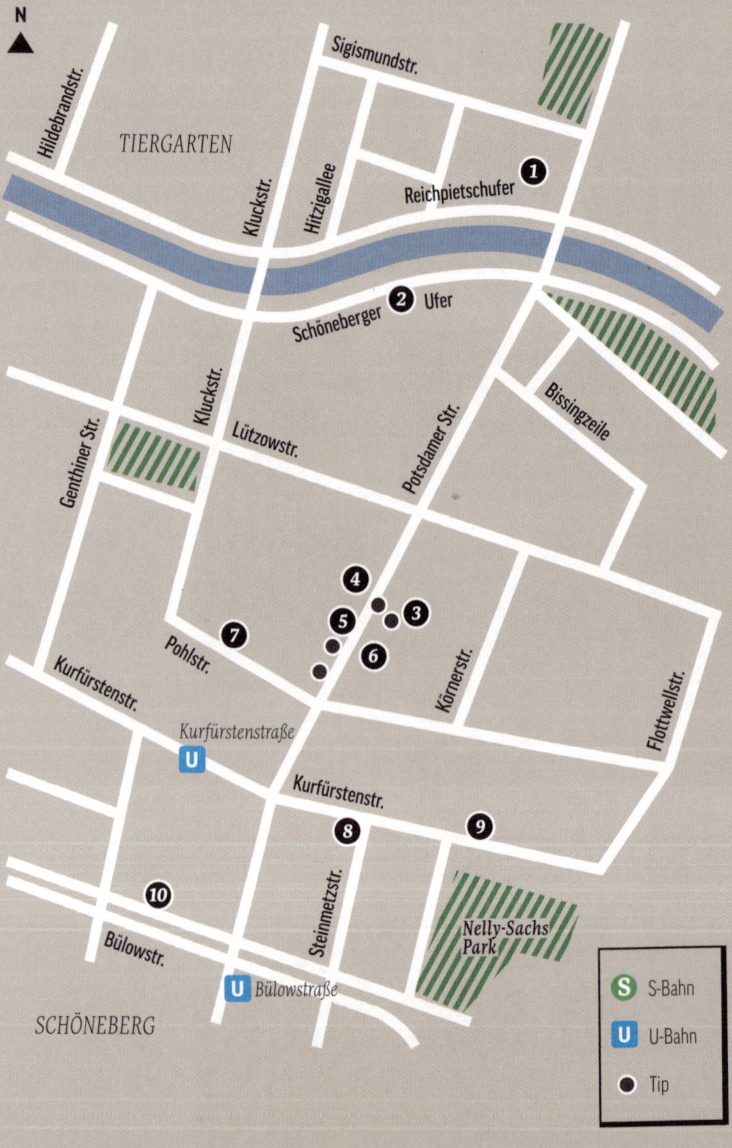
N
TIERGARTEN
Hildebrandstr.
Sigismundstr.
Hitzigallee
Kluckstr.
Reichpietschufer
1
Schöneberger
2
Ufer
Kluckstr.
Genthiner Str.
Lützowstr.
Potsdamer Str.
Bissingzeile
4
5
3
6
7
Pohlstr.
Körnerstr.
Flottwellstr.
Kurfürstenstr.
Kurfürstenstraße
U
Kurfürstenstr.
8
9
Steinmetzstr.
10
Bülowstr.
Nelly-Sachs Park
U
Bülowstraße
SCHÖNEBERG
S
S-Bahn
U
U-Bahn
Tip

THE ADVENTURE PLAYGROUND

For decades, the area around Potsdamer Platz was a cultural no man's land. In recent years, it has experienced a resurgence in popularity with the contemporary art community and their gallerists. This tour proves that not only artists but also their galleries require the occasional reinvention to stay creative.

No area in Berlin was as badly battered during and after WWII as Potsdamer Platz. Formerly one of Europe's busiest locales, extensive bombing caused much destruction to the buildings, which were later removed altogether to make room for the Wall and its surveillance infrastructure. Nearby Potsdamer Str., once a well-to-do residential area, became little more than a seedy thoroughfare. Neither the development of Mies van der Rohe's Neue Nationalgalerie and the nearby Kulturforum in the 1960s nor the area's masterplanned revitalisation at the hands of Italian architect Renzo Piano in the 1990s helped return Postdamer Str. to its former glory. However, rising rents in the Mitte district prompted a shift in the art world. In recent years, some leading galleries shifted to the area, many into the grand Bel Etage apartments that were once prized real estate.

Right The enormous space of Blain|Southern Berlin is the former printing room of newspaper Der Tagesspiegel. *Photo* Christian Glaeser

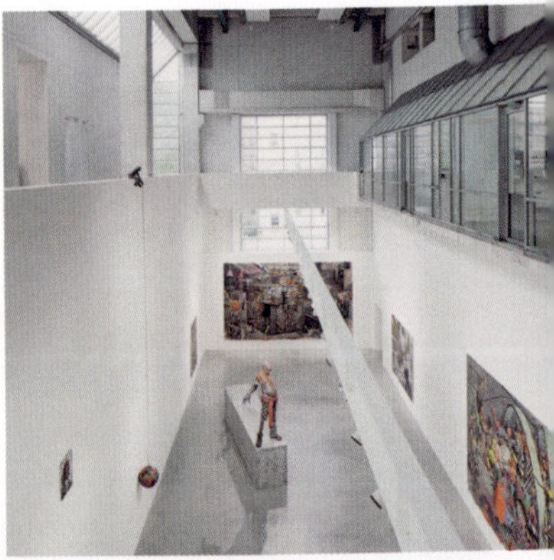

Below Installation view Angelika J. Trojnarski, 2011, Galerie Tanja Wagner, Berlin.

2

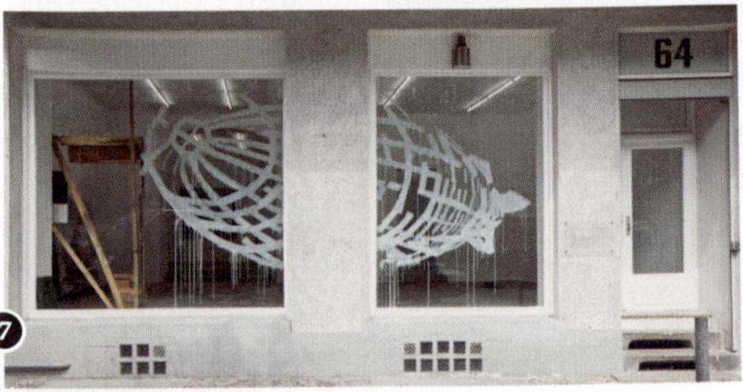

7

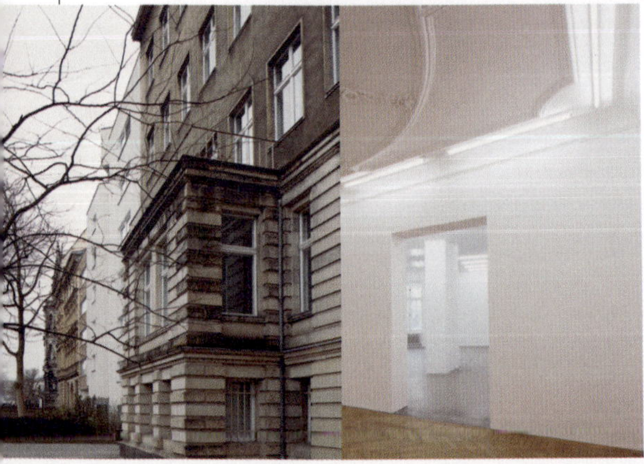

Left Who could guess that this unassuming residential building houses one of the city's most prestigous galleries?

This is Esther Schipper's apartment-cum-gallery, transformed by architect Arno Brandlhuber. *Photos* © Attilio Maranzano, courtesy of Esther Schipper, Berlin

3

Right Gregor Hylla's work at Tanya Leighton Gallery. *Photos* Courtesy of the artist and Tanya Leighton Gallery

8

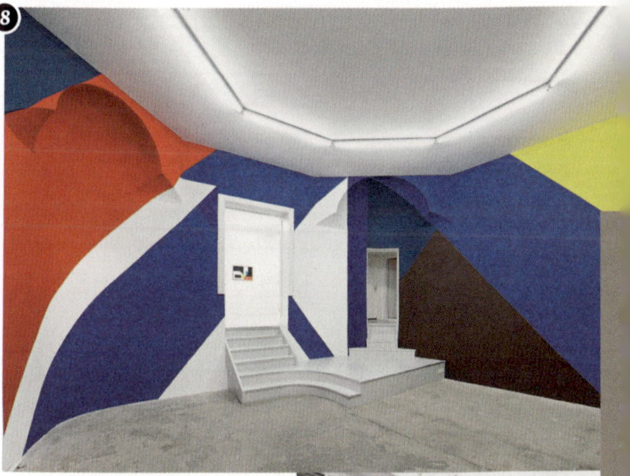

4

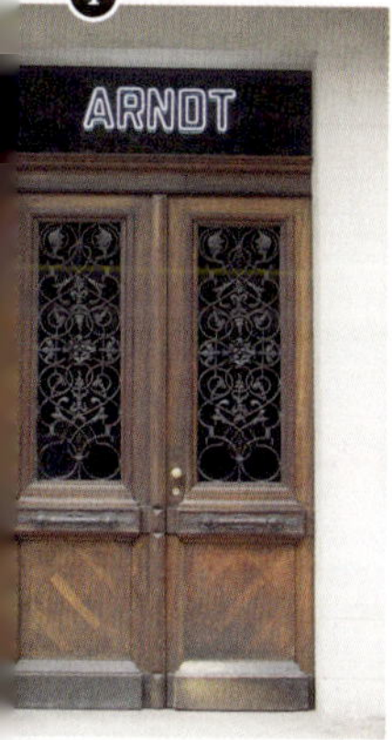

Above Discreet is *de rigeur* for the galleries around Potsdamer Str. *Photo* © Arndt Berlin

Right Street frontage of Tanya Leighton's gallery space, a former corner tavern (shelf structure by Sean Edwards).

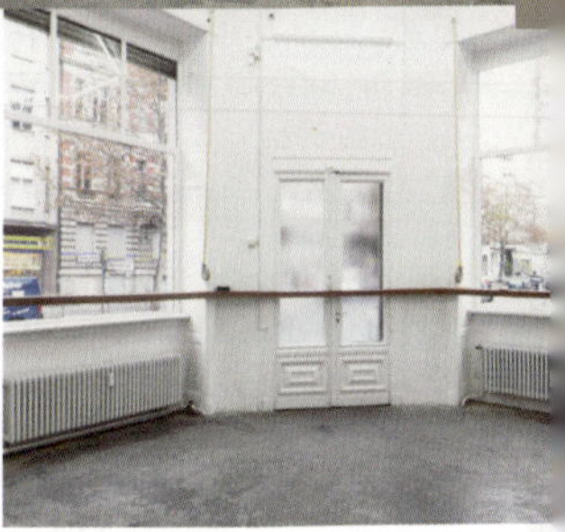

10

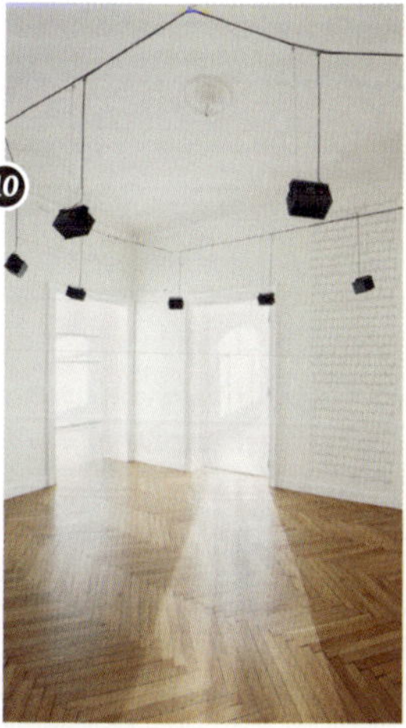

Left Sandra Peters' installation 'Interplay' at Kunstsaele Berlin.

❶ **Neue Nationalgalerie** *Kulturforum*

Potsdamer Str. 50, Tiergarten | Tue to Fri 10–18, Thu 10–22, Sat & Sun 11–18 | neue-nationalgalerie.de

It's an apt place to start the discovery tour. The New National Gallery, one of Mies van der Rohe's final designs, opened its doors to the public in 1968 as the 'gallery of the 20th century'. The minimalist pavilion, often described as a 'temple of light and glass', is in itself a work of art. The great hall at ground level – used for temporary exhibitions – presents a challenge to curators and exhibition designers due to its transparency and solid, dark ceilings. The museum's permanent collection is displayed in the basement. From 2015 the building will undergo substantial refurbishments by none other than British architect David Chipperfield, who also lent his skill to the Neues Museum (*see page 94*).

❷ **Esther Schipper** *Schöneberger Ufer 65,*

Tiergarten | Tue to Sat 11–18 | estherschipper.com

Across the river on Schöneberger Ufer you'll find the first Bel Etage gallery of this walk. One of the country's most respected gallerists, Esther Schipper was among the first to initiate the gallery migration from Mitte to this area, and once you enter the roughly 400sqm of former residential space, you'll understand her reasons. The location was refurbished with the help of architect Arno Brandlhuber (*see page 50*), who previously housed his offices here. Schipper has represented conceptual artists such as Thomas Demand, Carsten Höller, Liam Gillick and Ceal Floyer for more than two decades.

Tip ... While you are in the building, visit the **Wien Lukatsch** gallery on the third floor, which also houses an art bookstore in its impressive former residential space.

❸ **Blain|Southern** *Postdamer. Str 77 -78, Tiergarten | Tue to Sat 11–18 | blainsouthern.com*

London-based gallery heavyweights Harry Blain and Graham Southern opened their Berlin location at the recently refurbished former printing plant of one of Berlin's big newspapers, Der Tagesspiegel. The impressive halls – once filled with the sound of rotating machinery and the smell of newsprint – today provide space for giant art projects and unwieldy installations by artists such as British duo Tim Noble and Sue Webster or large-scale paintings by German Jonas Burgert. Even without the art, the building is worth the visit.

Tip ... You'll probably end up there anyway, but be sure to visit **Andreas Murkudis**' grand concept store (*see page 143*) on the ground floor of this building. Murkudis is intimately connected to Berlin's art world and has an extraordinary knack for starting the right business in the right place.

❹ **Arndt** *Potsdamer Str. 96 | Tiergarten | Tue to Sat 11–18 | arndtberlin.com*

Matthias Arndt has been running his Berlin gallery for 25 years. His location on Potsdamer Str. is his third, following two previous locations in Mitte. Today, Arndt himself is usually touring the globe, presenting established European artists and Asian newcomers in Southeast Asia and Australia. Meanwhile, his gallery, a former dance hall, regularly exhibits a selection of core artists such as Gilbert & George, Thomas Hirschhorn and Sophie Calle alongside Berlin-based newcomers.

Tip ... Milliner **Fiona Bennett** runs one of Berlin's veteran design labels. The British-born designer has been creating hats for a well-heeled international fan base since 1988. She opened a new salon here, (Potsdamer Str. 81-83), in 2012.

❺ **Die Tür** *Potsdamer Str. 98a, Tiergarten | Fri & Sat 14–18 | ajlart.com*

Well-hidden in the second courtyard of a posh residential building, you'll find one of Anna Jill Lüpertz' project rooms,

Die Tür. This and two other project spaces in the neighbourhood allow her artists to be flexible and work conceptually rather than having to focus on one space. The daughter of Markus Lüpertz, one of Germany's most famous contemporary painters, she focuses on young artists with a more unconventional practice.

Tip ... Another cultural business has made the leap from sanitised Auguststr. The bookstore **Do you read me?!** operates its venture **The Reading Room & Shop** (*see page 200*) here. Its program is inspired by the workings of an art gallery and features publication-related exhibitions and curated events.

❻ Klosterfelde *Potsdamer Str. 93, Tiergarten Tue to Sat 11–18 | klosterfelde.de*

Like its neighbours, Martin Klosterfelde's gallery also operated in a number of locations before settling in Potsdamer Str. Located on the first floor, the gallery stretches over a couple of *Altbau* rooms with creaky floorboards. Proving that art doesn't always need the White Cube, site-specific installations have included the work of German performance artist John Bock, who magically set the French doors and windows in motion, while Hanne Darboven's conceptual notes adorned the walls in strict geometrical patterns.

❼ Galerie Tanja Wagner *Pohlstr. 64, Tiergarten | Wed to Sat 11–18 | tanjawagner.com*

Tanja Wagner, a celebrated up-and-coming gallery owner, has also chosen Potsdamer Str. as the location for her entry into the art market. Situated in a 110sqm retail space on Pohlstr., she works with selected artists of her own generation who are not yet part of the circuit of larger galleries. She launched her gallery in 2010 with much promise and energy and continues to follow through with outstanding exhibitions and projects, so that the art world eagerly anticipates who else Tanja Wagner might unearth.

❽ **Tanya Leighton** *Kurfürstenstr. 156, Tiergarten | Tue to Sat 11–18 | tanyaleighton.com*

The corner of Kurfürstenstr. and Potsdamer Str. has fallen into disrepute because of the street prostitutes who work there, but that hasn't kept new gallerists away. Tanya Leighton, previously curator for video art at New York's Whitney Museum, shows international artists in a former corner tavern complete with beer cellar. Her affinity for the moving image is evident in many of her shows, often staged in collaboration with external curators.

❾ **Sommer & Kohl** *Kurfürstenstr. 13/14, Tiergarten | Wed to Sun 11–18 | sommerkohl.com*

A few doors down from Tanya Leighton, Salome Sommer and Patricia Kohl have established a gallery focusing on young contemporary art. Both trained in their craft at Neugerriemschneider, one of Berlin's most influential galleries, before setting up their rooms in the unpretentious space that was previously a bedspring factory.

Tip ... Nearby **Victoria Bar**, with its beautiful wood paneled walls, perfect drinks and nonchalant atmosphere, is a veritable institution and the point of call for all art folk in the area, especially after openings.

Potsdamer Str. 102
victoriabar.de

❿ **Kunstsaele Berlin** *Bülowstr. 90, Tiergarten Wed to Sat 11–18 | kunstsaele.de*

Magnificent spaces hide behind the dirty façades, döner stalls and dingy sex shops on Bülowstr. One of them is run by Kunstsaele Berlin as a combination of gallery, collection and salon lecture hall. The exhibitions consist of altering shows from the works of two private collections, Sammlung Bergmeier and Sammlung Oehmen, juxtaposed with minimalist and conceptual works from the program of Galerie Aanant & Zoo. On Wednesdays, the gallery holds Salon Populaire, a discourse on art and related topics.

MY CITY WITH

JOHANN HAEHLING VON LANZENAUER

Founder and Director of Circleculture Gallery for Urban Fine Arts

Inspired by the Street

When Johann Haehling von Lanzenauer and Dirk Staudinger started their gallery over a decade ago, Berlin was home to an unparalleled street art culture. Circleculture quickly became a hub for artists from this field. "Berlin's law enforcement is relatively relaxed and the many vacant spaces turned the inner city into an ideal playground for street artists, especially around the turn of the millenium. Today, many artists find more stimulation in producing studio work for museums and galleries. However, while their art isn't necessarily applied in an urban context, it still is inspired by urban subcultures," says Johann. Here are his recommendations for tracing street art in Berlin.

U *Weinmeisterstraße | Gipsstr. 11, Mitte | Tue to Sat 12–18*
circleculture-gallery.com

1 **"Don't miss Cuvrystr. in Kreuzberg. The entire wall space is covered by a collaborative work by French artist JR and his Italian colleague Blu.**
The mural was created as part of a 2007 street art show called Planet Process."

U *Schlesisches Tor*

2 **"Though much of the art is gone, many publications document the work created during the heyday of street art in Berlin.**
One of those books is a monograph created by Portuguese artist VHILS (Gestalten, 2011). Instead of painting on walls, he drills, chisels and scratches. One of his works can still be found on a wall near Schillingbrücke."

ALSO ... If you don't want to leave all of your discoveries up to chance, you'll find a number of street art tours on **urbanartguide.com**.

Guided tours are available via alternativeberlin.com or findingberlin-tours.com.

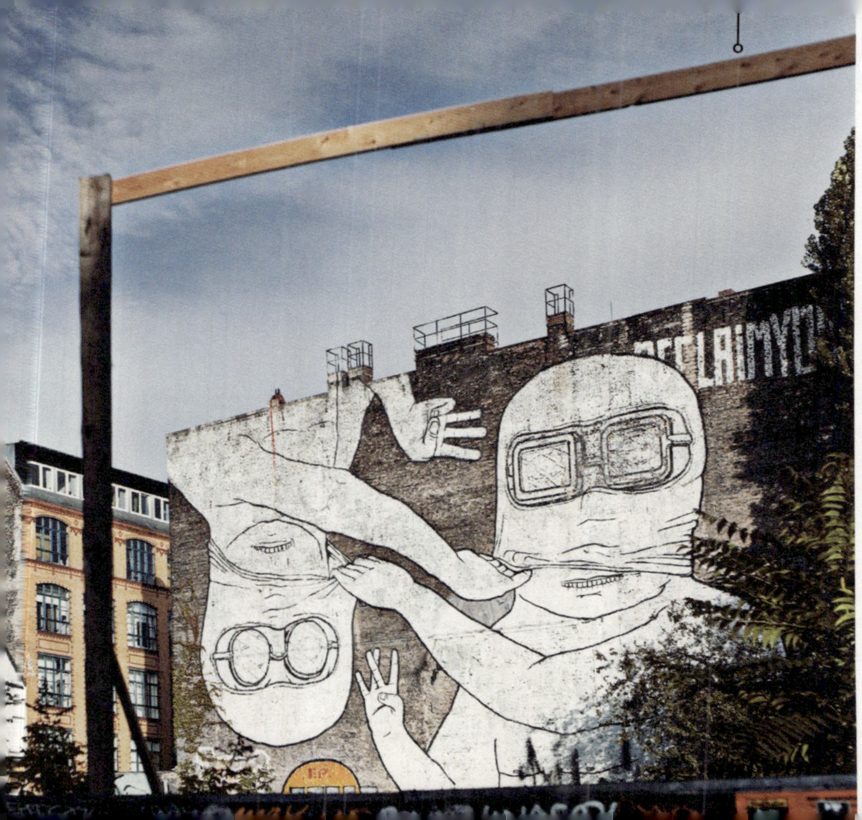

3 **"Due to the transience of street art, the work of Germany's most important street artist XOOOOX is perhaps best experienced in print.**

In early 2012, a monograph documenting ten years of his art in Berlin was released by local publisher Gestalten. His stencilled black and white models are often taken from advertising campaigns in fashion journals. If you keep your eyes open, you might also discover some of his artwork, most likely around Gipsstr. and Auguststr. in Mitte or on the Boros Bunker (*see page 92*)."

Left **The wall facing a vacant lot on Cuvrystr., Kreuzberg.** *Photo* **©joachimwagner.net**

THE INCUBATORS

The vast array of non-commercial project locations, or 'off-spaces', that often spring up as quickly as they vanish, are at the same time the underbelly and the motor of Berlin's art scene. This is a visit to six of Berlin's longest-standing, most dynamic project spaces.

Project spaces are usually started by artists taking advantage of Berlin's still-affordable rents and often involve many protagonists from all areas of artistic production. The exhibitions staged in the city's many such venues range from the mind-bogglingly amazing to the pitifully bad or entirely inaccessible. Artist-run spaces fulfill an important role in the artistic ecosystem: they maintain a dynamic discourse among artists, open channels for trading information, strengthening networks and – perhaps most importantly – serve as testing grounds for new ideas and as platforms for up-and-coming talent. While the lifespan of such venues appears rarely to exceed two years, a number of spaces have bucked this trend and continue strong thanks to the determination of their proprietors, an extraordinary curatorial approach, or both.

Lab for Electronic Arts and Performance (LEAP)

It takes some serious dedication to make a go of presenting an ongoing curated program for more 'difficult' art forms that include sound and performance. Thankfully the three founders of this combined project and studio space are not short on dedication. Located in a space they discovered from a train as it pulled out of Alexanderplatz station – inside the under-tenanted Berlin Careé shopping mall at Karl-Liebknecht-Str. – LEAP is usually only open for short periods to show performance pieces and installations. Despite its sporadic schedule, LEAP quickly shot to fame in certain circles thanks to their combination of fleeting art forms with a more traditional gallery approach.

S U ***Alexanderplatz*** | *Karl-Liebknecht-Str. 13 (Berlin Carré, 1st floor), Mitte*
check website for opening times | *leapknecht.de*

Essays & Observations

Below The Wilhelm Reich /Ayn Rand exhibition

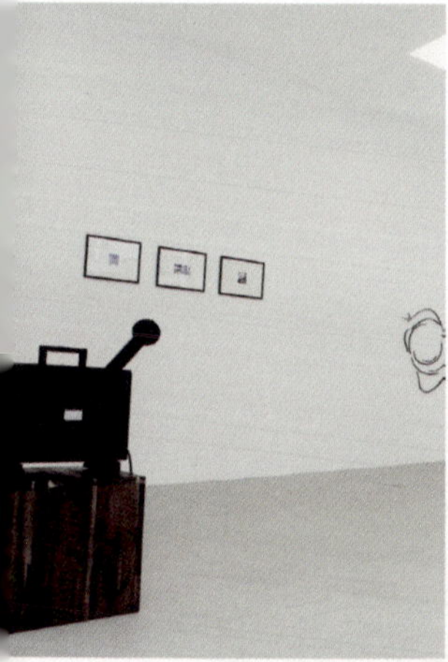

Located in an area that is increasingly popular with art lovers but not (yet?) art buyers, the gallery run by British artist Matthew Burbidge and his partner Sonia Ostermann challenges current curatorial practice and discourse. Since early 2010, the pair has investigated, discussed, collaborated, challenged and not least humoured the subjects of their investigation with shows that usually germinate from a curatorial theme, rather than completed art works. Exhibitions titled 'The Mistake' or 'Appropriation' carefully and thoughtfully tackle the particularities of the art world.

U ***Nauener Platz*** | *Maxstr. 1, Wedding* | *Sat 14–19*
essaysandobservations.com

REH Kunst

This space unites a number of very compatible concepts: art, mobile architecture and GDR nostalgia, though that last aspect is one that art historian, consultant and curator Valeska Hageney would rather not over-emphasise. The name is an acronym of the tongue-twisting but aptly descriptive word Raumerweiterungshalle (space extension hall), a mass-produced temporary structure that served all kinds of purposes in East Germany, from school extensions to wedding venues. At the height of production in the 1970s, thousands of REHs – which are extended through an accordion-esque mechanism and can be transported on the back of a truck – dotted the country. Hageney's REH, hauled to Berlin after having served as a GDR nostalgia store, is the perfect place to stage versatile solo exhibitions and group shows. The curved aluminium walls force artists and curators to engage with the space itself rather than simply positioning their work in a white cube.

S U ***Schönhauser Allee*** | *Kopenhagener Str. 17, Prenzlauer Berg | check website for exhibitions and times | valeskahageney.com/about-2/reh-kunst*

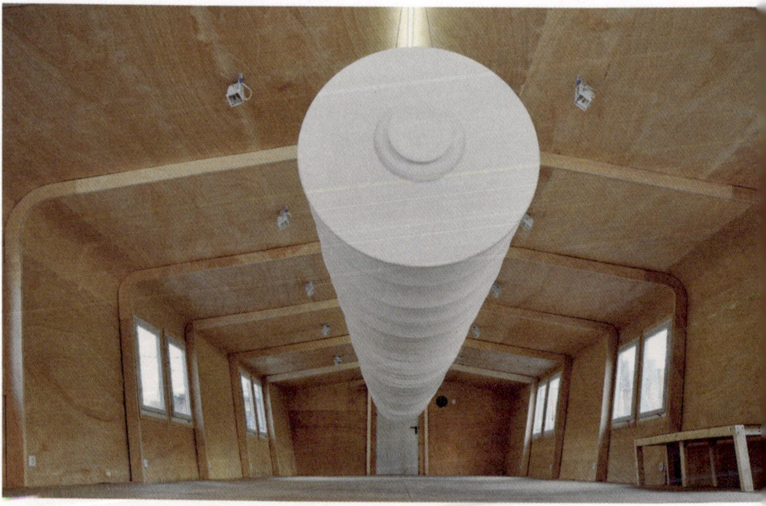

Autocenter

When practising artists Maik Schierloh and Joep Liefland opened an art gallery in an unused auto mechanic workshop in Friedrichshain, they didn't expect that a decade later it would be this city's longest running nonprofit project space. The duo wanted to do something different, something more extreme and, perhaps most importantly, something outside of the traditional structures of the art world. They're still sticking to their guns. With inexhaustible enthusiasm, the pair has channelled many now-established painters, sculptors, photographers and video artists, often from abroad, through their space on a high-frequency roster (no show is longer than three weeks). Until September 2012, the gallery was perched above a discount supermarket at the far end of Friedrichshain, but was on the move to a yet unknown location as this book went to print.

autocenterart.de

THAT BAR ON THE BOULEVARD

— *Maik Schierloh runs a second venture on Karl-Marx-Allee. Kosmetiksalon* ***Bar Babette*** *(no 36) used to be former East Berlin's most glamorous beauty parlour, situated in a purpose-built pavilion opposite the magnificent* ***Kino International*** *(no 33). Besides being a great place for a drink, the bar, is also a well-known art spot, featuring temporary exhibitions in its gallery space.*

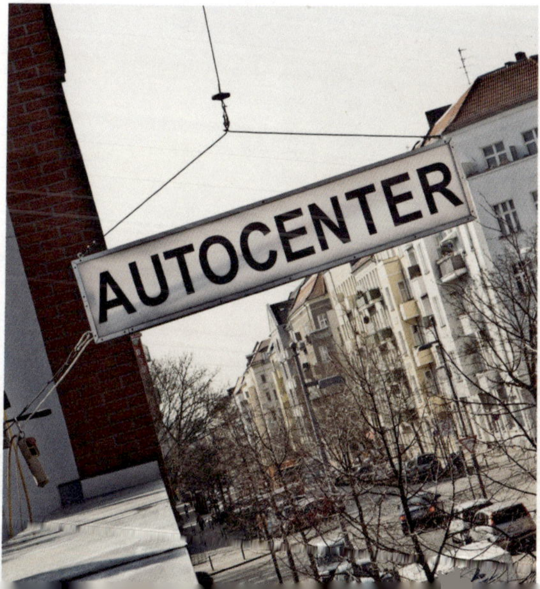

Left photo Roman März

Far left Installation view, Janine Eggert & Philipp Ricklefs: The Dynamic Sublime Device, REH KUNST, 2012.

Grimmuseum

The Grimmuseum is a very deceiving space indeed. First, its stately rooms have much more in common with the white-walled commercial art gallery than the ramshackle grittiness of your typical 'off location'. Secondly, its name refers neither to the authors of the gruesome but popular German fairy tales nor is its program a tribute to the painter Louise Grimm, who worked in this building and lent her name to the nearby street. Instead, Grimmuseum's mission is to create an interdisciplinary platform for the Berlin-based international art community, with a particular focus on curatorial practice. It's an incredibly prolific space, having shown over 150 artists in little more than two years.

U *Südstern* | *Fichtestr. 2, Kreuzberg* | *Wed to Sun 14–19* | *grimmuseum.com*

Below photo © Laura Gianetti, courtesy of Grimmuseum

Right Jens Nordmann, '012345689', 2011

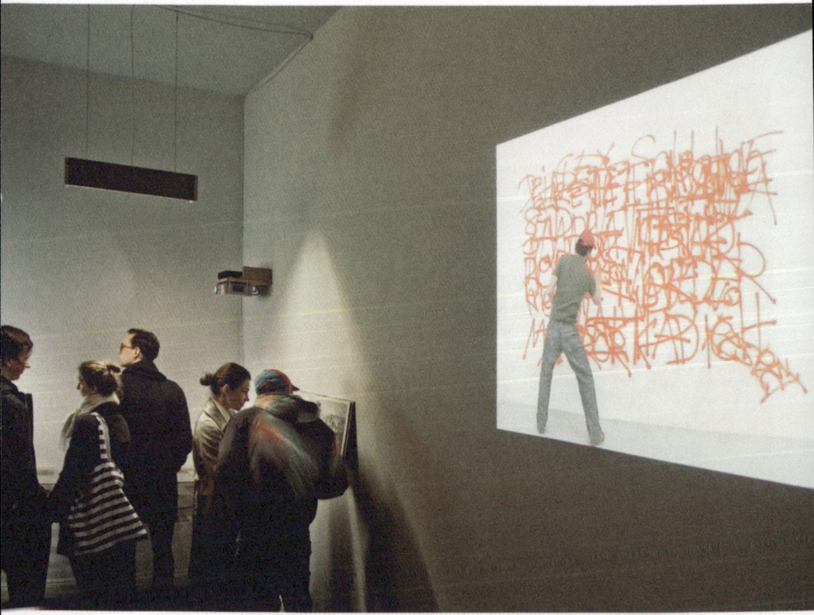

SOX

SOX, a roughly two by three metre display case situated on busy Oranienstr., is an an unusual art space. Formerly SOX36 (referencing the famous party venue in the neighbourhood), it was initiated by nine local artists in 2000. The original founders were intrigued by the possibilities of this small, unmanned space that is intimately connected to the neighbourhood, allowing passersby to engage with the art without having to overcome the threshold of a gallery. In 2010, two local artists took over as curators and continue SOX's protocol as a nonprofit venture with rotating exhibitions every six weeks.

Tip... To stay updated, get a copy of **BPIGS**, the 'Berlin Independents Guide', an artist run PR Network for exhibition spaces and art related venues in Berlin, with its affiliated online magazine.

bpigs.com

U ***Kottbusser Tor*** | *Oranienstr. 175* | *sox-berlin.com*

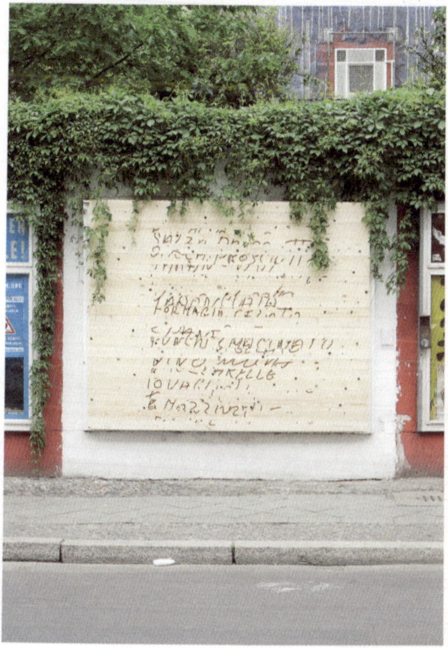

NICHE ART & ARCHITECTURE TOURS

— *This tour was put together by the three very well-connected ladies. Nele Heinevetter, Stefanie Gerke and Katharina Beckmann are art historians and an architect respectively. As the name of their business suggests, they believe that Berlin's creative energy is best explored in its niches. The trio offers private personalised tours around art and architecture locations in the city, including meetings with artists and gallerists.*

nicheberlin.de

ALWAYS IN FLUX

Sacred Art

One of the most ambitious recent moves in the art world was gallerist Johann König's acquisition of the former St Agnes church. The 50-year-old brutalist structure is situated in the increasingly creative no man's land beyond Moritzplatz in Kreuzberg. König plans to transform the main hall into an 800 sqm exhibition space displaying the works of his retinue of mostly conceptual, up-and-coming artists. The building, currently being restored and adapted by architect Arno Brandlhuber, is set to open in 2013, but is already hailed as Berlin's equivalent to the Tate Modern's Turbine Hall.

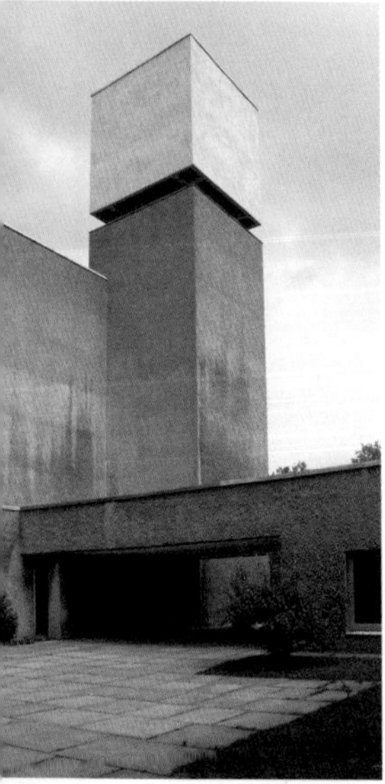

U *Moritzplatz* | **Alexandrinenstr. 118, Kreuzberg**
johannkoenig.de

Duve

A former industrial building not far from Johann König's church is home to a young gallery of international repute. Alex Duve, who settled in the neighbourhood in late 2012, represents about a dozen up-and-coming international artists. The gallery has an emphasis on international connections, especially with the New York market.

U *Prinzenstraße* | **Gitschiner Str. 94/94a (Entrance D, Floor 2), Kreuzberg**
duveberlin.com

Kwadrat

Martin Kwade's courtyard gallery is a classic example of a successful project-space-cum-art gallery. He represents a group of illustrious and ambitious artists, knows everyone in the art world and runs the 'Artists' Night' every Wednesday at King Size Bar, where he also pours the drinks on those occasions.

U *Kottbusser Tor*
Adalbertstr. 20, Kreuzberg | Fri to Sun 14–19
kwadrat-berlin.com

Cluster I

Berlin's vibrant art community tends to form clusters around particular districts or centres of artistic production. The area around Volksbühne, one of Berlin's significant theatres, is also a centre for the visual arts, and several respected galleries can be found in its surrounding streets. Places to look up are Christian Nagel's eponymous gallery, BQ, Zink and Croy Nielsen. These galleries also take turns exhibiting in a display case built into the Volksbühne building.
galerie-nagel.de | bqberlin.de | galeriezink.de croynielsen.de

Cluster II

Those interested in further exploring areas of artistic activity should venture to the area around Graefestr. in Kreuzberg and Friedelstr. on the border of Neukölln and Kreuzberg, where recent years have seen project spaces and galleries come and go at accelerated speed.

MD72

Galerie Neu's experimental branch MD72 is a destination in itself. The work of mostly conceptual artists is shown over two floors of beautiful formerly residential spaces.
U *Mehringdamm* | **Mehringdamm 72, Kreuzberg | Tue to Sun 12–18 | md72.com galerieneu.net**

Keeping Up

There are too many art-focused newsletters and blogs to mention, but here are some useful links:
berlinartlink.com
berlin-artparasites.com
berlinartjournal.com

Volksboutique Small Business

Art is at its most exciting when it treads new ground. In the case of New York artist Christine Hill, this means the combination of consumption and art. Her Volksboutique Small Business features a 4-metre long oak apothecary counter with an inventory of talismans. After conversation with the visitor, Christine assembles a 'care package' of objects. The result is a formidable keepsake.
U *Eberswalder Straße*
Choriner Str. 51, Prenzlauer Berg | Fri 12–18 volksboutique.org

Left St Agnes church
Photo Harald Rossa

Below Volksboutique Small Business – ready for business.
Photo Felix Oberhage

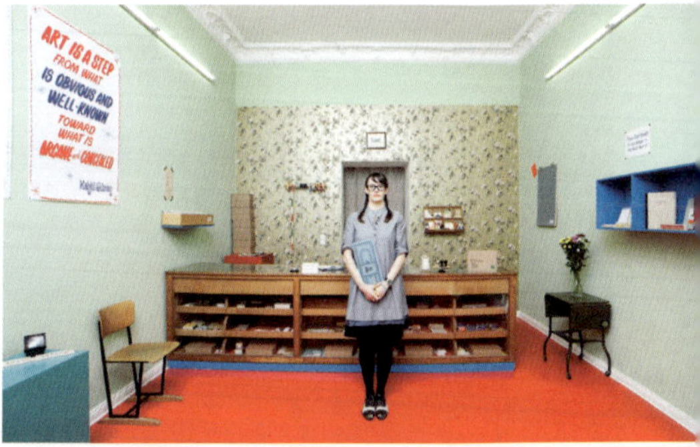

FASHION

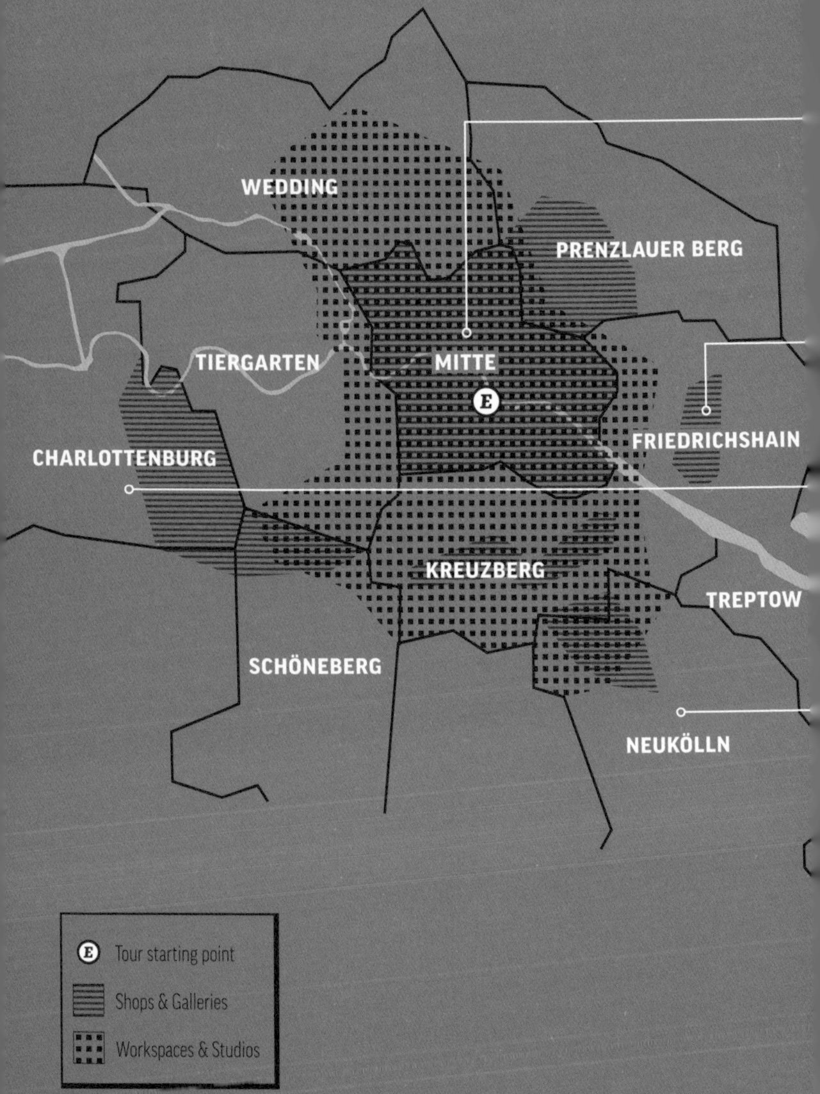
WEDDING
PRENZLAUER BERG
TIERGARTEN
MITTE
FRIEDRICHSHAIN
CHARLOTTENBURG
KREUZBERG
TREPTOW
SCHÖNEBERG
NEUKÖLLN
Tour starting point
Shops & Galleries
Workspaces & Studios

THE EPICENTRE

Mitte is Berlin's fashion centre, at least when it comes to shopping. Established local labels have clustered around Alte Schönhauser Str., Torstr. and Brunnenstr., while it's a little more commercial around Hackescher Markt. Since the fall of the Wall, a large effort has been made to restore Friedrichstr. to its former glory. As a consequence, this area is now home to some high-end global labels.

THE ROOKIE

If you are looking for the DIY aesthetic Berlin is famous for, head to the back streets of **Friedrichshain.** The area is also home to the studios of a few bigger fashion labels and up-and-coming talent.

THE PHOENIX

Charlottenburg's Kurfürstendamm was – in the old West – the place for shopping and entertainment. After being overshadowed by the 'New Mitte' for some time, the area is now becoming popular again, especially since ventures such as the anticipated 'Bikinihaus' are due to open in the near future and designers are rediscovering the neighbourhood as a venue for studios and stores.

THE LABORATORY

Currently Berlin's hippest *Kiez* (the Berlin word for neighbourhood), the streets surrounding **Neukölln's** Weserstr. are a laboratory for designers and hospitality ventures with a proliferation of stores floating new concepts.

OF THE CLOTH

THE INNER WORKINGS OF A MATURING FASHION METROPOLIS

If there's one thing that Berlin isn't short of, it's fashion schools. And where there are fashion schools, there is creative ambition – and where there's ambition, there's potential.

Berlin's nine fashion schools, which range from offering vocational training in textiles to prestigious university courses and branches of private international fashion academies, produce hundreds of graduates each year. While many migrate abroad or towards the textile industry in southern Germany, an increasing number of young designers have taken the Berlin plunge, starting their own labels or seeking employment within the city's burgeoning fashion scene. The years since reunification have seen a reignition of Berlin's self confidence as a creative metropolis, and over the past decade Berlin has grown from sartorial laboratory to fashion capital.

> ***"The recent decade has seen Berlin rise from sartorial laboratory to fashion capital"***

This renaissance is due to two fashion trade fairs. In 2002, the streetwear show Bread & Butter set up shop in Berlin after three seasons in Cologne, while the Premium fair lured labels, journalists and buyers to the city. In typical Berlin style, these events spawned an entire cottage industry of style projects and smaller shows. The international fashion media soon caught wind of these developments, shining a well-deserved spotlight on the city's designers. This book chronicles the development and particularities of this vital scene by introducing the most interesting fashion locations and a selection of the talent that calls Berlin home. The guided walk through Mitte features independent stores and leaves room for new discoveries, while two characters at the very forefront of Berlin fashion share their personal style highlights. The innovation doesn't stop at design – for those inclined towards a truly unique experience, this chapter highlights some 'retail experiments' whose operators put a Berlin twist on concept shopping.

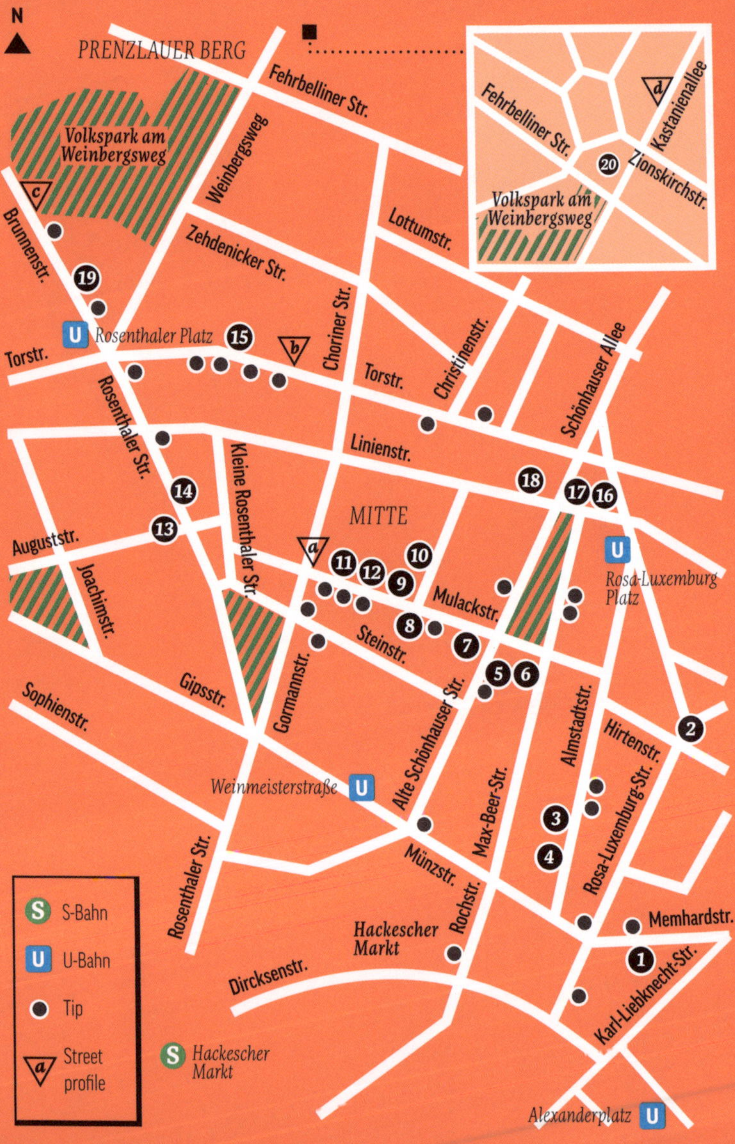
N
PRENZLAUER BERG
Fehrbelliner Str.
Volkspark am Weinbergsweg
Weinbergsweg
c
Brunnenstr.
19
Zehdenicker Str.
Lottumstr.
Choriner Str.
U Rosenthaler Platz
15
b
Torstr.
Torstr.
Christinenstr.
Schönhauser Allee
Rosenthaler Str.
Linienstr.
Kleine Rosenthaler Str.
14
18
17
16
MITTE
13
Auguststr.
a
11
12
10
9
Joachimstr.
Mulackstr.
U Rosa-Luxemburg Platz
8
Steinstr.
7
5
6
Gipsstr.
Gormannstr.
Alte Schönhauser Str.
Sophienstr.
Almstadtstr.
Hirtenstr.
2
Weinmeisterstraße U
Max-Beer-Str.
3
4
Rosa-Luxemburg-Str.
Münzstr.
Rosenthaler Str.
Hackescher Markt
Rochstr.
Memhardstr.
1
Dircksenstr.
Karl-Liebknecht-Str.
S Hackescher Markt
Alexanderplatz U
Fehrbelliner Str.
d
Kastanienallee
20
Zionskirchstr.
Volkspark am Weinbergsweg
S S-Bahn
U U-Bahn
Tip
a Street profile

FASHION STATEMENTS

Many of the city's maturing independent fashion labels and concept stores can be found in Mitte. A tour through the district provides a comprehensive insight into the evolution of Berlin's fashion scene.

As the name implies, Mitte is the geographical heart of the city – it is also Berlin's centre for shopping and design. Many Berliners now see it as a gentrified, overpriced destination frequented mainly by tourists on beer bikes. However, not long ago the district was a busy playground for the city's art, design, fashion and music avant-garde who set up semi-legal bars, galleries, stores and clubs, some of which have survived the district's rapid maturing and continue to be beacons of counter culture. Though there is little evidence of it today, this rebellious past formed the fertile ground on which independent designers felt comfortable enough to conduct their own experiments and to set up dedicated flagship stores.

1

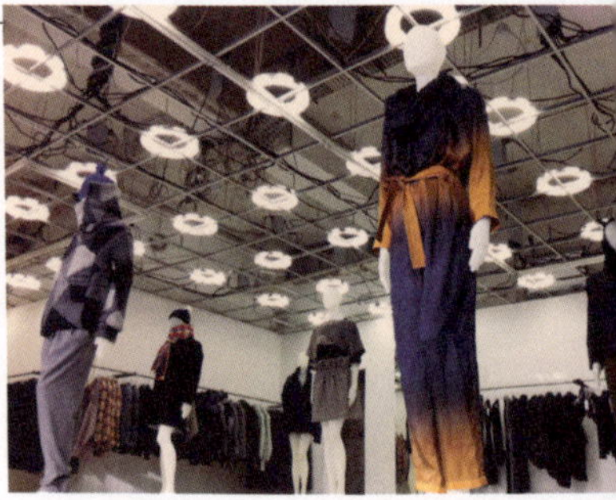

2

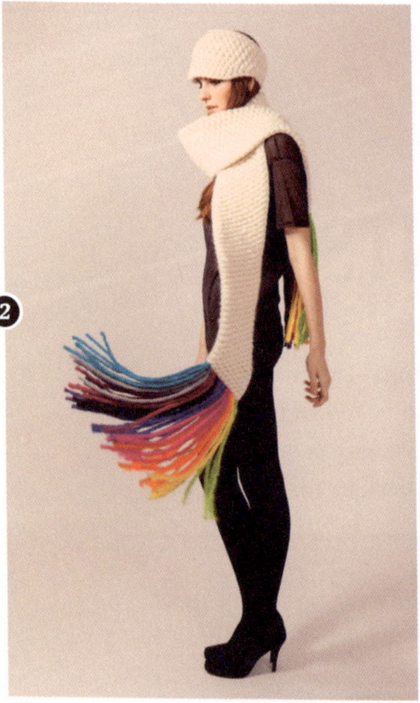

Left Rike Feurstein abandoned a career in law to apprentice in millinery in London and New York. Her studio and store opened in 2006. *Photo* Jan Bohl

Above An apt beginning for this tour, Jet specialises in Berlin designers. *Photo* Falk Weiss

3

Below A7 is a collective presentation space for a number of labels. *Photo* A7 shop

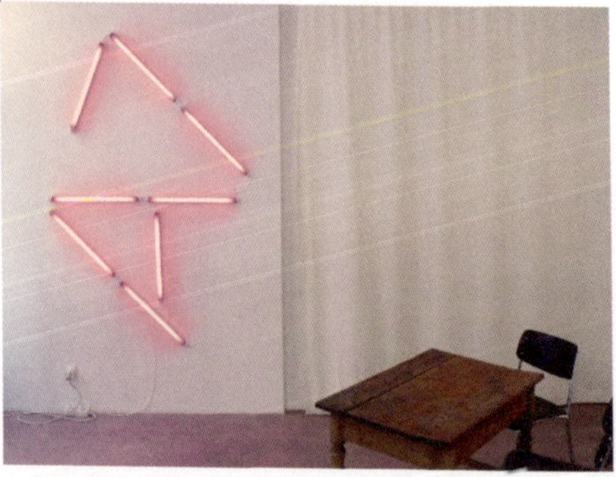

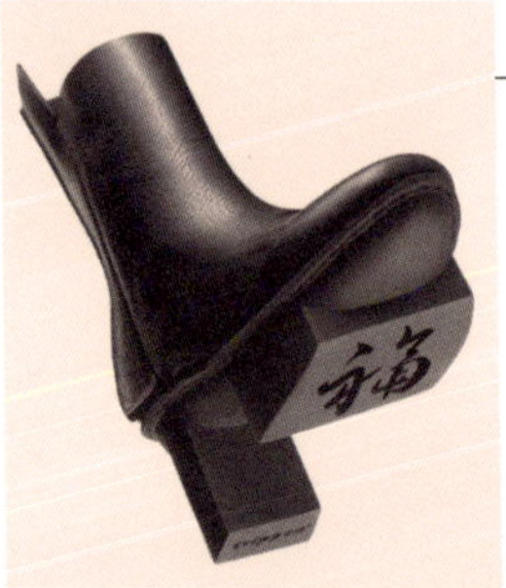

Above Trippen's style is distinguished by its avant-garde, at times Japanese-inspired shapes (pictured: 'Soul' from 'Happy Collection'). *Photo* © Jürgen Holzenleuchter, Ottensoos

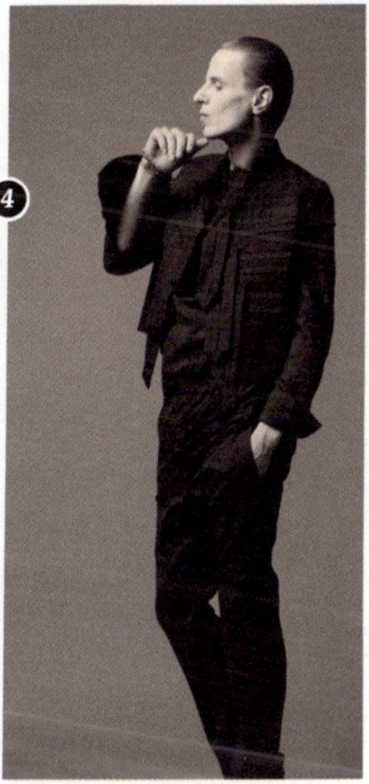

4

Right Lala Berlin is renowned for its distinctive, patterned cashmere creations. *Photo* Dan Lecca

9

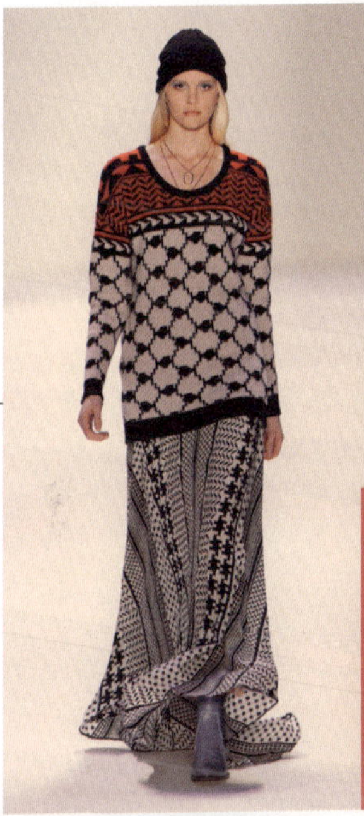

Left Actor Alexander Scheer models for Esther Perbandt. *Photo* Florian Kolmer

5

Right DSTM foregrounds sexiness in black. *Photo* Maxime Ballesteros

10

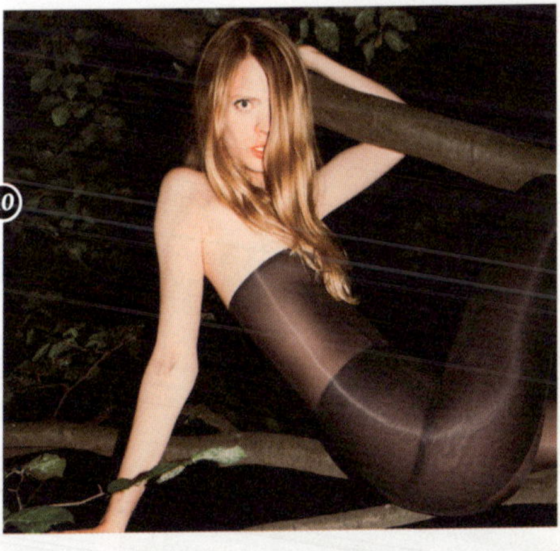

15

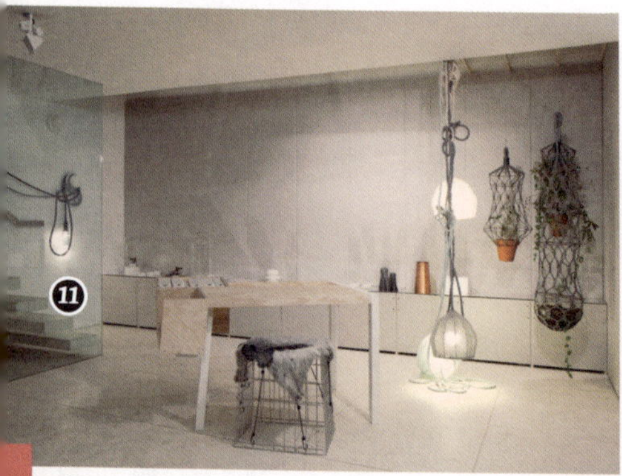

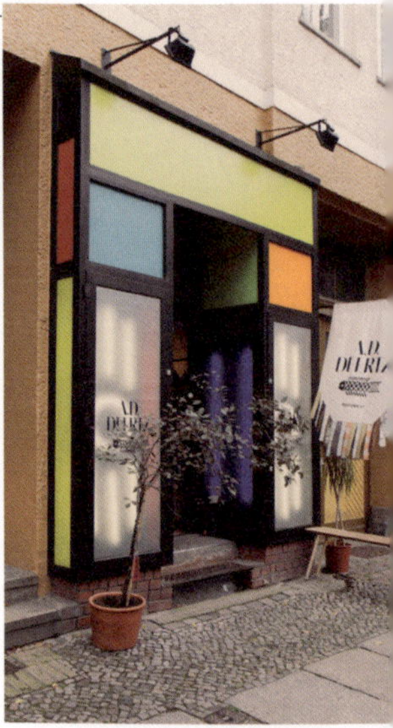

20

Above Baerck is a clothing store but also stocks the creations of product design oufit llot llov.
Photo Vera Hofmann

Above The colourful façade of A.D. Deertz on Torstr.

Below The L40 building on Linienstr., designed by architects Roger Bundschuh and Cosima von Bonin, is home to both Firmament and the Q by Umasan flagship store.
Photo Firmament

16 17

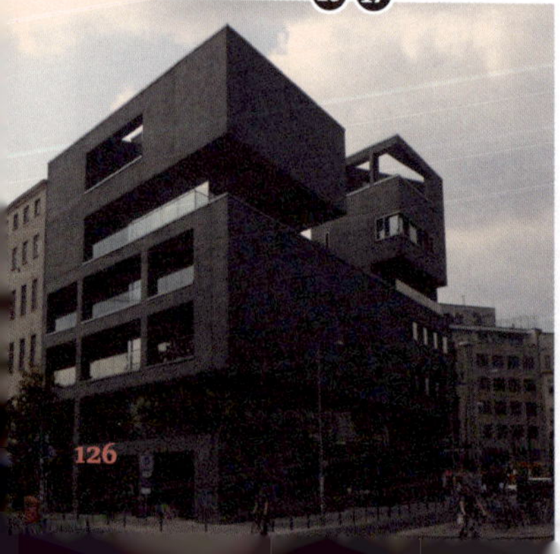

Right C.Neeon is a true institution in the Berlin fashion landscape (A/W collection 2012/13 "...girl with the black raven hair").
Photo Alex Kohout

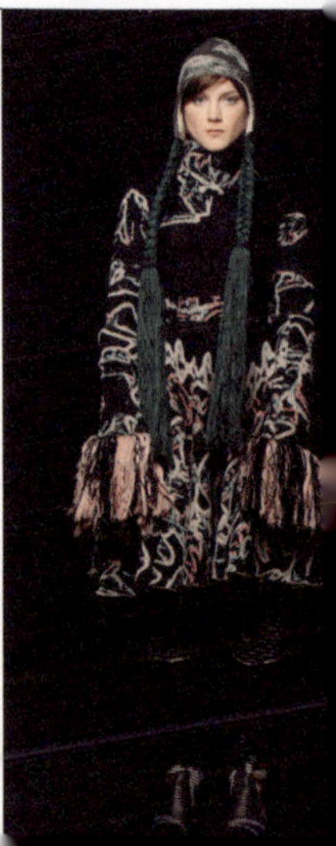

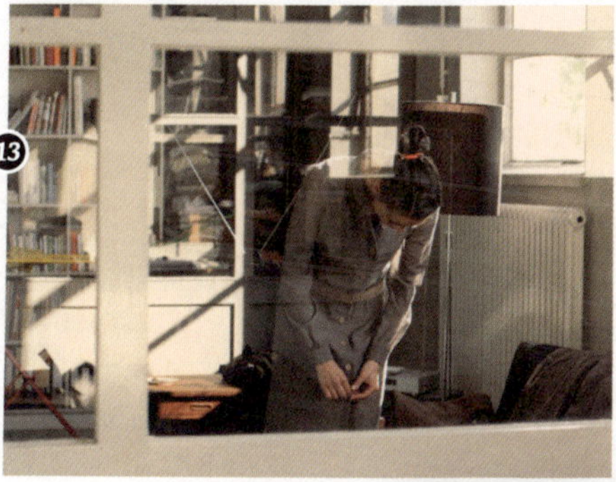

13

Left Wolfen's focus is on timeless, everyday pieces.

Below The Kaviar Gauche designers describe their work as 'modern glamour – luxury and casual avant- garde style with a relaxed attitude'. *Photo* C. Lecca

18

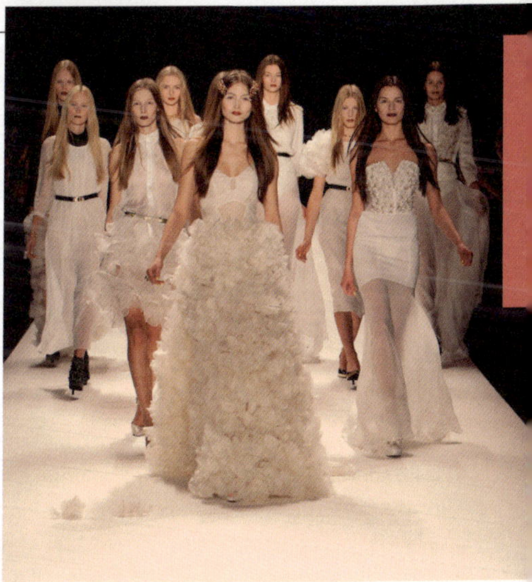

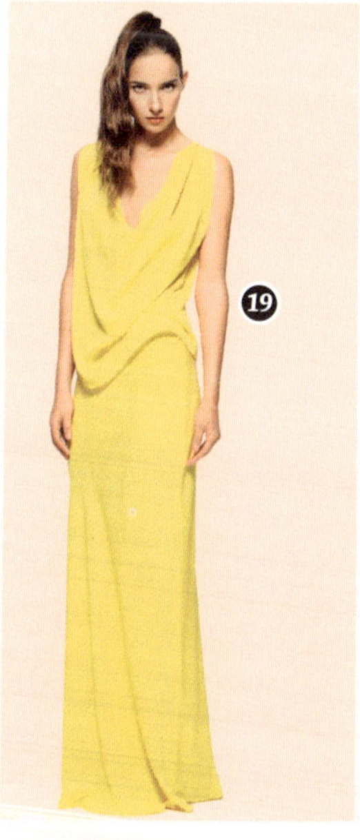

19

Left Antonia Goy's focus is on hand-picking high-quality materials to create luxurious womenswear. *Photo* Anton Andalus, aando-berlin.com

❶ **Jet** *Memhardstr. 1, Mitte | Mon to Sat 12–19*

Our tour starts near the commercial shopping malls at Alexanderplatz, at a little store that opened in late 2011. It's an apt beginning, since Jet specialises in representing Berlin designers. The neon-lit space with somewhat ramshackle charm provides a thorough insight into the breadth of styles produced by local fashion labels, ranging from streetwear to avant-garde.

Tip ... Across the road, the experimental luxury fashion store **Apartment** is concealed beneath a seemingly empty gallery space (*see page 141*). Also, **Ulf Haines** on the corner is a rare place to see the work of Antwerp-based designer **Stephan Schneider,** a professor at Berlin's University of the Arts.

❷ **Rike Feurstein** *Rosa-Luxemburg-Str. 28, Mitte Mon to Fri 12–19, Sat 12–18 | rikefeurstein.com*

Hat aficionados should take a small detour to a shopfront near Rosa-Luxemburg-Platz, Rike Feurstein's working studio. She is one of the few German milliners who aim to revitalise their craft with a contemporary, fashion-based approach. For Feurstein, that means doing away with the traditional decorative aesthetic. Instead, her concept relies on a strong form-meets-colour approach, producing bright yet minimalistic headdresses.

Also visit ... Rosa-Luxemburg-Str. 6 is the home of **Mykita,** one of Berlin's biggest success stories in product design (*see page 181*).

❸ **A7** *Almstadtstr. 7, Mitte | Wed to Fri 12-19, Sat 13–17 | a7berlin.de*

At the bottom end of Almstadtstr. sits A7, named simply after its address. A7 is a collaborative venture that functions as a presentation space and store for a number of local labels, including the label Tiedeken, part of the first wave of 'new Berlin designers' who launched around 2003. The label had a short break and lost part of its original name when Regina Tiedeken's business partner left. But in 2011, Tiedeken resurfaced with a more casual look that includes draped jersey dresses, knitted cardigans,

Also visit ... Art and architecture book lovers, drop in to **Pro Qm** (*see page 203*). Next door, the label **International Wardrobe** takes inspiration from traditional dress and folk art from far-flung places.

Almstadtstr. 50
Thu to Sat 10–20 | internationalwardrobe.com

printed shirts and large bags. Also part of the band of designers behind A7 is streetwear label Rob-Ert and bag and purse label Gretchen.

Refuel ... **Oliv**, on the corner, provides great café-style sustenance for the journey.
Münzstr. 8 | oliv-cafe.de

❹ Esther Perbandt *Almstadtstr. 3, Mitte*

Wed to Fri 10–19, Sat 12–18 | estherperbandt.com

Two doors down from A7 is the white, minimalist flagship store of local fashion celebrity Esther Perbandt. The Berlin-born, Moscow and Paris-educated designer has been creating her androgynous fashion for both sexes since 2004. During Fashion Week, she always enlivens the off-site calendar with her events and catwalk shows. Since cloning her distinctive bowl haircut on the models that presented her garments on the runway, she has become an easily recognisable fixture of the Berlin fashion community, as have her oversized bags and the signature chains adorning her clothes and accessories.

Tip ... Rochstr. boasts two stores of Danish label **Wood Wood** whose pieces are hugely popular in this city.
Rochstr. 3 & 4
Mon to Sat 12–20
woodwood.dk

❺ Trippen *Alte Schönhauser Str. 45, Mitte*

Mon to Sat 12–19 | trippen.com (Also: Hackesche Höfe, Hof 4 & 6 | Rosenthaler Str. 40/41, Mitte and Knaackstr. 26, Prenzlauer Berg)

This is a true Berlin design success story. The year 2012 marked 20 years since Michael Oehler and Angela Spieth started their shoe label, which now encompasses a number of overarching lines. Their 'form follows sustainability' approach means that all designs and materials are chosen to minimise the use of resources, while the shoes themselves are produced in a dedicated workshop about an hour's drive outside Berlin.

Tip ... **Wald**, which stocks many local labels, is near the intersection of Münzstr. and Alte Schönhauser Str.
Alte Schönhauser Str. 32c | Mon to Sat 12–20
wald-berlin.de

❻ **Atelier Awash Shop & Lab** *Max-Beer-Str. 31 | Mon to Sat 10–18 | atelierawash.com*

Anyone interested in a new take on menswear should drop in at Atelier Awash, the physical representation of eco label Banuq, which is designed in Berlin and sustainably produced in Italy. Artist-turned-designer Davide Garzoli uses materials such as hemp and linen and experiments with other eco-friendly production methods like vegetable-based dyes. The label's Italian influence is evident; where German fashion relies heavily on meticulously engineered pattern techniques, Banuq garments are all about materiality.

Refuel ... Casual Korean restaurant **Yam-Yam**, a popular spot to have a meal before heading out, is nearby.

Alte Schönhauser Str.6
yamyam-berlin.de

Pony Bar, also nearby, is a good place for people watching over a coffee or beer.

Alte Schönhauser Str. 44

❼ **Firma** *Mulackstr. 1, Mitte | Mon to Sat 12–19 firma.net*

The Firma flagship store is the first stop on style-heavy Mulackstr. Founded in 1998, the label is a veteran in this very young fashion metropolis. It is defined by almost obsessive accuracy and cool sobriety and is now supplemented by a line of cosmetics.

About the Street
Mulackstraße

The streets to the west of Alte Schönhauser Str. (Gipsstr., Steinstr., Linienstr., Gormannstr. and Mulackstr. in particular) constitute Berlin's centre for independent fashion. This evolution started in 2002, when the store of design label Bless opened its doors. Today, about a dozen fashion stores – among them the flagships of Berlin's most successful labels – line the street.

EXCURSION: VINTAGE

For all those who can't pass up last season's treasures, make sure to visit the following stores.

Das neue Schwarz
The store with one of Berlin's best vintage selections is located in the former flagship store of coveted product design/fashion hybrid Bless (*see page 179*).

Mulackstr. 38, Mitte
dasneueschwarz.de

In nearby Steinstr, you can find second season fashion by international stars like Bernhard Willhelm or Sonia Rykiel at **YUU.**

Steinstr. 26, Mitte | yuu-shop.de

Down the street, **XVII** sells vintage fashion and romantic one-of-a-kind accessories and objects.

Steinstr. 17, Mitte | xvii-store.com

Garments Vintage, not far from here, stocks an ecclectic mix of vintage designer fashion and is a satisfying stop for accessory hunters.

Linienstr. 204-205, Mitte
garments-vintage.de

8 Starstyling *Mulackstr.4, Mitte | Mon to Sat 12–19 | starstyling.net*

Starstyling occupies its own niche in the Berlin fashion scene, since a design philosophy underpinned by decoration is a big 'no' in Germany's design schools. But Starstyling, which started in 2000, has successfully been able to combine a decorative, fun aesthetic with casual fashion.

9 Lala Berlin *Mulackstr. 7, Mitte | Mon to Fri 11.30–19.30, Sat 12–18 | lalaberlin.com*

There's no going past Lala Berlin. Since Leyla Piedayesh first appeared on the scene in 2004 with a pair of modest knitted wristbands, her label hasn't stopped growing. A few knitted pieces became entire accessory collections, of which the bestselling items have always been soft, printed cashmere scarves. Now, Lala Berlin presents two collections a year at Berlin Fashion Week. Despite the shift from best-kept local secret to international fashion brand, the focus has not shifted away from high-end knits and cashmere continues to play a starring role.

10 DSTM - Don't Shoot the Messengers *Rückerstr. 10, Mitte | Mon to Sat 13–20*

Although DSTM's collections feature casual pieces, no other Berlin label is as emphatically sexy. Intrepid Canadian Jen Gilpin and New Zealander Kyle Callanan, who both settled in Berlin in 2008, propagate an image of the woman as vamp; high heels and skin-tight dresses play important roles, as does materiality in the form of glossy fabrics and softly shimmering silk. Leather is a recurrent material, used to shape the body and define contours, while silk delivers a flowing component and transparency. The DSTM portfolio is now complemented by a menswear range.

Optional ... At **Schwarzhogerzeil**, you'll find international avant-garde fashion alongside the work of local accessory and jewellery designers. Its 'off-season' sister store is a few doors down, recognisable by a macramé mobile at the door.

Mulackstr 28 & 23
Mon to Fri 12–19, Sat 12–18 , and Tue to Sat 14–18 respectively
schwarzhogerzeil.de

⓫ **Baerck** *Mulackstr. 12, Mitte | Mon to Sat 12–20 baerck.net*

Next awaits the bungalow-esque interior of Baerck, run by two of the four designers behind product design label llot llov (*see page 190*). Baerck exemplifies a defining characteristic of the Berlin creative scene – metamorphosis through flexibility. Instead of simply having an office, a studio, or an agency, Berlin creatives almost always have a project on the side. In the case of Baerck, the store initially started in the front room of the llot llov studio to sell Nia, a label run by one of its members. Since then, Baerck has grown organically into a one-stop shop for cutting-edge international style while housing a llot llov showroom in the basement.

Optional ... Two nearby stores cater to the posher clientele. **Hecking** not only sells accessories, but also some bags produced under Louise Hecking's eponymous label. **C'est Tout** focuses on fashion for special occasions with soft and feminine silk and jersey dresses.

Gormannstr. 8-9
hecking-shop.com

Mulackstr. 26
cestout.de

⓬ **Butterflysoulfire** *Mulackstr. 11, Mitte | Tue to Sat 14–18 | btfsf.de*

On a raised first floor, another veteran Berlin label presents versatile looks that range from medieval to avant-garde; wearers are required to tie, string or twine to fit snugly into creations made of heavy wool or solid jersey. Since starting out in 2002, Butterflysoulfire – which, according to its designers, is based on the questioning of art through fashion – has never experienced the hype that other labels have, but has consistently grown and evolved.

13 Wolfen *Auguststr. 41, Mitte | Mon to Fri 12–19, Sat 12–18 | wolfengermany.com*

Across Rosenthaler Str. sits the small Wolfen flagship store. This label unites two often contrasting concepts, fashion and idealism. Trained architect Jacqueline Huste started the label a decade ago, initially recruiting retired ladies in her hometown of Wolfen to knit the cardigans that have become the label's signature item. The Wolfen business model defies all established fashion rules. Rather than collections, there are series of simple, everyday clothes, all manufactured by local artisans or in Huste's studio and home in a former industrial building in Wedding.

Optional ... A small detour takes you to the shoe and accessories paradise **Le Coup**, featuring the up-and-coming shoe brand **Sydney Brown** as well as a range of independent international labels.

Steinstr. 16 | Mon to Sat 12–19 | lecoupshoes.com

14 PotiPoti *Rosenthaler Str. 66, Mitte | Mon to Fri 12–20 | potipoti.com*

Near Rosenthaler Platz you'll find the PotiPoti's flagship store, started by Silvia Salvador and Nando Carnejo, who swapped graphic design in their native Spain for fashion in Berlin. PotiPoti is the living example of Berlin's allure to the global creative scene. Having made the leap from backyard workshop to streetfront retail space, this label is one success story amongst many designers who leave after experiencing the first rough winter and little job prospects. PotiPoti's brightly patterned clothes are dominated by knitwear with strong graphic elements, manufactured in Spain. Its strong Iberian connection is also evidenced by other labels represented in the store.

⑮ A.D.Deertz *Torstr. 106, Mitte | Mon to Sat 12–20 addertz.com*

Optional ... Since launching her jewellery label in 2004, **Sabrina Dehoff** has refused to succumb to a signature style. The designer continually experiments with motifs, materials and combinations.

Torstr. 175 | Mon to Fri 12–19, Sat 12–18 sabrinadehoff.com

You can't miss A.D. Deertz thanks to its colourful façade and flying flag. Wibke Deertz has been making men's fashion since 2000. Just like Wolfen or Banuq, Deertz also freed herself from the shackles of the fashion calendar, producing a small series of ever-evolving 'classics' rather than bi-annual collections, sold almost exclusively through her own store. Her goal is to create fashion that looks like it's been part of the wearer's wardrobe for some time – because Berlin cool always involves a little patina.

b *About the Street*

Torstraße

No matter which aspect of Berlin design you seek, you'll end up on Torstr. This ugly four-lane thoroughfare may look nondescript at first, but the street's stores, restaurants and galleries are run by people who are invariably passionate about their work and happy to experiment with new concepts. They have ensured that it remains one of the most exciting areas in town.

Refuel ... There's plenty of opportunity to refuel along here, for instance at **Hartweizen.**

Torstr. 96 hartweizen.com

Optional ... Menswear store **Soto** (*see page 155*) is renowned beyond Berlin borders, while **Happy Shop** (*see page 142*), does away with established retail traditions.

⑯ Firmament *Linienstr. 40, Mitte | Mon to Sat 11–19 | firmamentberlin.com*

Just off Torstr., the monolithic L40 building (named after its location) is a small paradise for guys who refuse to grow up. In-house label Firmament is devoted mainly to screen printed shirts while the rest of the stock – including special editions by a number of sneaker brands – complements its aesthetic.

Optional...Superficial features a selection of shirts by Asian designers and Berlin newcomers.

Torstr. 102
Mon to Fri 12–20
superficial-berlin.com

⑰ Q by Umasan Flagship Store & Showroom *Linienstr. 40, Mitte | Mon, Wed to Sat 12–19 | umasan-world.com*

Right next door to Firmament is the flagship store of the vegan label by twins Sandra and Anja Umann. Inspired by yogic law, Q does without leather and all other animal-derived textiles such as wool and cashmere. The range includes sportswear as well as jackets and dresses in a straightforward colour scheme. Q's form, function and pattern are determined by human anatomy and kinesiology.

Also visit ... a few other interesting design addresses such as, **Appel Design Gallery** (*see page 172*) and **Möbel Horzon** (*see page 180*).

Tip ... As you continue, you may also come across the **Kaviar Gauche vintage store**, a testament to the fact that Berlin fashion is really growing up.

Brunnenstr. 6,
Mon to Sat 12–19
kaviargauche.com

⑱ Kaviar Gauche *Linienstr 44, Mitte | Mon to Sat 12–19 | kaviargauche.com*

Kaviar Gauche is an integral part of the young German fashion scene. Where other designers strive to be understated and conceptual, this label seeks to create a sense of eye-catching elegance. Known for its flowing dresses with emphasis on the waistline and well-appointed accessories, Kaviar Gauche has crossed over into the world of high fashion and has branched out into bridalwear on top of its prêt-à-porter range.

⑲ Antonia Goy *Brunnenstrasse 5, Mitte antoniagoy.com*

As you make your way back to Rosenthaler Platz, turn right into Brunnenstr. to find Antonia Goy's restrained flagship store, an extension of her studio and home. The Paris-trained designer continues to establish a large international network, whether to show her work (in Paris), to produce it (with artisans in Poland) or to sell it (like many German designers, she enjoys much popularity in Japan). Her work is always of exceptional quality, which is not a given in a city where many designers produce and finish their garments themselves.

About the Street

Brunnenstraße

This street goes through a significant transformation on its way from Mitte to Wedding. The lower end has become a bustling hub for fashion stores and other design-related businesses. Up the hill, as the street becomes less glamorous, you will still find the occasional art gallery.

Optional ... There's a definitive streetwear edge to the **Civilist Service** store nearby, and exhibitions, collaborations with international labels and other events ensure that this space is more than just a shop.

Brunnenstr. 13
civilist-berlin.de

20 C.Neeon *Kastanienallee 55, Mitte | Mon to Sat 11–21 | c.neeon.de*

C.Neoon has been around since the days when Kastanienallee was a true fashion mile. When textile designer Clara Leskova and fashion designer Doreen Schulz joined forces after their graduation from Kunsthochschule Weissensee School of Art, it did not take them long to win the acclaimed fashion competition Hyères in 2004. The wave of international attention that followed helped put Berlin on the avant-garde fashion map. It seems that this was also the birth of a design partnership now typical of Berlin: nowhere else does the two-girls-one-fashion-label concept seem to have gathered so much traction. In recent years, things have become a bit quieter around C.Neeon. Without reinventing themselves or promoting a new trend, they instead consistently develop their style of wild patterns and innovative cuts with eye-catching elements.

Tip ... C.Neeon isn't the only remnant of past avant-garde days; **Temporary Showroom** (*see page 145*) is another veteran institution on this street.

Optional ... Near Rosenthaler Platz, on the way towards Prenzlauer Berg, another store, **Adrett,** devotes itself entirely to Berlin and German fashion.

Weinbergsweg 23,
Mon to Sat 12–20
adrett-berlin.de

About the Street:
Kastanienallee

This 2km strip was once Prenzlauer Berg's major art and party artery. After the fall of the Wall, the area was popular with students and artists who snapped up the inexpensive and often vacant apartments in run-down buildings. The rapid transformation from decrepit thoroughfare to bustling party strip and later to a popular shopping mile has earned Kastanienallee the nickname of 'Casting Alley'. Today, most of the fashion-related businesses located here are limited to printed T-shirts or Berlin souvenirs but there are some notable exceptions.

SEBASTIANO RAGUSA

Stylist

Invisible Forces

Stylists are the unsung heroes of the fashion world, responsible for transforming a designer's vision into a look that's fit for everyday life – or into a different context altogether. Even within this eccentric species, Sebastiano Ragusa is one of a kind. With a shaved head, an imposing stature and a personal penchant for eccentric clothing, Sebastiano knows how to dress himself (and others) to make a grand entrance. Born in Stuttgart to Sicilian parents, he arrived in Berlin in 2008 armed with a degree in fashion journalism and has since pursued his love for style by working with local designers and as fashion director at Derzeit, an independent daily publication for Berlin's Fashion Week. These are his suggestions for a high-style afternoon.

sebastianoragusa.com

1 **"Butterflysoulfire is a typical Berlin success story: two fashion audodidacts who came up with a perfect plan and haven't stopped since.** While other Berlin fashion brands have come and gone, Butterflysoulfire celebrated its 10th anniversary in 2012 and has become a well known brand abroad – in Asia, for example – where their work has lots of fans."

U ***Rosenthaler Platz | Mulackstr. 11, Mitte | Tue to Sat 14–18 | btfsf.de***

2 **"Pastpresent is a combination of a gallery, studio and menswear shop that plays an important role in the Berlin fashion scene. It is well-heeled with a bit of a gothic feel, and not only is it 'off Mitte', but it is also off the beaten track.** Berlin is home to many different tastes and styles. Pastpresent is one of those places that perfectly embodies the spirit of the city – it's well worth the pilgrimage!"

U ***Heinrich-Heine Straße | Köpenickerstr. 96, Mitte | Mon to Sat 14–20 | pastpresent.de***

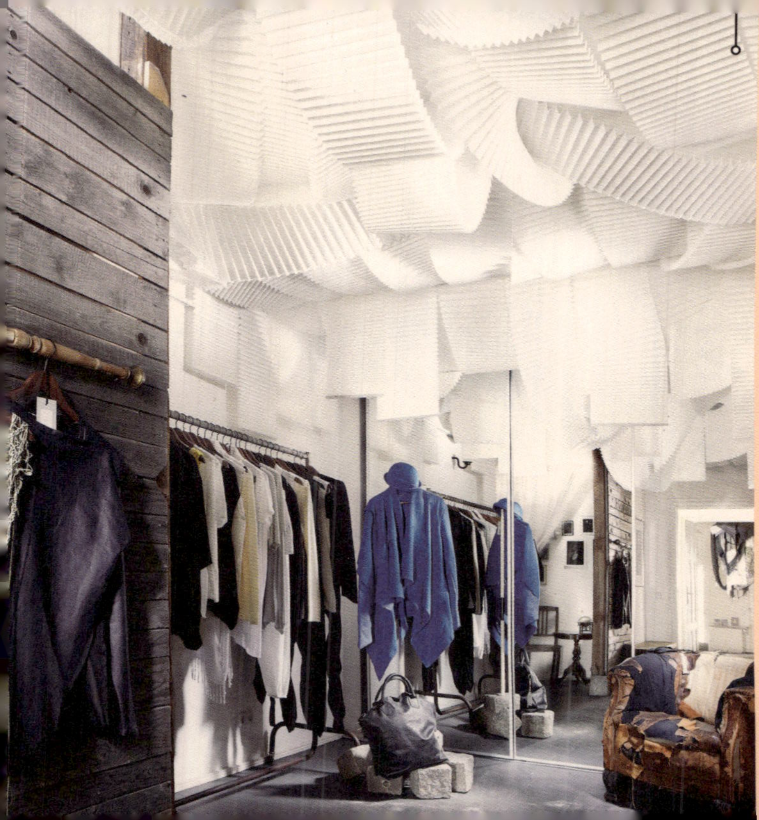

3 **“Nightboutique is a veritable fashion institution. The concept – a kind of sales party with vintage treasures and fashion installations – would probably never work anywhere else in Germany.** What originally started as an event has now turned into a showroom by appointment where contemporary high fashion like Comme des Garçons and Maison Martin Margiela is matched with vintage pieces.”

U ***Friedrichstraße | Georgenstr. 35, Mitte by appointment only | nightboutique.net***

TIPS ...

Mamecha, Japanese Green Tea Café – with great attention to detail.

Mulackstr. 33, Mitte | Mon, Wed to Sat 12–20, Sun 14–20 | mamecha.com

Möbel Olfe, a good place to start the night – loud music, mixed crowd.

Reichenberger Str. 177, Kreuzberg Tue to Sun from 18 | moebel-olfe.de

Left The Butterflysoulfire store
Photo Laura Deschner

THE RETAIL EXPERIMENT

Sometimes a shop isn't just a shop. It's a source of inspiration, a work of art, an experiment with counter-culture or an academic enterprise. Those who run these places are curators of consumption, at times true pioneers who reconceptualise the way we engage with shopping. Berlin, with its abundance of affordable space and its DIY spirit, is the perfect location to develop a new angle on fashion retail.

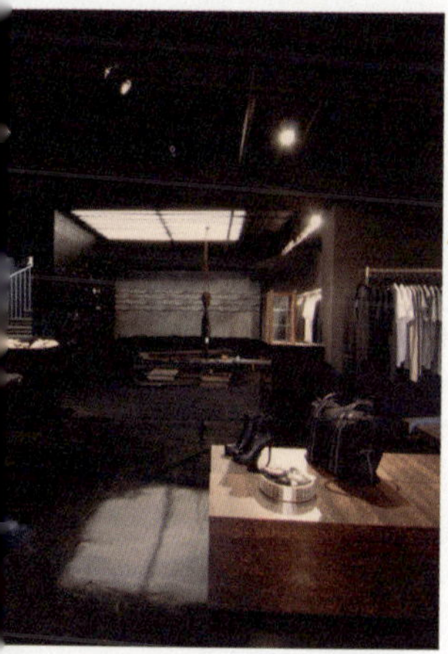

Photo Ira Wirth -Widarzik

Apartment

This is perhaps Berlin's most radical fashion store, where the 'luxury' label not only applies to fashion but also to the retail space – much of Apartment is simply unoccupied. A large bouquet of flowers is the only sign of habitation upon entry. A spiralling staircase leads to the basement, where black is the dominant colour and extends to carpet, floor, furniture and the fashion (Rick Owens amongst others). Cash, Apartment's second season store, is around the corner on Rosa-Luxemburg-Str.

U S ***Alexanderplatz*** | *Memhardstr. 8, Mitte | Mon to Fri 11–19, Sat 12–19 | apartmentberlin.de*

Darklands

ROVING AROUND

— *In a city that's always in flux, pop-up stores and nomadic ventures are the norm. Blogs like* ***lesmads.de, stilinberlin.de*** *and newsletters* ***ceecee.cc*** *and* ***sugarhigh.de*** *keep you abreast.*

Black is the dominant shade at Darklands, a store that reflects Berlin's resistance to being just fashionable. Opened by Canadian Campbell McDougal in 2008, Darklands' distinguishing feature is its nomadic nature. The store has previously resided in the cool quarter of Mitte as well as in a basement between clubs and galleries near Hauptbahnhof, far from the trendy fashion destinations. Many of Darkland's labels are not found elsewhere in Berlin. In early 2012, Darklands shifted to a hidden courtyard in Tiergarten and also started stocking womenswear.

U ***Hauptbahnhof*** | *Heidestraße 46–52, Building 7, Tiergarten Mon to Sat 12–19 | darklandsberlin.com*

Happy Shop

Since 2002, Mischa Alexandra Woeste has been steadily campaigning to brighten up the image of Germany's and Berlin's fashion universe, which wouldn't usually be described as 'happy'. Woeste's first strike was to create jubilant womenswear under the tongue-twisting name 'Smeilinener'. In 2011, she extended her crusade for positive thinking with 'Happy Shop', a temple to contemporary fashion, stocking international labels and accessories selected by Woeste and creative director Mark Windekilde. The container-shaped building was purpose-designed by Woeste's husband's architecture firm Fingerle&Woeste.

U ***Rosa-Luxemburg-Platz*** | *Torstr. 67, Mitte* | *Tue to Sat 11–19*
happy-shopberlin.com

RETAIL THEATRE

— *Happy Shop is more stage set than store, literally. It features a fly system modeled on that of a theatre; all displays can be swiftly whisked away to make room for fashion shows, exhibitions and parties.*

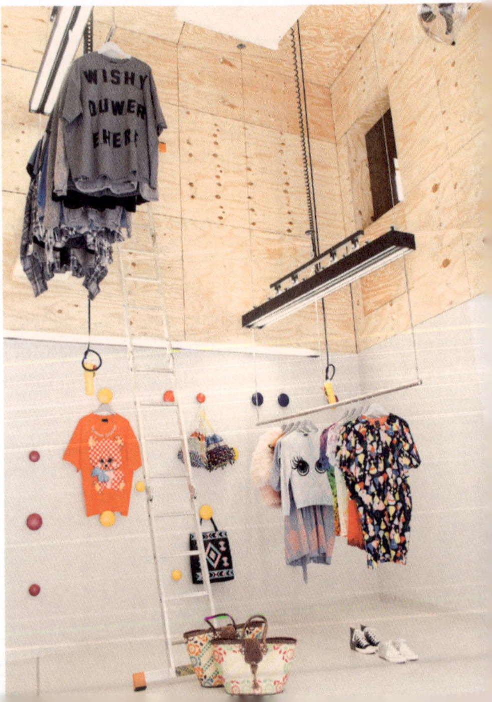

Right photo Leifur Wilberg

Far right photo CS Digital, architecture and interior design by AAS Gonzalez/ Haase

Murkudis

There's no question about it: Andreas Murkudis runs Berlin's most striking fashion store. The enormous volume of space inside this former newspaper printing plant suggests that the person behind it must be bold in their approach to business and sophisticated with regard to taste. That Andreas Murkudis is a true pioneer became even more evident in late 2011, when the retail maven moved his three stores from one of Berlin's best addresses in Mitte to the rather nondescript Potsdamer Str. Murkudis' concept works. His well-heeled fans are inspired by the hand-picked selection, which includes the international fashion establishment such as Dries van Noten alongside accessories from local newcomers like jeweller Kiki Dieterle.

OBJECT AS SUBJECT

— *The compound that was formerly the printing facility of Berlin's newspaper* ***Der Tagesspiegel*** *is now a vibrant hub for art galleries. Murkudis has found the ideal environment for presenting fashion and objects as cultural artifacts, rather than mere consumer goods.*

U *Kurfürstenstraße* | *Potsdamer Str. 81, Tiergarten* | *Mon to Sat 10–20*
andreasmurkudis.com

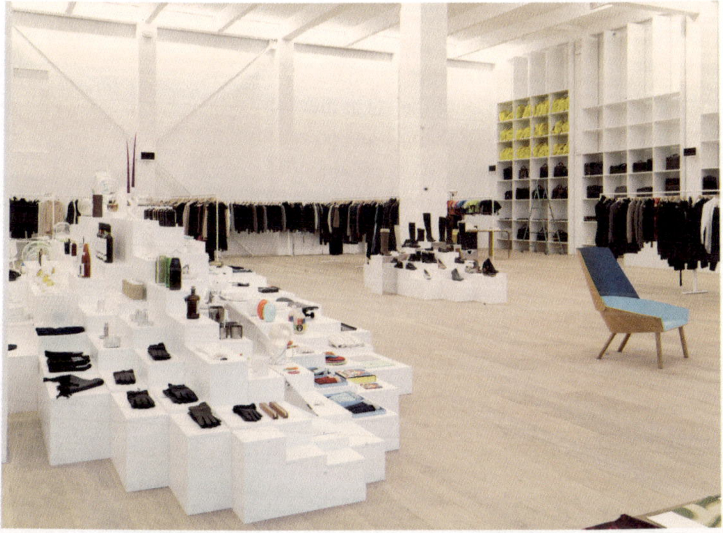

Voo

In 2011, even grungy Kreuzberg got a hip concept store. Situated right in the middle of the former heart of counter-culture on Oranienstr., Voo's 300sqm space in a former industrial warehouse is now also home to a café (*see page 230*) and hosts fashion parties, readings, concerts and runway shows. Relatively unrenovated, the atmosphere is industrial chic meets vintage charm. Featuring as much clothing as it does other accessories including candles, pens, books and socks, Voo is a concept store in the very sense of the definition, but reflects the sartorial sensibilities of the casual Kreuzbergian.

U ***Kottbusser Tor*** | *Oranienstr. 24, Kreuzberg* | *Mon to Sat 11–20*
vooberlin.com

Tip ... The store was founded by Yasin and Kaan Müjdeci, who also own the popular **Café/Bar Luzia** nearby.
Oranienstr. 34 | *luzia.tc*

Photo below © Oukan, Achim Hatzius

Oukan 71

This charity-cum-concept store is a welcome addition to Friedrichstr., which has become a commercial shopping mile since the fall of the Wall. Natalie Viaux and Huy Thong Tran Mai started Tokyo Gakudan in July 2011, presenting the work of young Japanese fashion labels in Berlin to help creatives affected by the events in Fukushima earlier that year. However, instead of closing after a few months, what started out as a project is now a permanent space complete with the occasional reading and exhibition.

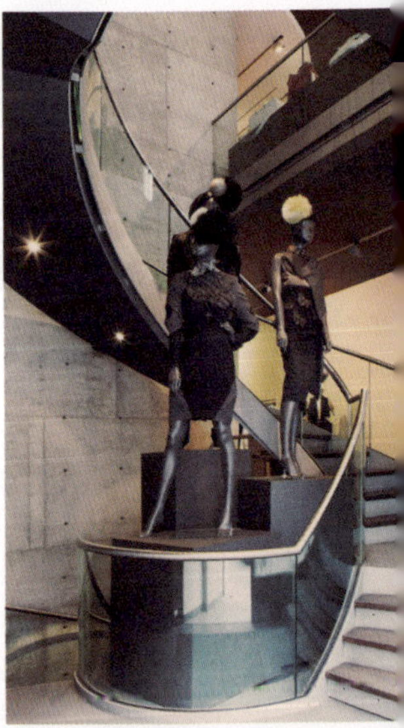

U ***Stadtmitte*** | *Kronenstr. 71, Mitte* | *Mon to Sat 12–20*
oukan71.com

Temporary Showroom

It's all in a name at Temporary Showroom, although 'temporary' refers only to the changing schedule. Their corner location on Kastanienallee – which was a centre for counter-culture in the post-Wall days but is now the ultimate showcase for gentrification – has been stalwart of avant-garde style since it opened. In 1999, its director Martin Premuzic rented the space with some friends and used it for parties and exhibitions. He gradually shifted to representing German and international labels in search of retailers. Today, the building, like most others on this street, has been entirely renovated. Temporary Showroom represents 10 to 15 independent, mostly Scandinavian labels.

Tip ... Once **Fashion Week** comes around, Temporary Showroom returns to its roots as an agency. It stocks yet-to-hit-mainstream labels from all around the globe and is open only to press and buyers.

Photo below
Achim Hatzius

U ***Rosenthaler Platz*** | *Kastanienallee 36a, Mitte* | *Tue to Sat 11–19* | *temporaryshowroom.com*

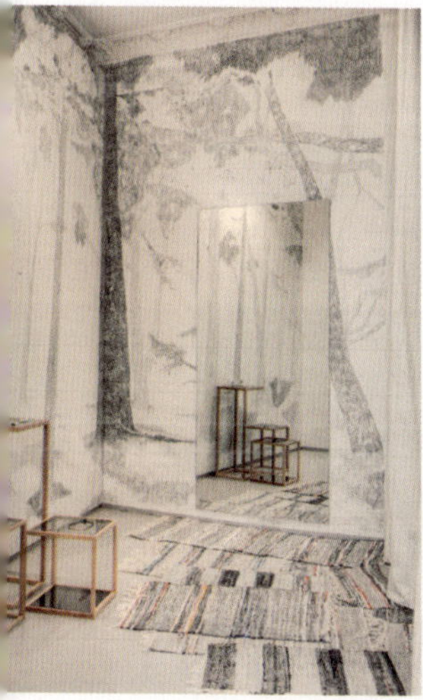

Konk

Don't underestimate the importance of this diminutive store. Founded in 2003, Konk is ancient by Berlin standards, yet it hasn't stopped being ahead of the pack. The store was initially the flagship for the first label by Ettina Berrios-Negrón (*see page 150*), which she then ran with a partner. Inspired by the burgeoning Berlin fashion scene, the duo slowly introduced other local fashion and jewellery designers into the shop's collection and Konk blossomed into a destination for new German fashion. Ettina sold the shop to Edda Mann in 2012 but the concept remains.

U ***Rosenthaler Platz*** | *Kleine Hamburger Str. 15, Mitte* | *Mon to Fri 12–19, Sat 12–18* | *konk-berlin.de*

BEHIND THE SCENES WITH

Frank Leder

Frank Leder is one of Berlin's most unusual designers, as he engages – happily, critically and not entirely without irony – with German culture and traditions. Where other designers prefer to forgo national stereotypes and are a little uneasy on the subject, this designer reinterprets and dissects the traditional working uniforms of butchers, mailmen and forest rangers into wearable, beautifully constructed collections for men and women. His studio, located in an expansive Bel Etage apartment in Charlottenburg, shows that his fascination with the subject stretches beyond his work in fashion.

frank-leder.com

Photos this page & next Max Zerrahn

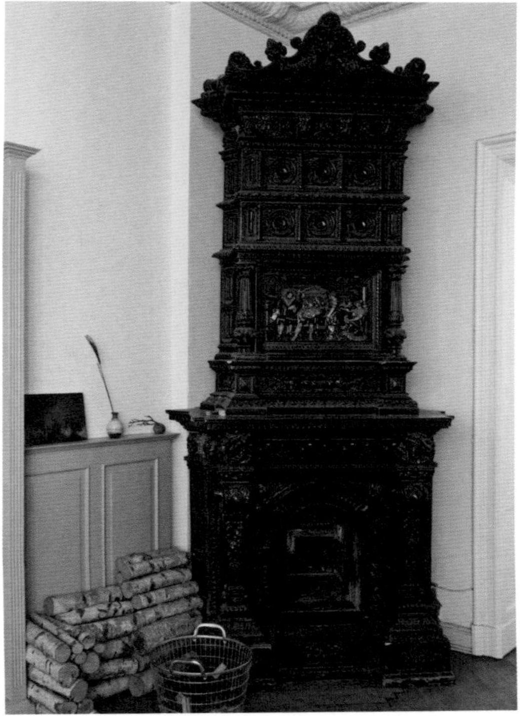

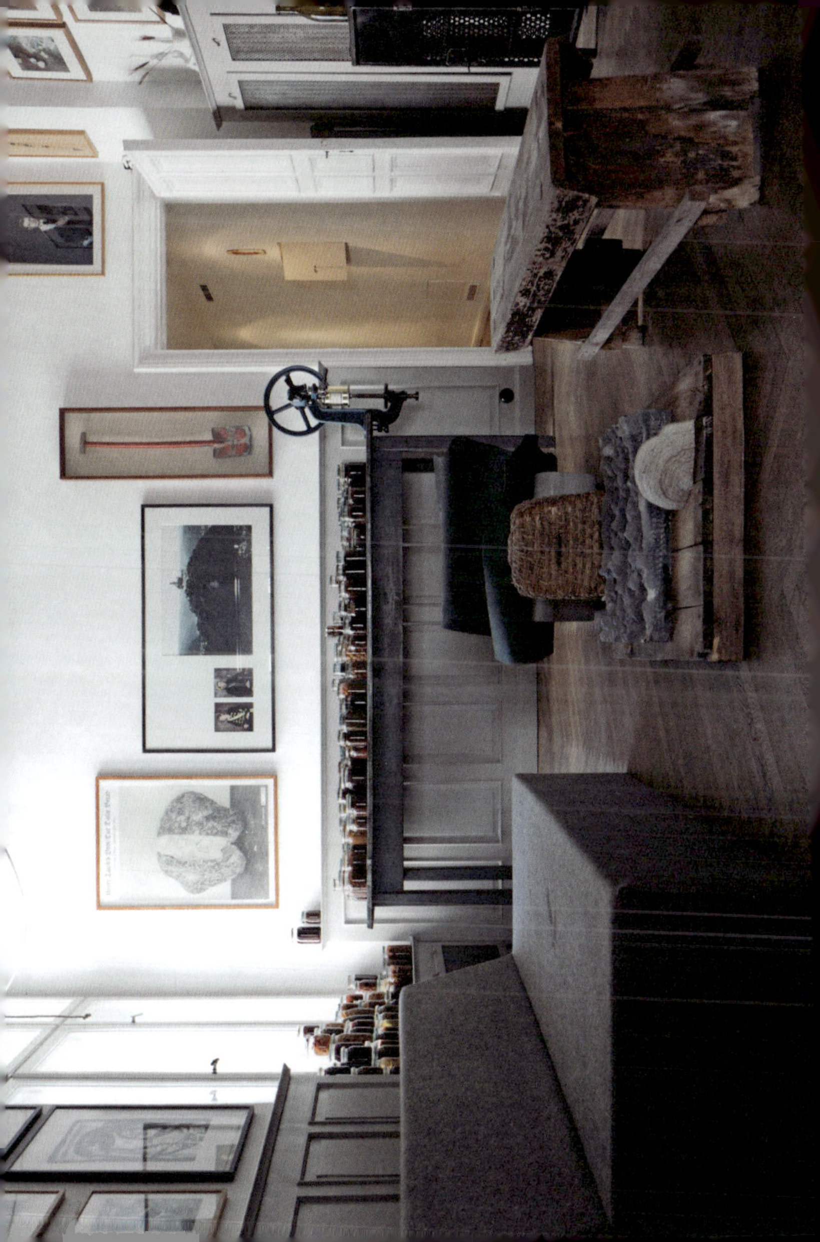

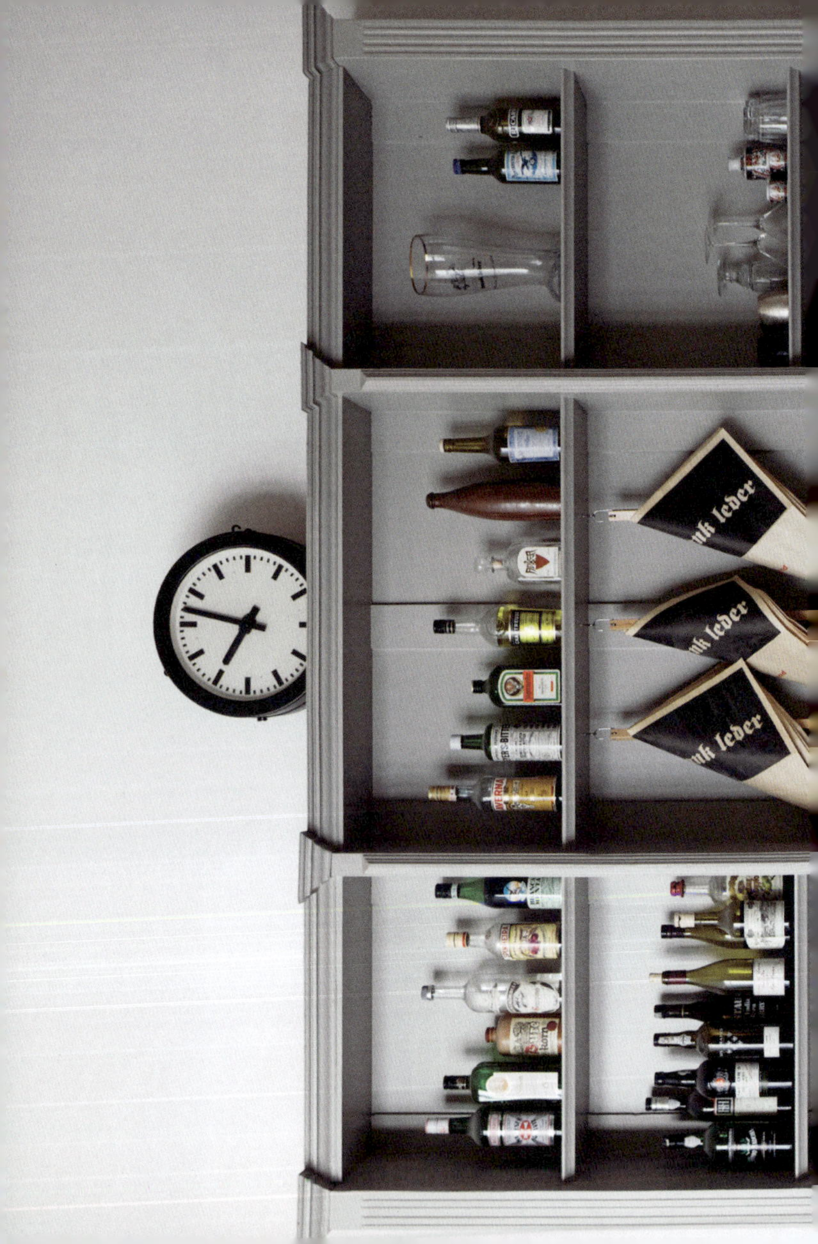

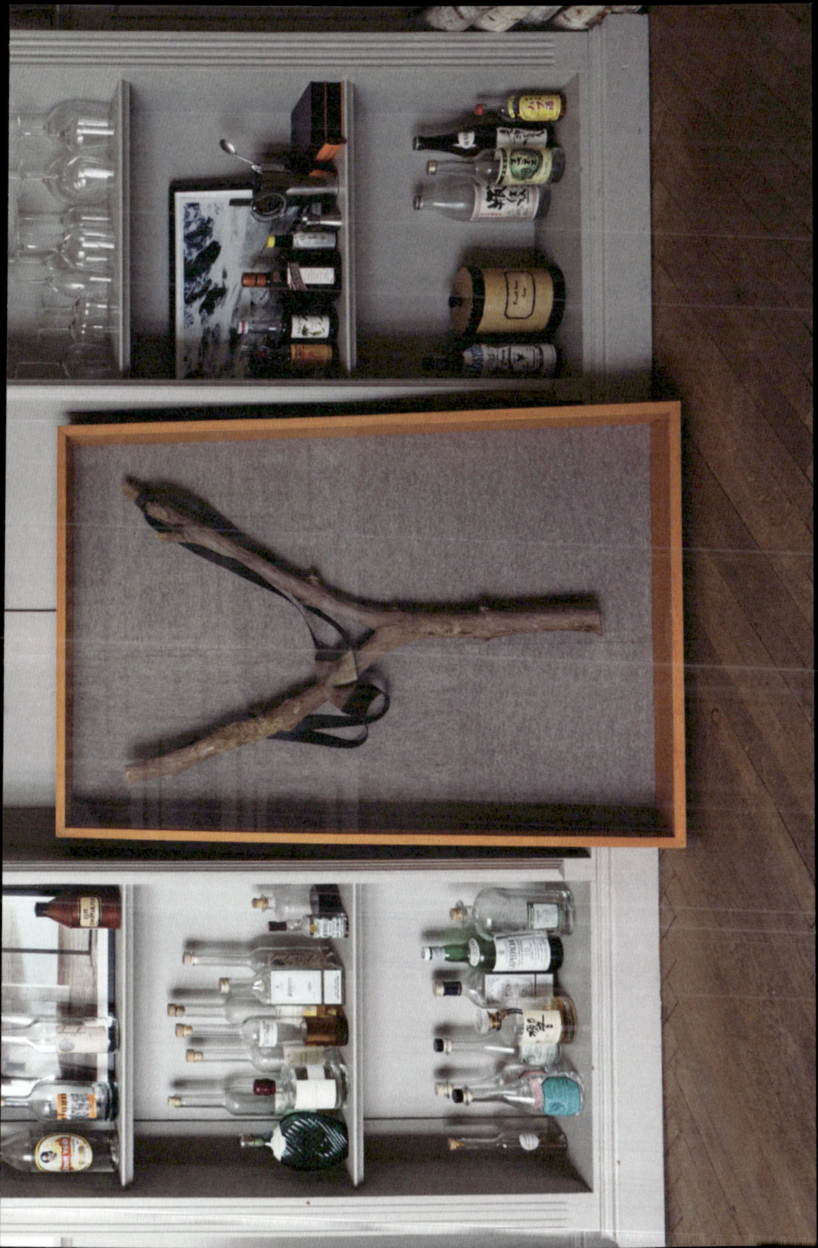

MY CITY WITH

ETTINA BERRIOS-NEGRÓN

Fashion Designer

Material World

Ettina Berrios-Negrón knows, and is known by, everyone in the Berlin fashion scene, having founded Konk, a destination for new Berlin and German fashion, in 2003. In 2010, she launched a new label, Thone Negrón. Leaving Konk in good hands, she opened a small, elegant salon in quiet Schröderstr. to display her collection, which ranges from layered skirts to long dresses made of materials like silk, cotton or wool. Ethnological influences, colour combinations and small details highlight each piece of her collection. Ettina knows where to go both for style inspiration and for hands-on research. Here are her recommendations for fashion lovers and designers.

U *Rosenthaler Platz | Thone Negrón Salon | Schröderstr. 13, Mitte | Thu & Fri 12–18 and by appointment | thonenegron.com*

1 **"The Starstyling shop is an experience, like a tiny Disneyland. It's a label with a sense of humour. You can browse for hours and always find something. There's a surprise around every corner.**
With a founding year of 2000, Starstyling is a true dinosaur in Berlin's maturing and fast-growing fashion community and is still an important example of casual, creative, and high-level Berlin fashion. The designers combine a sense of humour with curiosity."

U ***Rosa-Luxemburg-Platz | Mulackstr. 4, Mitte starstyling.net***

2 **"This unassuming shop in Kreuzberg is a port of call for Berlin fashion designers.**
Knopf Paul stocks every kind of button you can imagine. Be polite and patient! If you follow the rules, you will be treated like a king, even if you only buy a 30 cent snap."

U ***Gneisenaustraße | Zossener Str. 10, Kreuzberg Tue & Fri 9–18 Wed & Thu 14–18 | paulknopf.de***

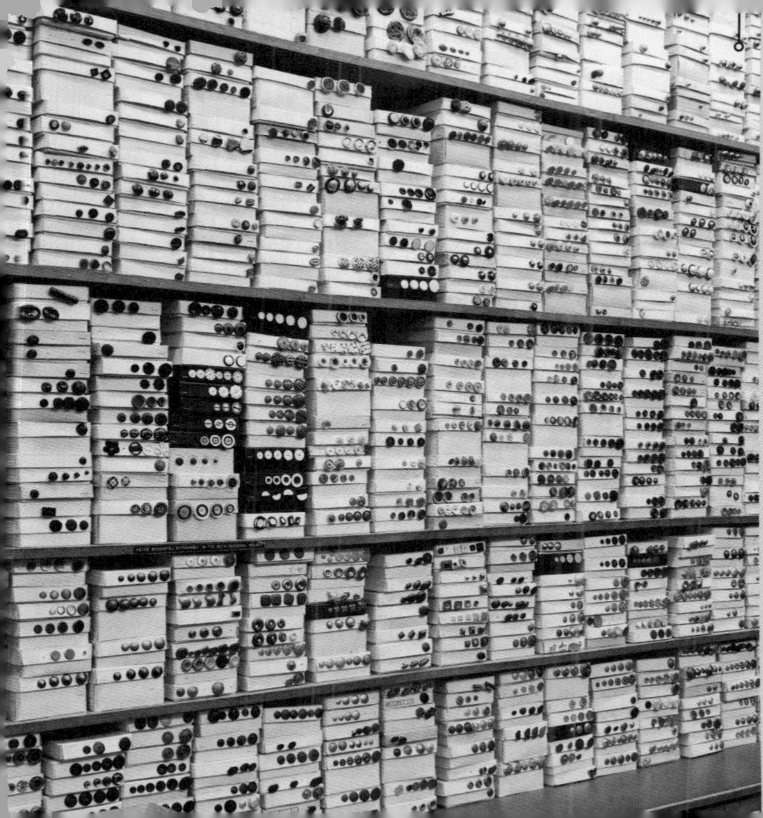

3 **“The Wilhelm Rüther Hobbyshop is one of many long-established specialty stores.”** Stocking just about everything needed by the budding fashion designer, it’s best to come here if you’re ready to be surprised.

U ***Eisenacher Straße | Goltzstr. 37, Schöneberg Mon to Fri 10–18, Sat 10–16 | hobbyshop.de***

TIP ...

“**Molinari & Ko** offers classic Italian cuisine for lunch and dinner and has a great outdoor area.”

Riemannstr. 13, Kreuzberg | Mon to Fri 8–0.30, Sat & Sun 9–0.30

“The market on **Winterfeldtplatz** in Schöneberg is the perfect place to meet up with friends and to buy produce and fresh flowers.”

Winterfeldtplatz, Schönberg | Wed & Sat mornings | winterfeldt-markt.de

Photo Max Zerrahn

STORES & STORIES

Rita In Palma

High-fashion accessories produced by Turkish women in Neukölln? The idea is not as far-fetched as you'd imagine. Accessory label Rita in Palma's crocheted collars, pendants and scarves are a neighbourly affair, made by immigrant women in the *Schillerkiez*, far off the beaten fashion track. Growing the local economy has taken Rita In Palma global – their pieces have been spotted around the necks of stylemakers the world over.

U *Leinestraße* | Kienitzer Str. 101, Neukölln | Mon to Fri 12–16 & by appointment ritainpalma.com

Right Rita in Palma's Araba scarf.
Photo Fabian Frost

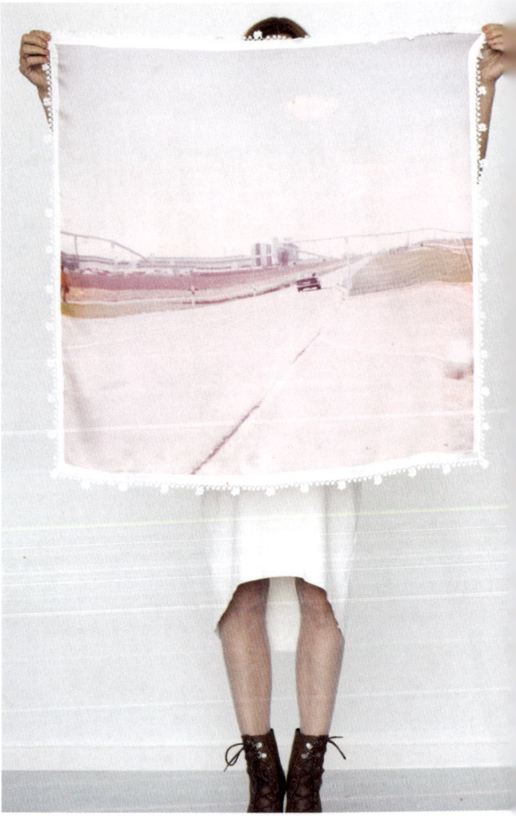

Slowmo

The siblings behind Slowmo, Melchior Moss and Felicia Moss-Kraus, live and work by the conviction that "organic is not a fad, it's a commitment." Slowmo's fashion is 100 per cent organic and fair trade and is produced as locally as possible, sewn in a small factory in Tempelhof and silkscreened in Berlin-Friedrichshagen. Their streetwear-style casualwear occupies a special niche in Berlin's fashion scene.

U S *Warschauer Straße* **Libauerstr. 16, Friedrichshain | Sat 12–17 slowmo.eu**

F95

For years this permanent offshoot of the Premium Fashion Fair was located in Friedrichshain, just off the shopping radar. In 2011, F95 found a more central home at Gleisdreick, across the street from the exhibition halls that host its parent event. With a interior featuring baroque armchairs and carpets from Schlosshotel Gerhus in Grunewald, their new space puts the 'concept' in concept store.

U *Gleisdreieck* | **Luckenwalder Str. 4-6, Kreuzberg Mon to Fri 12–20, Sat 11–18 | f95store.com**

Alfred

Leather is designer Carmelo Tadeschi's material par excellence. For Alfred, his Berlin-based label, he turns the finest Italian leather into Cubist bangles, flashy belts and simple bags. The pieces are produced in Berlin, Italy and Morocco.

U *Stadtmitte* | **Leipziger Str. 66, Mitte | by appointment only | aaalfred.de**

Zeha

Having trod the streets of Berlin through the 20th century, Zeha shoes have stories to tell. The brand was founded in 1897 and grew through the years to become the official sport shoe of the GDR. Revived after the fall of the Wall, the label's shoes are designed and produced locally, lending metropolitan style and a retro feel to everything from sport shoes to boots and heels.

U *Rosenthaler Platz* | **Brunnenstr. 195, Mitte Mon to Fri 12–20, Sat 11–19**

U *Senefelder Platz* | **Prenzlauer Allee 22, Prenzlauer Berg | Mon to Fri 12–20, Sat 10–18**

U *Gneisenaustraße* | **Friesenstr. 7, Kreuzberg | Mon to Fri 12–20, Sat 10–18 zeha-berlin.de**

Department Store Quartier 206

Berlin's answer to the upscale department store culture of other European metropoles is the Department Store Quartier 206, situated on Mitte's Friedrichstr. Home to many small boutiques, Quartier 206 is an immersive shopping experience complete with a small piano bar for mid-browsing breaks. The Cabinet store is an especially hip destination.

U *Stadtmitte* | **Friedrichstr. 71, Mitte | Mon to Fri 10.30–19.30, Sat 10–18 quartier206.com**

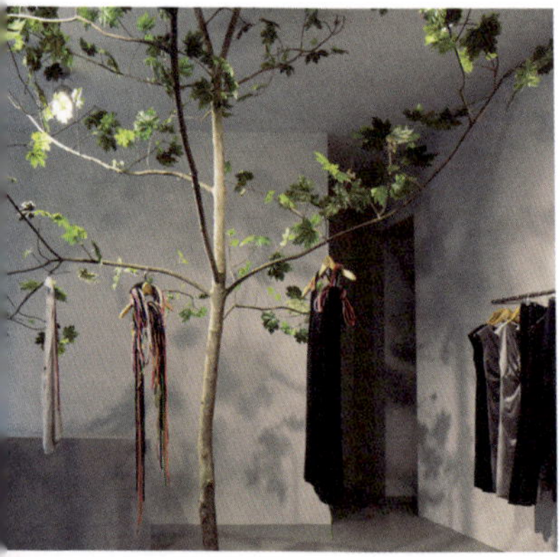

Anuschka Hoevener

Trained in New York, London and Halle, designer Anuschka Hoevener has used her Berlin base to build a network of stores, garnering an international following. Her fashion thrives on attention-grabbing details: crimped seams, coloured flaps, and spherical knits add a harmonious flight of fancy to tailored, wearable pieces.

U *Rosenthaler Platz* | **Linienstr. 196, Mitte**
Tue and Wed 14–18, Thu to Sat 12–19
anuschkahoevener.de

The Corner

Fashion in Berlin runs the gamut from DIY to the very heights of haute couture. For those whose tastes fall nearer the latter, there is The Corner, a temple to high style, with three locations and a seconds store.

U *Französische Straße* | **Französische Str. 40, Mitte (MenStore) Markgrafenstraße 45, Mitte | Mon to Fri 10.30–19.30, Sat 10.30–19**
U *Uhlandstraße* | **(Outlet) Knesebeckstr.32, Charlottenburg | Mon to Fri 10.30–18.30 Sat 10–18**
U *Adenauerplatz* | **Wielandstr. 29, Charlottenburg**
thecornerberlin.de

Adddress

Clocking up its 10th year in business, Adddress was one of the labels that marked the beginning of Berlin's rapid development towards a fashion city. Founder Andreea Vrajitoru honed her skills in reputed international design studios before setting out on her own. Adddress pieces can be found in its centrally located store in Mitte and at L'Etage, of which Vrajitoru is co-founder.

U *Weinmeisterstraße* | **Weinmeisterstr. 12–14, Mitte**
adddress.de
U *Senefelder Platz* | **L'Etage, Kollwitzstr. 45, Prenzlauer Berg | Mon to Sat 11–19**
letage.de

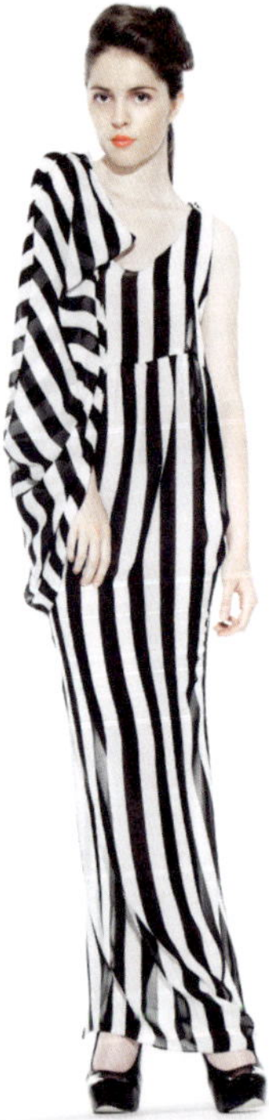

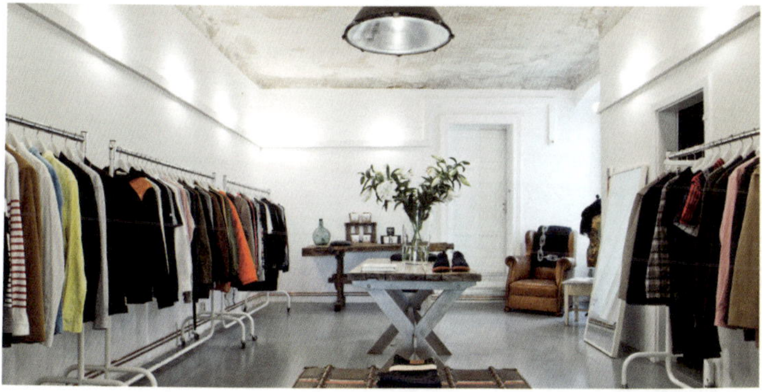

Top left Anuschka Hoevener moved from busy Kastanienallee to the quieter pace of Linienstr.
Photo Adrian Sauer

Bottom left Dress from the Adddress spring/summer collection 2012.
Photo Franziska Prütz

Above For many style-conscious males, Soto is the one-stop shop in this city. The online store caters to non-residents.
Photo Robert Wunsch

SOTO

Boasting the finest in menswear from around the world, including names like Patrick Ervell and Band of Outsiders, Soto ('South of Torstraße') has become a destination for fashion-conscious Berliners and visitors alike. With a name that plays on the concept of New York and London's hip SoHo neighbourhoods, and 'Le Berlinois', a locally-inspired winter accessory line, Soto's modern dandyism and international flare melds perfectly with its location at the junction of cool Mitte and bourgeois Prenzlauer Berg.
U *Rosa-Luxemburg Platz* | **Torstr. 72, Mitte | Mon to Sat 12–20 | sotostore.com**

cHkA & Styleserver

Berlin fashion pioneers Styleserver were among the first to introduce local designers to the outside world via the internet, setting off the fashion fever that has engulfed the city. Now that many designers have opened their own online shops, Styleserver has changed its tactic: their Prenzlauer Berg store cHkA (so named because the letters 'chka' were left on the façade when Anuschka Hoeveners vacated the premises) carries a selection of local and international designer items, and customers who order online can have their purchases delivered to cHkA for fitting.
U *Rosenthaler Platz* | **Kastanienallee 47, Mitte | Mon to Sat 12–20 | styleserver.de**

OBJECTS & VISUAL DESIGN

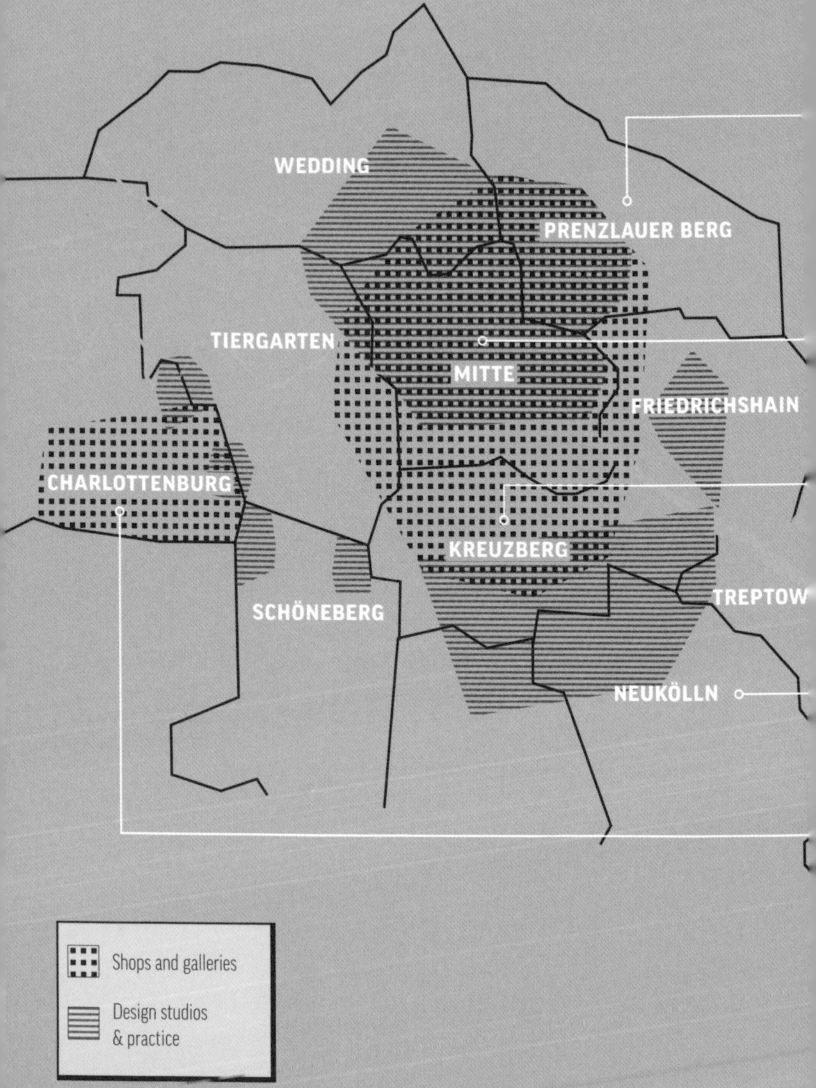
WEDDING
PRENZLAUER BERG
TIERGARTEN
MITTE
FRIEDRICHSHAIN
CHARLOTTENBURG
KREUZBERG
TREPTOW
SCHÖNEBERG
NEUKÖLLN
Shops and galleries
Design studios
& practice

THE VILLAGE

Prenzlauer Berg has come a long way since images of its grey, run-down streetscapes circled the world after 1989. Now, the students and artists that populated the district have grown up, and the bars and nightclubs have made room for cafés and an abundance of small stores, especially those of jewellers, furniture and product designers.

THE DISPLAY CASE

Home to plenty of independent fashion stores, **Mitte** is the place to seek out showrooms and galleries presenting the work of the city's more established designers.

THE PLAYGROUND

As the home and favourite destination of Berlin's creatives, **Kreuzberg** also features many stores and galleries, especially around Oranienstr. and, increasingly, the area surrounding Moritzplatz. Many temporary happenings such as exhibitions and pop-up stores can be found here.

THE PETRI DISH

Though they are few and far between, any design experiments are likely to be found in **Neukölln** thanks to the low rents and increasingly hip clientele.

THE GRAND DAME

Designers and artists of a more established generation – think high-end jewellery and vintage furniture – have been trading in the west of the city, predominantly in **Charlottenburg**, for decades.

TO BE OBJECTIVE

THERE ARE AS MANY WAYS TO PRODUCE, PRESENT AND SELL DESIGN AS THERE ARE DESIGNERS IN THIS CITY

You don't have to go far to find someone who will tell you that this city is great to live in but a terrible place to make money. In a twist on the old adage, though, desperate times have made for creative measures.

You could probably count on two hands the product design studios in this city that employ crowds of designers to deliver commercial products. Instead, Berlin's design world is a sea of individuals and small outfits responsible for an astounding volume of ideas and objects. Eschewing established parameters, the city's design scene presents an incredibly diverse, detailed, and impossible to define landscape, where many small stores and galleries have a short lifespan and design collaborations form around projects, many of which never make it past the conceptual stage.

"Berlin's design world is a sea of individuals and small outfits responsible for an astounding volume of ideas and objects"

Anyone seeking inspiration in this environment is in for more than they bargained for. The unique status of creative design in the city, where ideas deemed impossible are brought to fruition and unusual creative alliances produce international waves, bolsters the innovation endemic to Berlin and pushes the frontiers of design. This chapter makes an attempt at a loose-form categorisation of the many issues, themes and motivations surrounding Berlin design in order to help the reader understand, trace and explore its practices. Design can be explored from any number of angles in the city, from institutions and individuals reinterpreting traditional workmanship to galleries and roving projects firmly anchored in the here and now and individuals whose passion for objects has lent itself to the creation of private museums, stores and showrooms. There are bookstores devoted to every crack in the landscape of creative endeavour, as well as niche businesses dedicated to the traditional, the social and the innovative aspects of design – or all of them rolled into one.

OUR PARTNER

ETSY

Truly innovative design benefits from the exchange of ideas and skills amongst a community of like-minded people. Few understand this as well as the team behind Etsy, the international online marketplace for unique, hand-made design items. Knowing that every creative endeavour has to start somewhere, Etsy allows its designers to float new ideas and work directly with their customers, as well as being a reliable sales platform once a small design business is established. Here are six Berlin designers who have expanded their business ideas with Etsy.

etsy.com

Verena Schreppel

Living in the busy multicultural Neukölln neighbourhood of Rixdorf has inspired Berlin native Verena Schreppel's jewellery. Each ring, necklace or set of earrings produced by the designer implies a sense of motion, either in the flow or weave of the piece itself, or in its form – her international bias is revealed in a series of rings, earrings and cufflinks meticulously cut into the shape of individual continents and the familiar form of the Berlin city boundaries.
verenaschreppel.etsy.com | verenaschreppel.com

Top Right The Knit Kid's cotton tops

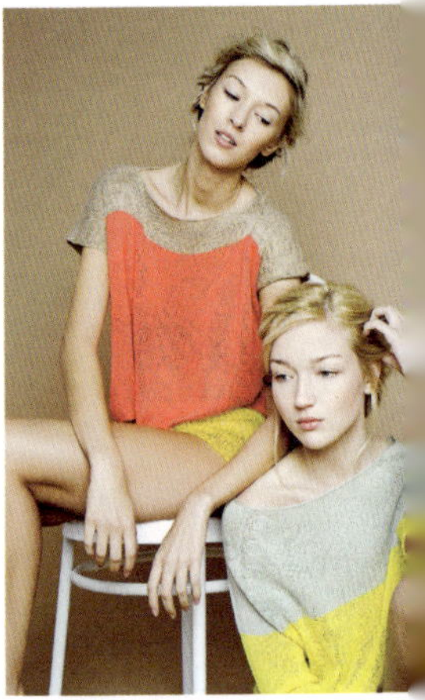

The Knit Kid

Proving that sometimes all you need to succeed is your two hands, Sabrina Weigt, aka The Knit Kid, produces beautiful, simple and stylish dresses, scarves, collars and shrugs from the tips of her knitting needles. The Wedding-based designer's contemporary sensibilities are reflected in her custom-made pieces' silhouettes and colour palette, with varying knits and wools uniting to form an eye-catching, casual elegance.
theknitkid.etsy.com
the-knit-kid.de

Aempersand

From her Alt-Treptow studio, Aempersand's Anna-Magdalena Wendt produces classic mens- and womenswear with a contemporary twist. Privileging quality materials and workmanship, her designs focus on the details. Simple, form-fitting pullovers support draped shawls and collars, while pants, skirts and dresses draw the eye with their careful lines and pleats, creating understated, easygoing, and eminently wearable ensembles.
aempersand.etsy.com
aempersand.de

Below Ena Light; the designer refers to it as 'haute couture' for light bulbs'.

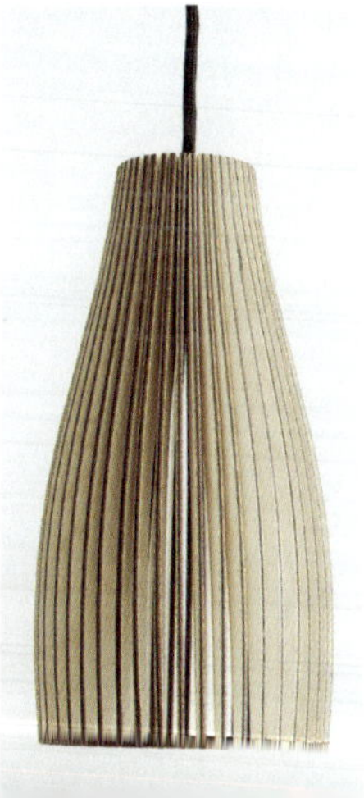

WertWerke

WertWerke's Sascha Czerny creates sinks and washbasins from concrete and wood in his workshop in Blankenfelde. These unpretentious and durable design objects mould the functionality of the bathroom sink into a conversation piece.
wertwerke.etsy.com
wertwerke.de

Below Luchta 1.2 is a 'sandwich' from concrete and plywood.

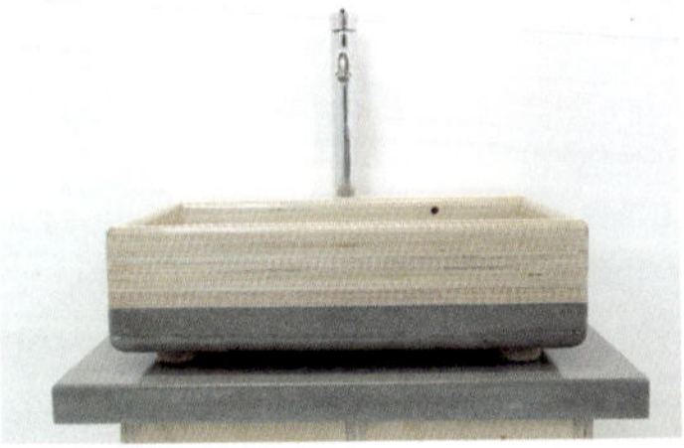

Smallcaps

Sabrina Sundermann's passion for typography shines on her letterpress-printed cards and notebooks. Travel is a recurring theme, and her Berlin notebooks are adorned with ink stamps of recognisable monuments. Sabrina also teamed up with a friend to create a city guide called 'Hello Berlin'.
smallcapsberlin.etsy.com
smallcaps-berlin.de

iumi

Architect Paul Girardet produced his first iumi lamp as a gift for his sister. Paul, who lives in Prenzlauer Berg, confers with his friends and family for design assistance, and the lamps arrive to buyers flatpacked, ready to be assembled. Their sleek styling and warm glow reflects the individual stories behind each lamp, a departure from mass-produced designer housewares.
envelampa.etsy.com | iumi.de

ON SHOW

This is a city of museums big and small. Those who take their time will find many unusual destinations devoted to design and the greater creative cause.

According to official statistics, most visitors to Berlin will patronise at least one of the city's museums, which range from the shrines devoted to old and new art on Museum Island to the more niche locations concerned with the ubiquitous *currywurst* or the history of hemp. The city seems to yield a museum for almost everything, but even the most devout museum-goer won't be able to visit them all. Here is a shortlist of destinations that cater specifically to the distinguished design lover.

Buchstabenmuseum – Museum of Letters

Type designers rejoice: here's a destination that recognises typography's role in documenting changes in society, culture, business and the urban environment. Like many of Berlin's most exciting gallery locations, this one originated with a single individual. Barbara Dechant, a Viennese-born graphic designer, had always collected individual letters. She teamed up with her friend Anja Schulze to rescue public type displays from store façades and train stations as Berlin underwent its rapid processes of renewal. The pair provides a home to these retired signs so they can continue to tell their stories. Today, the museum resides in a largely defunct shopping mall, a quiet enclave just steps from the bustle of Alexanderplatz.

U ***Alexanderplatz*** | *Karl-Liebknecht-Str. 13, Mitte (First Floor, Berlin Carré Shopping Mall)* | *Thu to Sat 13–15* | *buchstabenmuseum.de*

Photo Andre Stoeriko

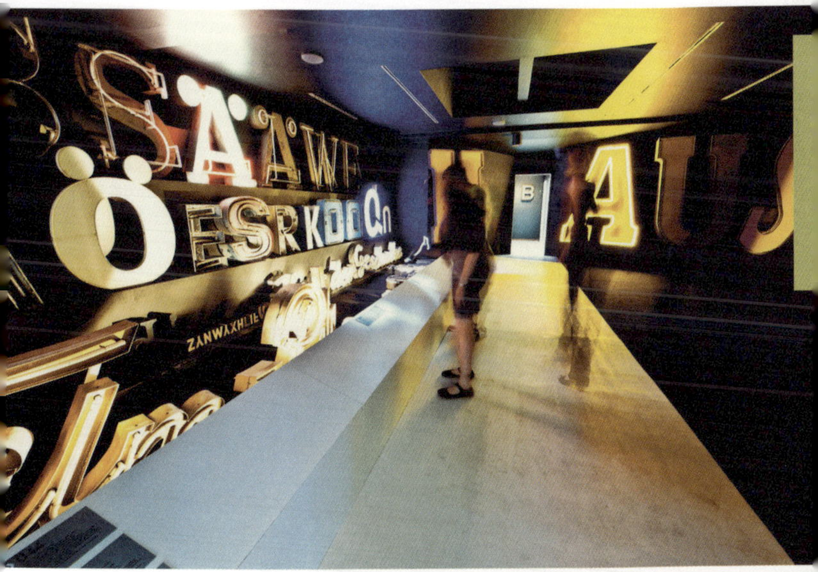

Museum der Dinge – Museum of Things

At the beginning of the 19th century, when the term 'design' still hadn't acquired its current significance or inflationary use, a few dozen influential architects, artists, craftspeople and business people decided to pool their knowledge and resources to further the development of craft and 'the culture of the object'. They named their alliance the Werkbund. Over time, it accumulated an archive that today comprises about 20,000 objects and almost twice as many documents. This collection forms the basis of what is on display at the aptly-titled 'Museum of Things' in a former factory building on Kreuzberg's busy Oranienstr. Design classics and no-name objects with cultural significance are given equal billing, and excellent temporary shows, focusing mostly on contemporary design, are always a highlight.

Tip ... Don't miss the tucked-away 'Frankfurt Kitchen' display, the original inbuilt kitchen that transformed modern kitchen design.

U *Kottbusser Tor* | *Oranienstr. 25, Kreuzberg* | *Fri to Mon 12–19 or by appointment* | *museumderdinge.de*

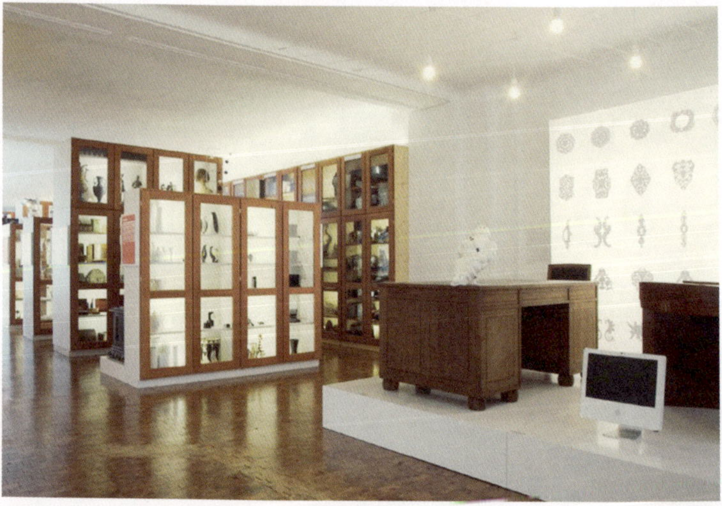

Direktorenhaus

Hidden away, though in a very central location, you'll find one of Berlin's most exciting gallery and event venues operating on the blurry line between design and art, Direktorenhaus. Once home to the administrative offices of the State Mint, it was revived in 2010 by the dynamic couple behind the popular Illustrative Festival, an event that has been bringing together illustrators from all over the world in three cities annually since 1996. Katja Kleiss and Pascal Johanssen discovered the venue on a walk through the area and threw open the doors to their first exhibition before the ink had dried on their temporary lease agreement, when just one floor of the stately office building had been renovated. Among its busy schedule of exhibitions – where one-off, art-inspired objects by local designers are a recurring theme – Direktorenhaus also hosts a number of other events, among them 'Taste', a festival addressing the equally blurry line between design and food.

U ***Klosterstraße*** | *Am Krögel 2, Mitte* | *Open by appointment*
direktorenhaus.com

Left View of the permanent exhibition at Museum der Dinge. *Photo* Armin Herrmann © Werkbundarchiv – Museum der Dinge

Below Benjamin Hubert's solo exhibition 'Materiality' at Direktorenhaus.

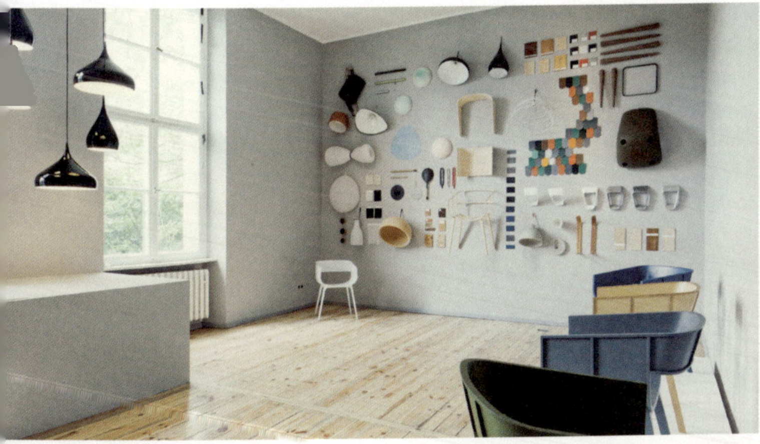

Computerspielemuseum – Computer Games Museum

Are there still people sneering at the idea that computer games can, and do, make a significant contribution to cultural development? The Computer Games Museum reforms the ignorant – and those who think they witnessed the birth of digital gaming just because they owned a Commodore 64 – by tracking the the development of its subject back to the 1950s. Just like the Buchstabenmuseum up the road, Computerspiele Museum's foundations rest on an incurable passion for the subject, private funding, and countless hours of voluntary toil.

Tip ... Over 3000 functioning artifacts and more than 20,000 games can be experienced first hand.

U ***Weberwiese*** | *Karl-Marx-Allee 93a, Friedrichshain* | *Daily 10–20 (closed Tues)* | *computerspielemuseum.de*

Kunstgewerbemuseum, Kunstbibliothek und Kostümbibliothek – Decorative Arts Museum, Art Library and Costume Library

Situated between the noisy entertainment buzz of Potsdamer Platz and the quieter pull of the New National Gallery, Germany's oldest decorative arts museum will have the object lover agog. Featuring much more than historic gold and silverware, the museum's enormous array of objects – frequently acquired through large bequests – also includes Art Nouveau pieces and Bauhaus furniture. The adjacent Kunstbibliothek, with its hundreds of thousands of documents, books and magazines, offers an equally exhilarating experience. It also includes the 'Lipperheidesche Kostümbibliothek', comprising thousands of books and documents relating to fashion history.

U ***Potsdamer Platz*** | *Entry on Matthäikirchplatz, Mitte* | *(The Decorative Arts Museum is closed for renovations until early 2014)* | *Tue to Fri 10–18, Sat & Sun 11–18* | *smb.museum*

Designtransfer – University of the Arts

The Universität der Künste (UdK) is Europe's biggest university devoted solely to all facets of visual and performing art, from abstract painting to the French horn. UdK's design program, which includes fashion, visual communication, industrial design, media arts and architecture, is famous beyond the city's borders and first choice for Germany's art-inclined university entrants. Though the institution's reputation is no secret, it offers few occasions to peek behind the curtain at what's happening here. The Designtransfer gallery, tucked away on the ground floor of a building on the Charlottenburg campus, provides one such rare opportunity. The gallery's program consists of curated exhibitions corresponding to current themes in design, as well as public lectures and seminars.

Below Intallation by Buenos Aires-based design studio Remolino. *Photo* © designtransfer

Tip ... Once a year, the University opens the doors of its studios, workshops and exhibitions spaces for one hugely popular weekend.

udk-berlin.de

U ***Ernst-Reuter-Platz*** | *Einsteinufer 43-53, Charlottenburg* | *Check website for opening times* | *designtransfer.udk-berlin.de*

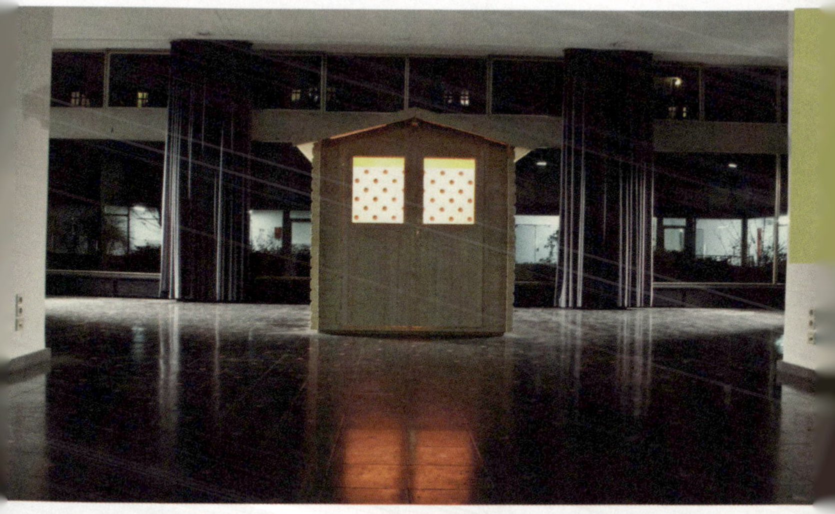

THE COLLECTORS

In other cities, galleries specialising in design and furniture are easy to pigeonhole as either 'commercial' or 'experimental'. But Berlin's small but vibrant scene of galleries with a design focus defies easy categorisation.

That design, art and architecture share many common themes is nothing new. A more recent global phenomenon has designers connecting with modes of production previously reserved for art. They now produce their work especially to be shown in galleries, creating one-a kind pieces alongside their mass-manufactured work for corporate clients. Unlike other European design metropoles like Paris or London, Berlin lacks an established community of design galleries, but it is not devoid of interesting people and locations engaged with the curation and exhibition of contemporary pieces, new concepts and vintage classics.

Helmrinderknecht

THE TALENT

— *Although not always present in Berlin, the Helmrinderknecht line-up of designers includes a veritable Who's Who of Berlin's design establishment (think* ***August Hermann Weizenegger*** *or* ***Osko+Deichmann****) as well as discoveries with promise, like* ***Judith Seng****.*

When Swiss national Martin Rinderknecht and Petra Helm decided to start their own project after working in fine art, they realised Berlin didn't really need another art gallery. Their mutual respect for design provided the inspiration for their eponymous space. The location, amongst some of the city's most respected fine art galleries in Mitte, opened in 2009 with a solo show by Spanish designer Martí Guixé, who divides his time between Barcelona and Berlin. Helm and Rinderknecht approach their mission just as an art gallery would – working with select groups of designers, some established and others just starting out – but insist that the objects displayed must be functional. The pair left their permanent location in 2011 to continue operations as a roving outfit, staging exhibitions in various cities such as Zürich and, in autumn 2012, Vienna. Their base, however, continues to be Berlin.

Photo Robert Rinderknecht

helmrinderknecht.com

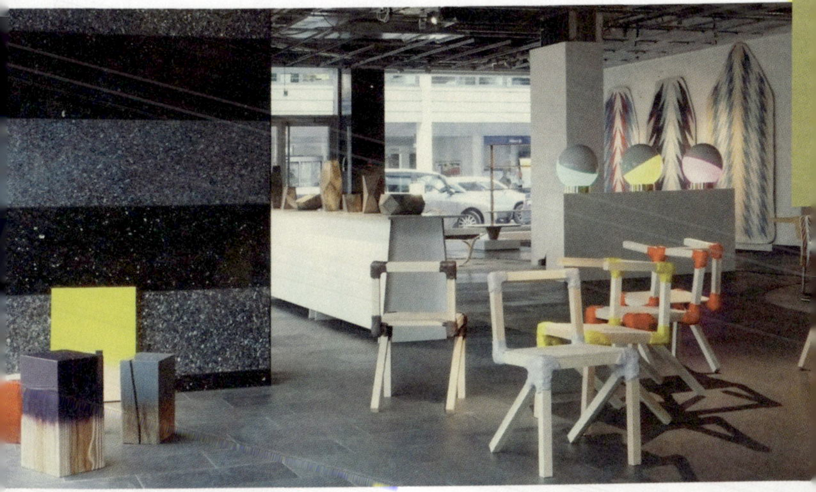

Appel Design Gallery

Tilmann Appel's gallery has become a stalwart address to view, buy and learn about contemporary design. The vintage design enthusiast and avid collector opened the space in 2005, when Torstr. was a gritty thoroughfare rather than an artery of cool. Though roughly a quarter of the items are sourced from his extensive personal collection, Appel has now shifted his attention to contemporary design and collaborations with local design businesses and international galleries. He is particularly focused on uncovering surprising or little-known facets of design culture, like the furniture designed by industrial designer Dieter Rams.

U ***Rosenthaler Platz*** | *Torstr. 114, Mitte* | *Tue to Sat 12–18 and by appointment* | *appel-design.com*

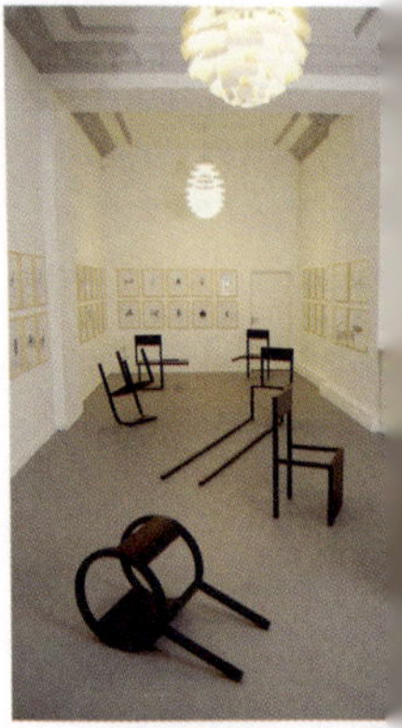

Above The exhibition 'Extraordinary Seats' *Photo* © Appel Design Gallery

Karena Schüssler

Besides cultivating a successful career designing accessories for fashion labels, Karena Schüssler had always been an enthusiastic collector of classic and unique design pieces. What started as an obsession while she lived in Paris finally turned into a business in 2009 when Schüssler opted both for a location change and a career shift, the result of which was the opening of her gallery in Berlin-Charlottenburg. Here, she presents mostly unique pieces and limited-edition work by contemporary designers, listing local names alongside internationally celebrated talent.

U ***Uhlandstraße*** | *Uhlandstr. 45, Charlottenburg* | *Wed to Fri 14–18, Sat 12–16* | *karenaschuessler.com*

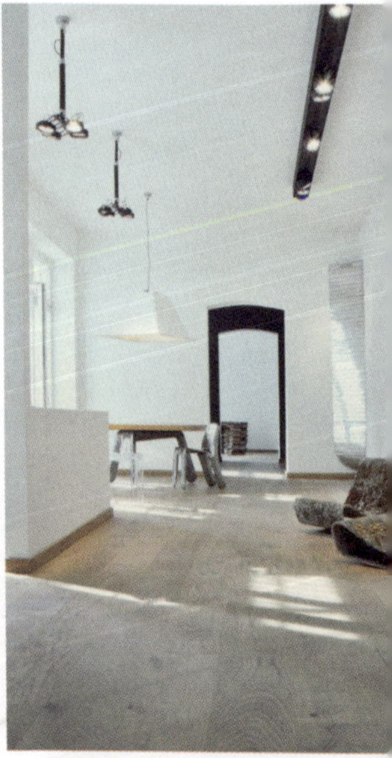

Hans-Peter Jochum

OBJECT CULTURE ...

— *Those interested in historical objects and furniture will find many destinations in Berlin including private collections, galleries, stores and public institutions with a specialty focus. For instance, the* **Bröhan Museum** *in Charlottenburg specialises in art and objects from the periods of Art Nouveau, Art Deco and Functionalism.*

broehan-museum.de

For over 30 years, Hans-Peter Jochum's gallery has been known as a reliable destination to view and buy 20th century classics, sourced from all over the world. Jochum himself is a design detective who is not scared to travel far and research extensively to present the perfect piece with a perfect story. Temporary exhibitions - often including work by contemporary designers - are staged nearby.

U ***Uhlandstraße or*** *S* ***Savignyplatz*** | *Bleibtreustr. 41, Charlottenburg (Entry Mommsenstr.) | Mon to Fri 14–18, Sat 11–16 | Exhibitions Knesebeckstr. 54, Charlottenburg | Wed to Fri 14–18, Sat 11–16 | hpjochum.de*

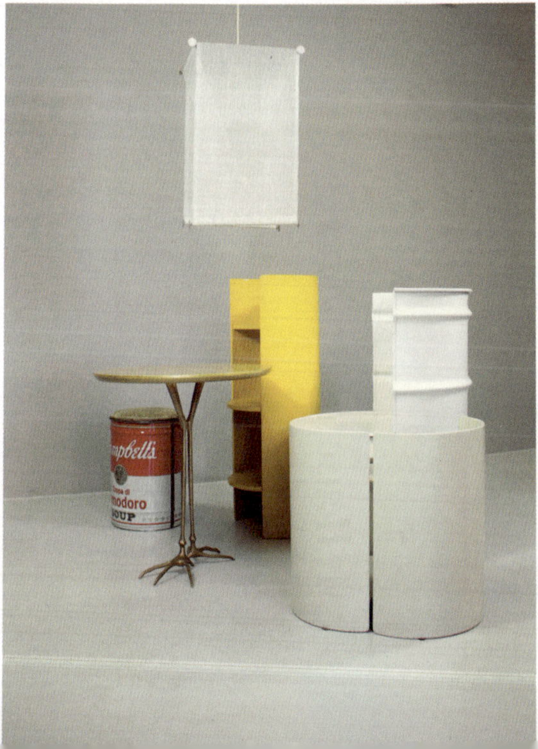

Right Dino Gavina's work *Photo* © Hans-Peter Jochum Galerie

Left Karena Schüssler's rooms *Photo* Courtesy Angelika Dacqmine

DR ANNEMARIE JAEGGI

Director of the Bauhaus Archive

My House the Bauhaus

The Bauhaus was the most important art and architecture school of the 20th century and one of the cradles of modernism. Although the Bauhaus existed for a mere decade and a half – from 1919 to 1933 – its impact was profound. Today, its legacy is spread all over the world in the shape of buildings and furniture that were either designed at the Bauhaus or inspired by its influence. Berlin is home to the Bauhaus Archive, which presents Bauhaus graphics, products and architecture drawings. We've asked the Archive's director Dr Annemarie Jaeggi to recommend other sites in the city that illustrate the Bauhaus' impact, philosophy and legacy.

U *Nollendorfplatz | Klingelhöferstr. 14, Schöneberg | Wed to Mon 10–17, closed Tue | bauhaus.de*

1 **"A number of the Bauhaus' defining characteristics are reflected by my selection of locations, three buildings designed by the directors of the Bauhaus. Although the Bauhaus itself was not an architecture school as such, each of the Bauhaus' three directors were practising architects, and observing these buildings closely means engaging with their basic design philosophy.**

One of six UNESCO Cultural World Heritage listed modernist housing estates in Berlin is the **Großsiedlung Siemensstadt**. The residential compound was built between 1929 and 1931. The dwellings were designed by a handful of prominent modernist architects who referred to themselves as the 'Ring', among them Hans Scharoun and Walter Gropius, the Bauhaus' first director. While the entire estate is a showpiece for social housing, it is particularly interesting to observe Gropius' contribution in comparison to that of his peers. His section of the compound, in

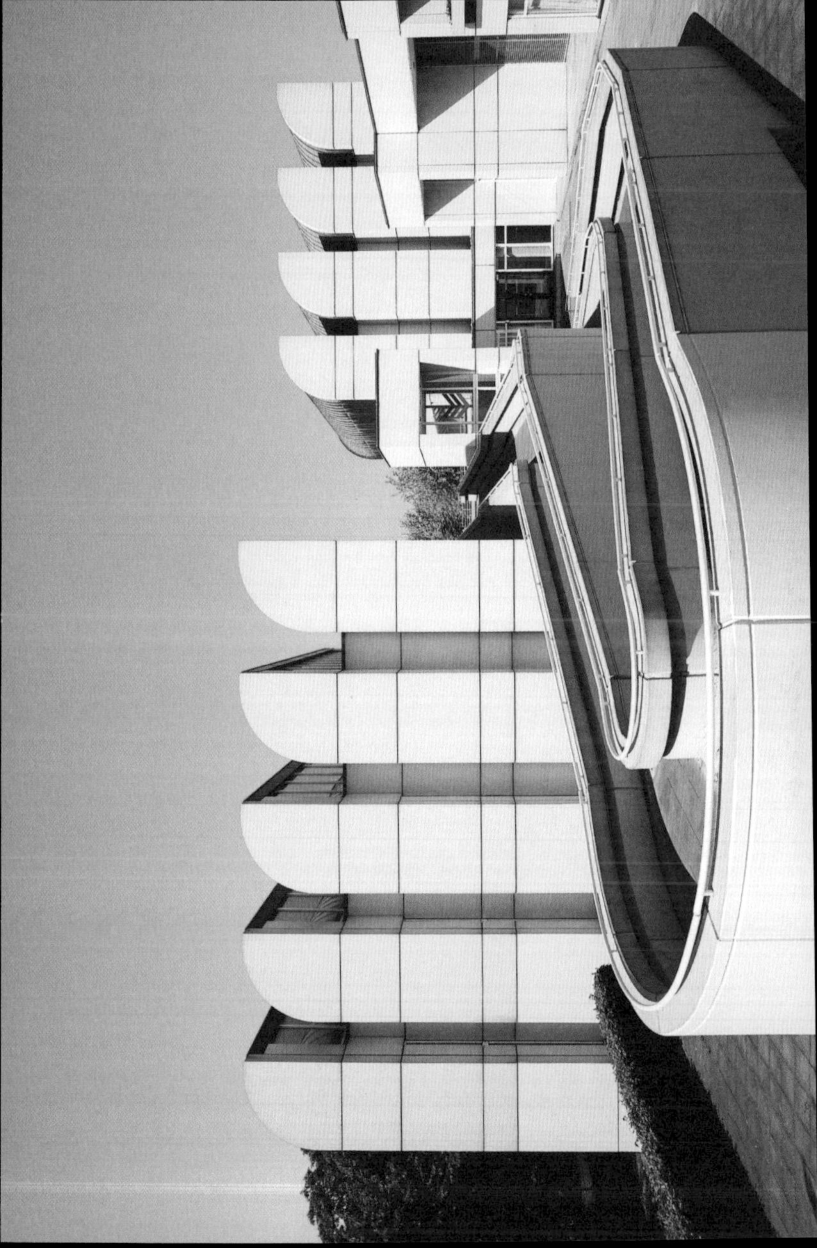

contrast to some other buildings on the site, is austere and adheres to strictly functional criteria."

Start your exploration at Infostation Siemensstadt
U *Halemweg or Siemensdamm*
Goebelstr. 2, Spandau | Sun 13–18

TIP … Tours of the area can be arranged through the specialist architectural tour operator **Ticket B.**

ticket-b.de

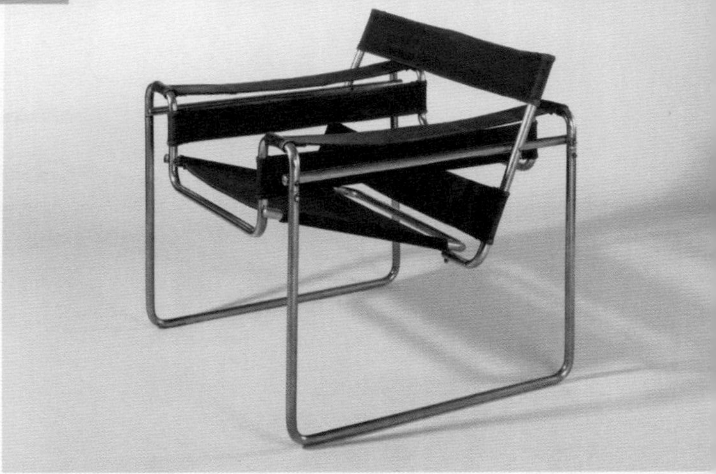

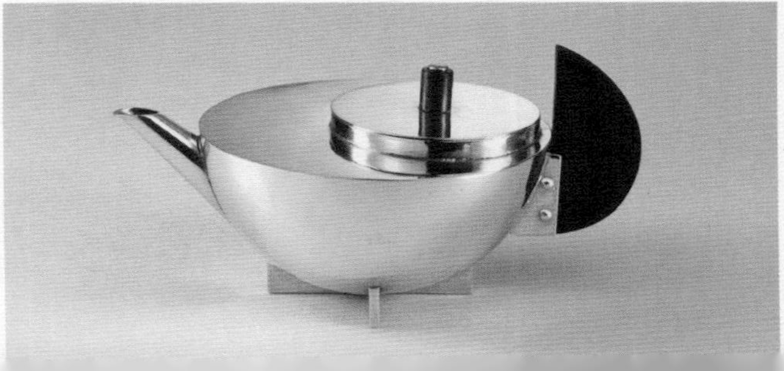

Previous page Bauhaus Archive / Museum of Design in Berlin by architects Walter Gropius, Alex Cvijanovic and Hans Bandel. Bauhaus Archive Berlin
Photo Karsten Hintz

Top right Marcel Breuer's popular steel tube armchair, designed 1926. Bauhaus Archive Berlin *Photo* Fotostudio Bartsch

Bottom right Brass teapot designed by Marianne Brandt, 1924. Bauhaus Archive Berlin *Photo* Gunter Lepkowski, © VG Bild-Kunst, Bonn 2012

2 "The heritage-listed Bundesschule von Bernau, an institution for adult education that opened in 1928, was designed by the second director of the Bauhaus, Hannes Meyer, together with his often overlooked business partner Hannes Wittwer.

In many ways, the conception and construction of this building embodies the philosophy of the Bauhaus school with a focus on the actual process of building over the finished product. The school's students were actively involved in all parts of the process, from the design to the furnishings, using the building itself as an opportunity to learn. The restrained, functional structure includes dorms, cafeterias, classrooms and a gym hall. It has been carefully and beautifully restored and still serves educational purposes."

Hannes-Meyer-Campus 9, Bernau bei Berlin · baudenkmal-bundesschule-bernau.de

3 "Landhaus Lemke, a residential building by a lake in Lichtenberg on the fringes of Berlin's inner city can easily be reached by tram from Alexanderplatz.

Built in 1932-33, the project was completed in the same year that the Bauhaus school closed its doors. Anyone who visits Mies van der Rohe's small, squat clinker brick building is taken by its perfect proportions and the meticulous execution of the architect's 'less is more' principle, which creates an ideal cohesion between the building and its surrounding environment. Initially designed for a private client, the building shared the turbulent fate of many of Berlin's architectural jewels. After its residents left in 1945, it was used as a garage by the Red Army, then as a storage and services facility by the GDR government before it was listed as a heritage site in the 1970s. It was finally restored and opened to the public in 2002. There is also a regular program of art exhibitions."

Oberseestr. 60, Hohenschönhausen
miesvanderrohehaus.de

A NICHE OF THEIR OWN

Three of the city's most established design locations tell the story of a design community that celebrates all who defy definition or venture where no one else has before.

Berlin is widely known as a place for design experimentation. However, professional object and product designers who take the plunge and open a retail store or gallery are few and far between and many promising initiatives are short-lived. On the other hand, some gallery/store hybrids have been around for years and reveal much of Berlin's design folklore.

Bless

THE SPLITS

— *It's a frequently recurring model in Berlin: the non-location-centric design collaboration. One part of the team basks in the creative freedom and experimental spirit of the German capital, while another enjoys the buzz (and at times the clients) of another creative metropolis.*

There really is no other local design label – product, fashion or otherwise – that has produced inspiring work as consistently as Bless. Trained fashion designers Ines Kaag and Desiree Heiss have been working from separate locations (Berlin and Paris) since they started out in 1995. The pair's unorthodox designs almost always re-interpret products. Why not use a vacuum cleaner as a stool when it's not in use? If you carry your bike lock around your waist like a belt, isn't it a fashion accessory? The label's flagship store on Mulackstr. was known and loved beyond Berlin's borders and its closure was interpreted by many as a powerful signifier of the demise of Mitte's independent, experimental design scene. But in 2010 the Bless ladies made it clear that they haven't given up on Berlin. They opened the 'Bless home', which presents their work in the more private setting of Ines Kraag's old apartment.

U ***Eberswalder Straße*** | *Oderberger Str. 60, Prenzlauer Berg (3rd floor, backhouse) | Check website for opening times | blessberlin.com*

Photo Bless

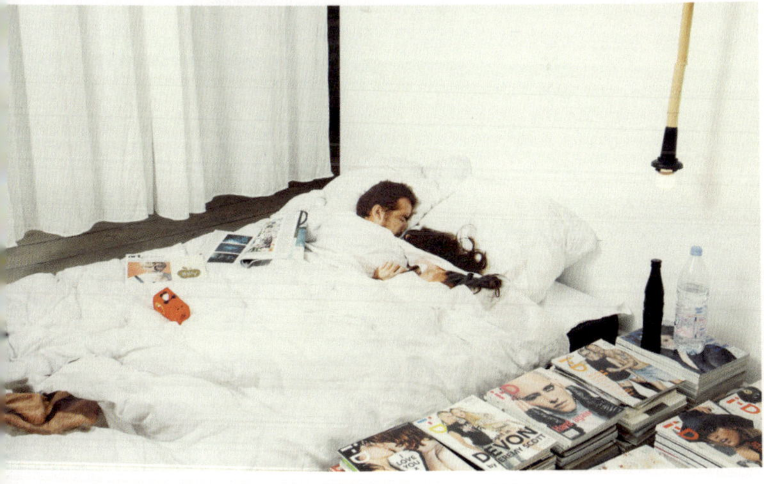

Moebel Horzon

Rafael Horzon defies easy definition. Since arriving in Berlin over two decades ago, he started a booming art gallery, founded his own university, a separation agency, set up an apple cake factory, began a business that proposed to clad all Berlin buildings in the same material, started a fashion label that took the country by storm with such designs as the 'head-tie' and then funnelled the grammar of all languages into a single, easy-to apply linguistic formula. Horzon was an integral figure of Mitte's 1990s crowd of now internationally successful writers, artists, curators and other hard-to-define characters. Today, Horzon runs a store where he sells exactly two products; a shelf that you'll find in any self-respecting Berlin creative person's living room, as well as his own book.

Tip ... **Rafael Horzon's** aptly-titled Das Weisse Buch (The White Book, available only in German and now French) is a tongue-in-cheek memoir that not only chronicles the author's life over the past two decades, but is also an excellent portrait of the boiling cauldron of madness that was Mitte in the 1990s, tracing the many developments that lead to Berlin's status as one of the world's popular creative cities.

U ***Rosenthaler Platz*** | *Torstr. 106, Mitte* | *modocom.de*

Photo André Zulkowski

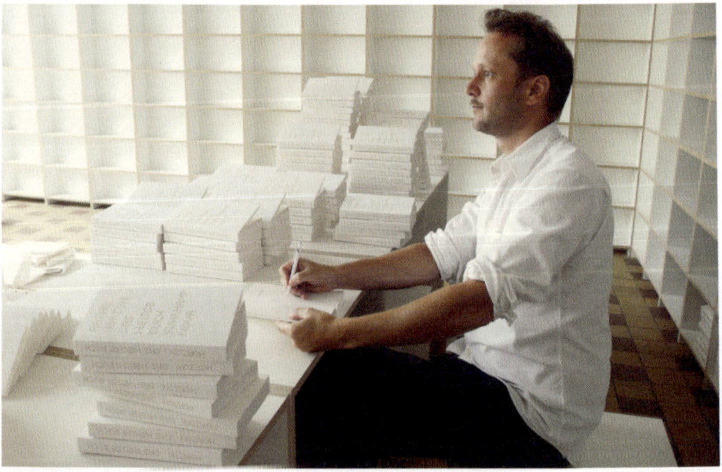

THE SPECTACLE — *Berlin has become a small but significant global hub for avant-garde eyewear. Besides* ***IC! Berlin*** *with its store on Max-Beer-Str. (no 17, ic-berlin.de), the much praised* ***Whiteout & Glare****, also opened nearby (Rosa-Luxemburg-Str. 49, whiteout-glare .com).* ***Lunettes Kollektion*** *on Torstr. (no 172, lunettes-kollektion .com) features vintage frames alongside its own range.*

Mykita

This Berlin success story began in 2003, the year that saw many local labels – predominantly in fashion – outgrow their fledgling stage and develop into professional companies. Mykita's group of four founders included University of the Arts design graduates Harald Gottschling and Philipp Haffmanns. The latter had previously started another eyewear outfit, IC! Berlin, probably the first Berlin label that attracted the attention of Hollywood stylists. Mykita, so named after the location of its headquarters, which was once home to a daycare centre ('Kita' in German), was the natural progression of this first foray into eyewear. Mykita's frames are still produced by hand in a four-storey factory warehouse in Mitte, with much emphasis on innovation and collaborations with other designers, such as Bernhard Willhelm and Alexandre Herchcovitch.

U S ***Alexanderplatz*** | *Rosa-Luxemburg-Str. 6, Mitte* | *Mon to Fri 11–20, Sat 12–18* | *mykita.com*

Photo MYKITA/PR

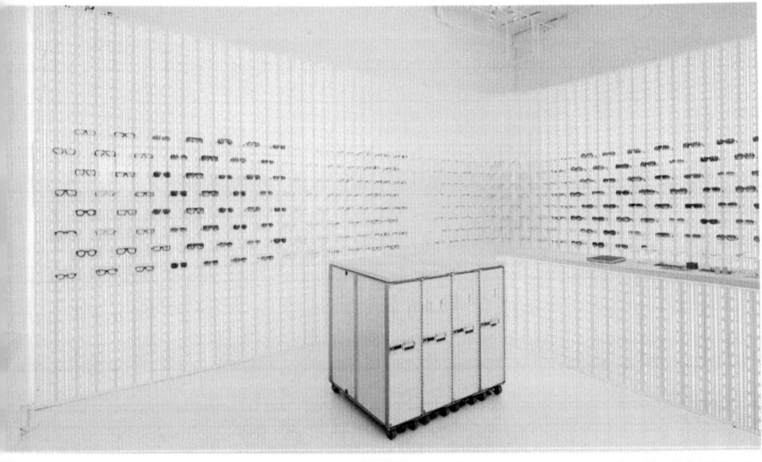

BEHIND THE SCENES WITH

Mark Braun

One of Berlin's most successful young product designers, Mark Braun manages to straddle the divide between the 'author designer', whose work bears a recognisable personal style, and the more commercially viable practice of the gun for hire. His studio in a shared artist compound near the Kreuzberg end of Alt-Treptow is a hands-on workshop where tinkering with materials and producing prototypes takes centre stage.

markbraun.org

Right **Prototypes of the 'Lift' occasional roto mould table.**

Following pages **Impressions of the studio.**

Photos **Max Zerrahn**

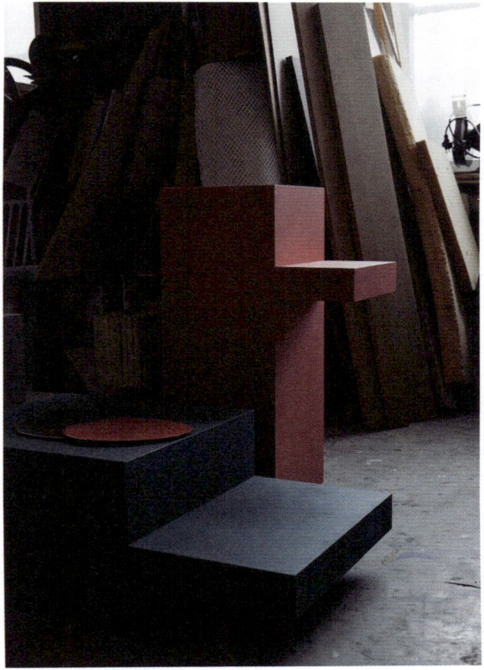

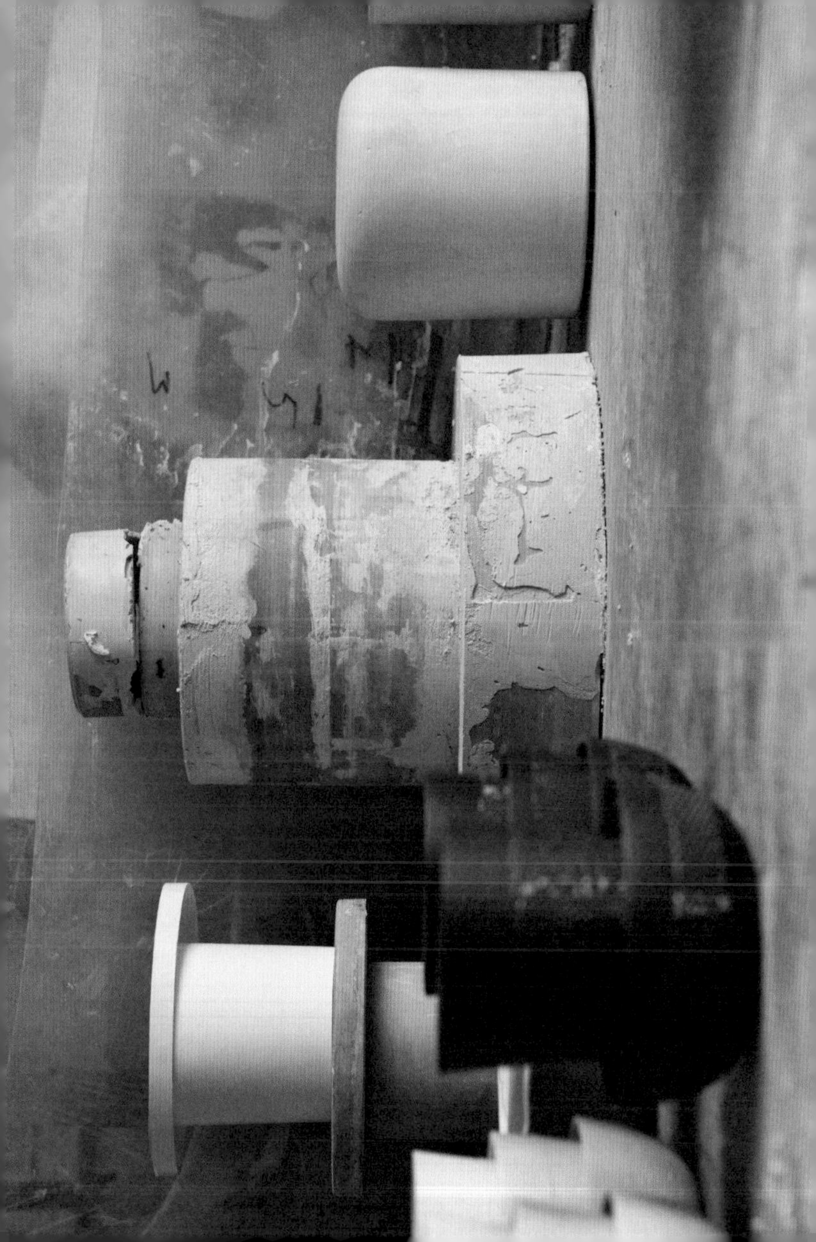

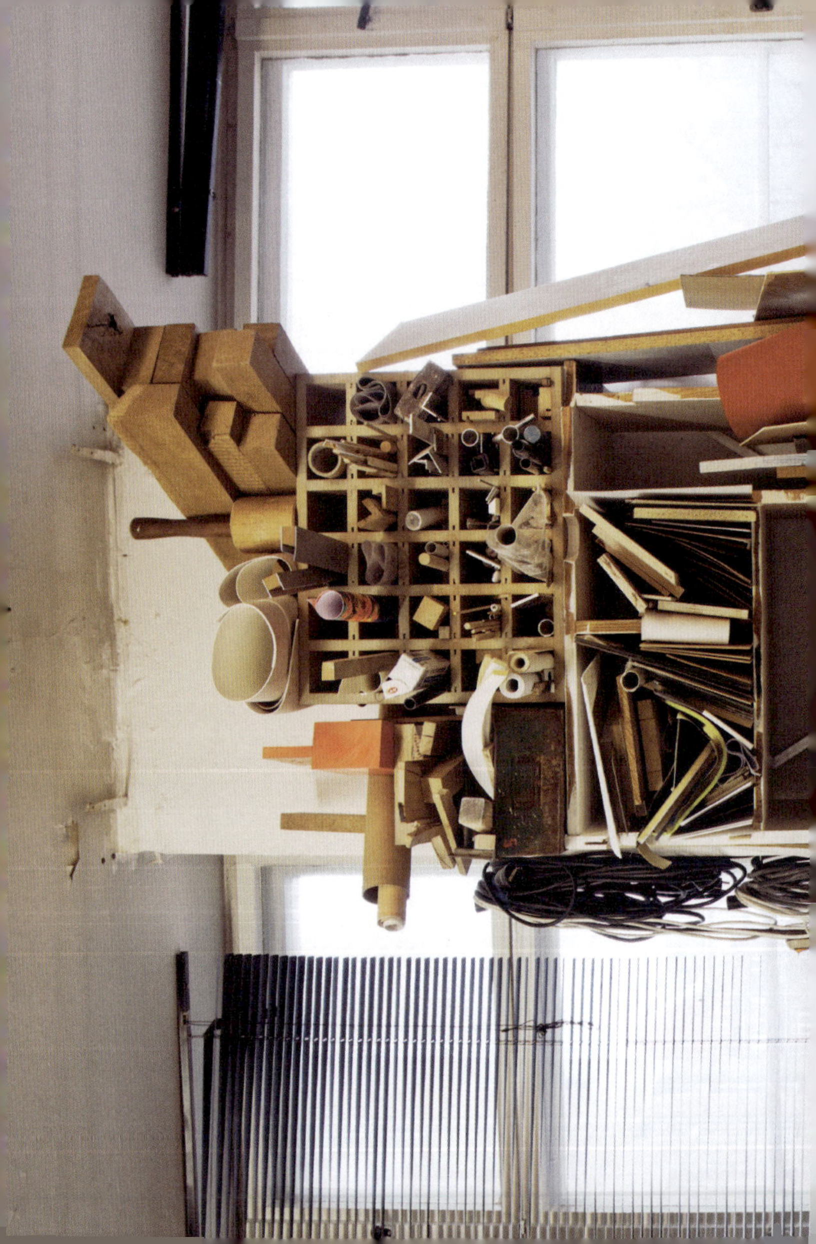

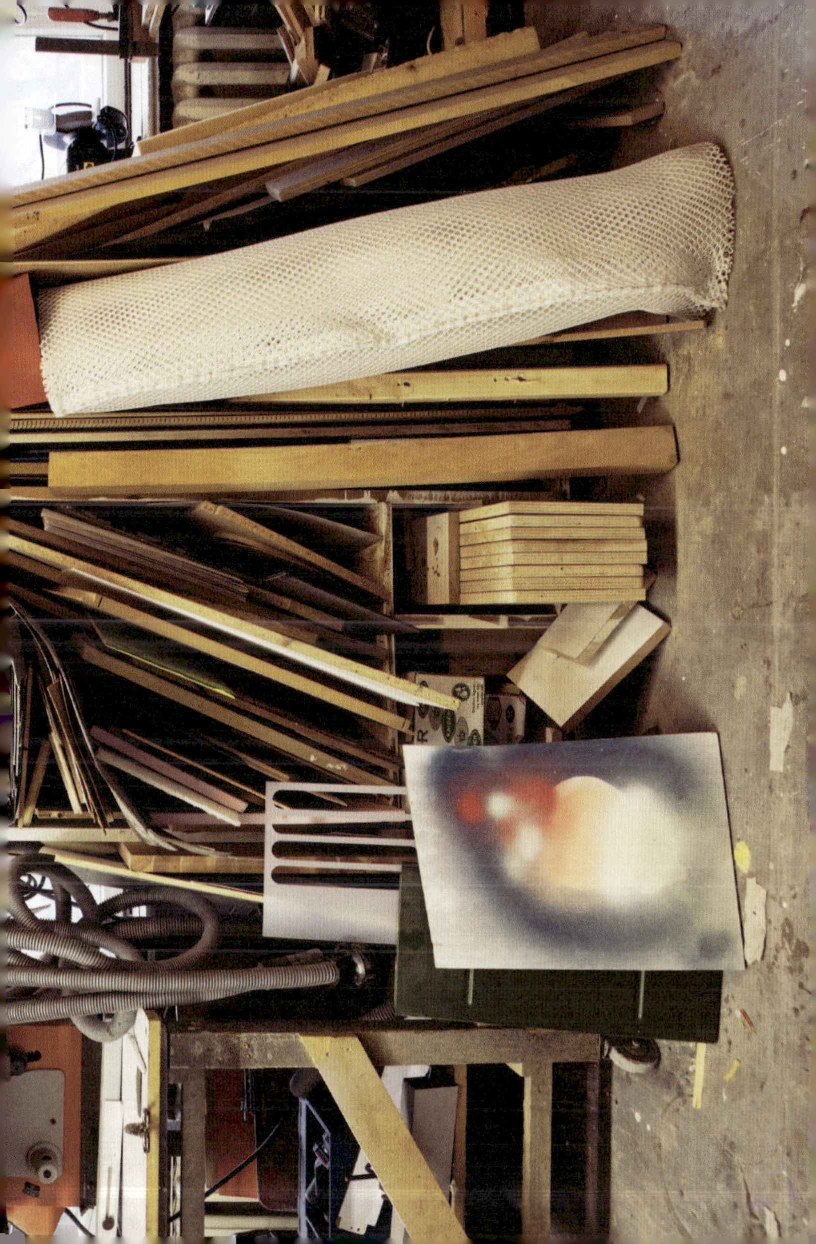

ALL THAT GLITTERS

Germany's capital doesn't have its own academy or university for jewellery design. But thanks to the extraordinary working conditions in the city (yes, we'll say it again: it's all that space), Berlin has nonetheless become a haven for jewellery galleries and artists.

Berlin boasts an entire spectrum of possibilities in jewellery, from exclusive galleries to studio workshops that double as exhibition spaces. There are three camps within the jewellery community; the first being those galleries and artists who take their inspiration from the art world, refusing to succumb to the dictatorship of wearability and practicality while maintaining strong links to Germany's renowned jewellery academies. The others run more traditional gold and silversmithing practices, producing wearable, immaculately executed interpretations of classical beauty. And then there are those retail shops typical of Berlin, where the work bench is part of the display space, and the process and product are visible in equal parts.

THE 'AUTHOR JEWELLER'

— *Always a step ahead when it comes to technical vocabulary, what the English language describes simply as 'contemporary jewellery' is known in German as 'author jewellery',* Autorenschmuck. *Like many German adjectives, the word is heavy with meaning, highlighting the creator's role in the process of making precious objects to wear on the body. Unlike traditional gold and silversmithing, this kind of jewellery isn't defined by the value of the materials used, but by the artists' engagement with their medium.*

Oona

Oona is one of the foremost addresses for 'author jewellery' in the city. Understanding and executing jewellery as a form of artistic expression, the work displayed at Oona is mostly produced as limited edition pieces exploring the boundaries between jewellery and wearable art. Applying an unrestrained formal vocabulary while taking inspiration from the likes of film, architecture and fashion, Oona's circle of artists includes Berliners like Amelie Riech, who creates wearable pieces from ceramics, and internationally renowned sculptural jeweller Svenja John as well as labels like German-Japanese outfit PE/AH, who take a geometric, fashion-oriented approach.

U ***Rosenthaler Platz*** | *Auguststr. 26, Mitte | Tue to Fri 14–18, Sat 13–18 | oona-galerie.de*

Photo Till Bortels

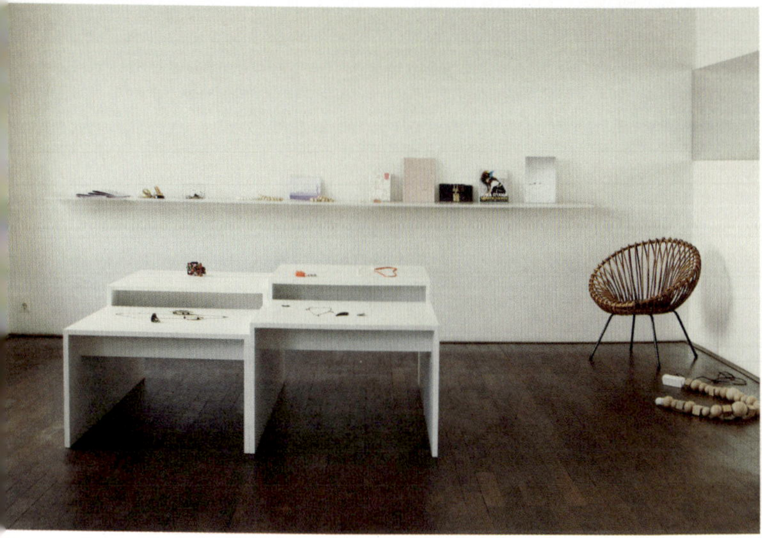

Schmuckfrage

This gallery is one of the proverbial good things that come in small packages. Its diminutive exhibition space presents a diverse crop of works by nearly 30 artists whose stylistic spectrum ranges from conceptual pieces to perfectly executed interpretations of classic silversmithing. Driven by his own curiosity and passion, owner Stephan Plessner is himself a veritable encylopedia of knowledge when it comes to both the history of jewellery and its contemporary practice and application.

U ***Rosenthaler Platz*** | *Brunnenstr. 187, Mitte | Mon to Sat 12–18, (closed Wed) | schmuckfrage.de*

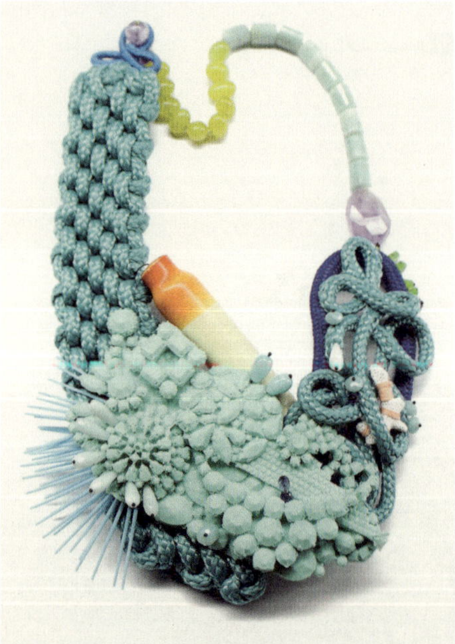

Tip ... Nearby, jeweller **Ruth Temur** has set up her combined workshop and gallery. Many of the artists she exhibits studied at the prestigious, tradition-oriented school of design in the southern German town of Pforzheim.

Veteranenstr. 27, Mitte | Tue to Fri 12–19, Sat 12–17 | temur-schmuck.de

Another exciting address featuring a very international set of contemporary jewellers is nearby **G96-New Values**. Here, a conceptual and playful approach takes centre stage, and not all of the artisans are traditionally educated jewellers.

Knaackstr. 96, Prenzlauer Berg | Mon to Sun 14–21 | g96-newvalues.com

COOP GOLD

— ***Coop Gold*** *is a union of artists and trained gold and silversmiths who offer basic courses and workshops on all aspects of jewellery making. Many late arrivals to this art form receive their induction here while hobby jewellers can hone their skills and connect with the scene.*

Planet Modulor* | *Prinzenstr. 85, Kreuzberg* | *coopgold.de

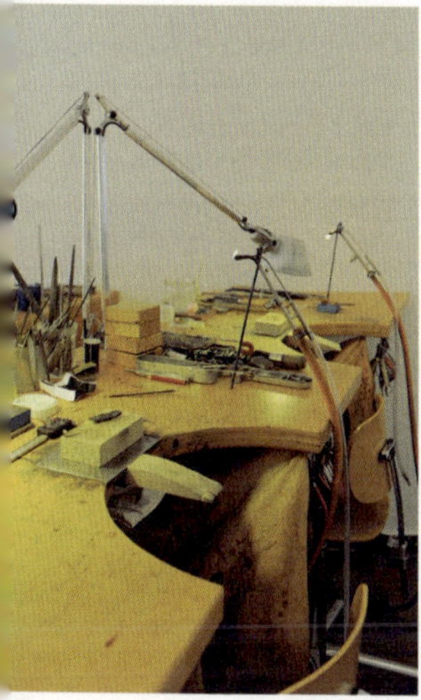

Werkstattgalerie

If you are looking for more established, traditional galleries, the western part of Berlin is the place to start your search. Any such journey should begin at the Werkstattgalerie, the perfect symbiosis of classic and contemporary jewellery practice. Master jeweller Rosemarie Brodhag has long been a fixture on the scene; she still trains younger jewellers and has a knack for discovering exciting up-and-coming talents. Unsurprisingly, her group of artists reads like a Who's Who of the German jewellery scene.

U ***Spichernstraße*** | *Meierottostr. 1, Wilmersdorf* | *Tue to Fri 10.30-18.30, Sat 10.30-15* | *die-werkstattgalerie.de*

Tip ... Of all the galleries listed here, **Schmucksalon Krüger** probably corresponds best to the Berlin image of DIY charm. But don't be fooled, this is an established space focused on only using resources mined under fair and transparent conditions.

Falckensteinstr. 45, Kreuzberg
opening hours vary
swchmucksalon-krueger.de

Tip ... A more recent addition to the fold, **Noon** does not focus solely on jewellery, but takes a contemporary, interdisciplinary approach.

Dresdenerstr. 26, Kreuzberg | *Wed to Fri 11-19, Sat 12-18* | *noonberlin.de*

Fritz

Over in Kreuzberg, goldsmith Manuel Fritz' gallery on Oranienplatz is a veritable institution. Led by his own instincts and tastes rather than an elaborate curatorial vision, Fritz shows a broad spectrum of work, from the products of rookie designers to refined objects in precious metal or gaudy pieces by experimental newcomers.

U ***Kottbusser Tor*** | *Dresdenerstr. 20, Kreuzberg* | *Mon to Fri 10–19, Sat 12–16* | *schmuckfritz.de*

Above Rosemarie Brodhag's work bench.
Left Denise Julia Reytan's necklace 'Samoa', 2010. Her work is available at Schmuckfrage.

LLOT LLOV

Design Collective

The Spontaneous City

llot llov is an unusual design conglomerate, even by Berlin's experimental standards, though the four trained designers of differing backgrounds met the typical Berlin way – late at night at a party. That was in 2005. Before long, two of the four were operating an experimental store-cum-gallery that has now matured into one of Berlin's most fashion forward shops. Meanwhile, the team began creating products together and soon set up their own production and distribution network. Their favourite Berlin places combine the spontaneous and surprising aspects of the city with its colourful and multi-cultural history.

llotllov.de

Below The former Teufelsberg listening post.
Photo Andreas Jüttemann

1 **"Up on top of a mountain of WWII rubble, the Teufelsberg, sits what used to be America's biggest set of artificial ears. At the lofty height of 80 metres, the US military erected three bulbous and hardly discreet antennae in the shape of geodesic domes, which served as listening posts to eavesdrop on communication inside the territory of their Cold War opponent.** Today, the abandoned station – a long-time favourite destination of urban explorers who didn't mind scaling the barbwired fence – is open to the public via tours. It also affords amazing views over Berlin."

You can find out more and book tours at berlinsightout.de.

S *Berlin-Grunewald*

2 **"A special place for a Sunday outing is the Preußenpark in the well-groomed district of Wilmersdorf. Some time in the 1990s, women from Berlin's Thai community started to set up hawker-style food stalls here.**

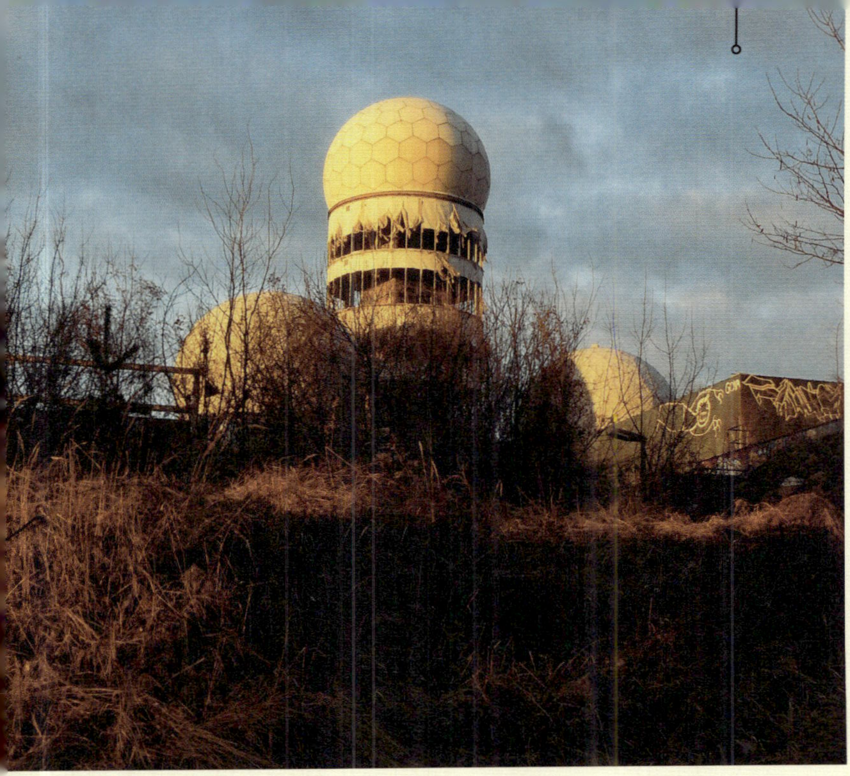

This phenomenon has grown into a weekly tradition. All transactions happen at ground level, and diners set up their picnic blankets between the vendors, which turns it into a very informal eating experience."

Ⓢ *Fehrbelliner Platz or Konstanzer Straße*

3 "**Berlin is famous for its flea markets, particularly those at Mauerpark and Boxhagener Platz.**
We especially love flea markets where finding real treasures still means trawling through boxes of useless junk and entirely unsorted deceased estates. The flea markets we're particularly fond of are in Wedding, Neukölln and Schöneberg. Aunt Google will help you find them."

TRUE VALUES

You don't need to have lived in Berlin for years to realise that commercial interests don't usually rank among the highest priorities of those opening a store or a design business here. More important is authenticity and the love of a good experiment.

Berlin is not a place where polished retail ventures rub shoulders, as the city's wealth is scarce and people's values lean towards self-fulfilment over the accumulation of material riches. Rather than looking for the best in international product retail, Berliners tend to seek the best in ideas. The original concepts emerging from the city may not always be perfectly executed but they are guaranteed to rest on a solid ideological foundation.

VIA Werkstätten

Opened in Prenzlauer Berg eight years ago, VIA Werkstätten is a social enterprise with a focus on innovation and design. Unlike other sheltered workshops, VIA Werkstätten actively seeks communication and collaboration with the city's designers and up-and-coming creative talent, such as graduates from the Weissensee Art Academy, to create products with a design bend. The results are not only distributed to other retailers, but are also available in VIA Werkstätten's own store, Blumenfisch, situated on the cusp between design conscious Mitte and reasonably affluent Prenzlauer Berg.

U ***Senefelder Platz*** | *Schönhauser Allee 175, Prenzlauer Berg*
blumenfisch.de, via-werkstaetten.de

Below A workshop held at VIA Werkstätten as part of the participatory design project 'able' (able-berlin.de). *Photo* Isabelle Dechamps

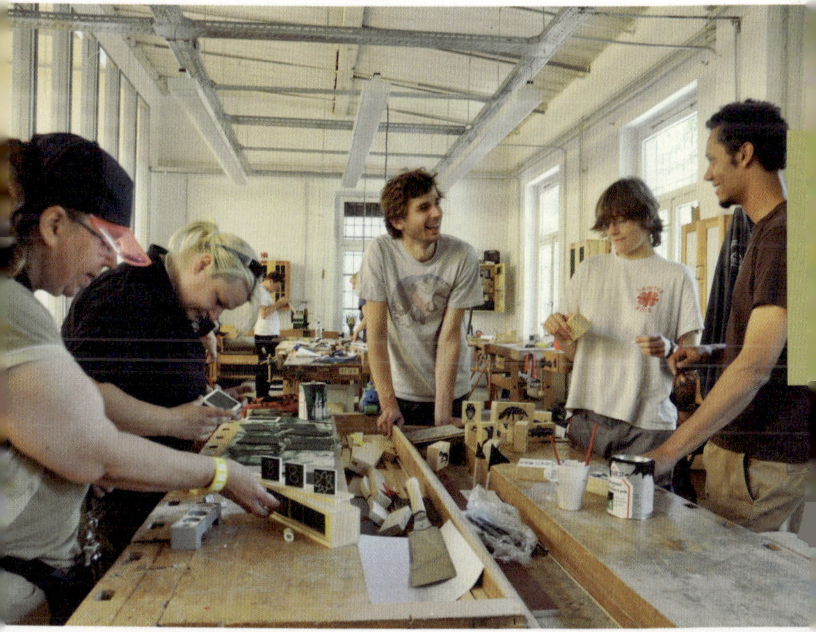

Die imaginäre Manufaktur (DIM)

The 'imaginary manufactory', which combines traditional craftsmanship with a social cause and modern design, is on display in the historic store of the former Institute for the Blind in Kreuzberg. The store was already selling brushes and baskets made by blind people when, in 1998, designers Oliver Vogt and Hermann Weizenegger had the idea to imbue this traditional institution with new life and a new mission. Together with design students, employees of the Institute and people with disabilities, the studio set out to create new, attractive and contemporary products that wouldn't jeopardise the existing business model. Today, more than 70 international designers have been invited to create new objects and DIM products are sold in museum shops in San Francisco, London and Tokyo.

U *Kottbusser Tor | Oranienstr. 26, Kreuzberg | Mon to Fri 10–19, Sat 11–16*

Wertvoll

Few shop owners take their mission as seriously as the ladies behind Wertvoll, a small empire devoted to the cause of sustainable and ethical clothing and products. Aware that it is sometimes difficult for customers to understand what 'ethical' clothing actually means, Wertvoll's proprietors developed their own labelling system to mark each product in their store as either 'recycled', 'handmade', 'fairly produced', 'ecological' or 'donation', meaning part of the money you spend will go towards a worthy cause or project.

U *Senefelder Platz (or Tram on Greifswalder Str.) | Marienburgerstr. 39, Prenzlauer Berg | Mon to Fri 10–20, Sat 10–18 | wertvoll-berlin.com*

Schoener waers wenns schoener waer

Impossible to pronounce for a non-native, this store's name (meaning 'it would be nicer if it was nicer') is much more complicated that its nature. Located on the Bermuda Triangle of creative altruism {sharing the noisy Moritzplatz roundabout with the beloved Prinzessinengarten (*see page 52*) and the gigantic Planet Modulor (*see page 205*)}, this self-described 'concept store for sustainable design' specialises in just that. Its proprietors, University of the Arts graduates Nicole Bednarzyk and Sylke Rademacher, also stock many locally designed sustainable products.

U ***Moritzplatz*** | *Oranienstr. 58a, Kreuzberg* | *Mon to Fri 12–19, Sat 12–16*
schoener-waers.de

SchubLaden

Turning useless objects into something new is a pursuit to which a number of designers and makers in this city have subscribed to. One of the most original and successful followers of this school of thought is furniture designer Franziska Wodicka, who runs her own store in Kreuzberg with her label SchubLaden. The idea is simple enough: Wodicka rescues unused or single drawers and remodels them into sideboards or other containers.

Photo Nina Straßgütl

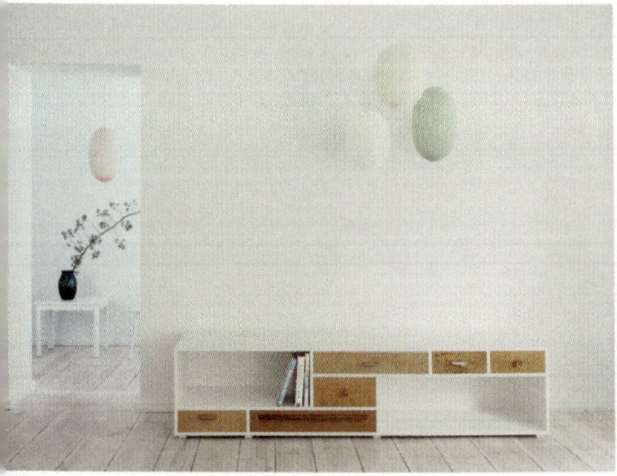

U ***Südstern*** | *Körtestr. 26, Kreuzberg* | *Tue to Fri 11–19, Sat 11–16*
schubladen.de

BEHIND THE SCENES WITH

Daniel Heer

Few designers manage to combine age-old traditional workmanship with contemporary product design as successfully as Daniel Heer. Born in Switzerland into a family of master saddlers and upholsterers, he continues to refine his craft of making precious mattresses and cushions from horse hair, complemented by a range of leather accessories, in a studio in Kreuzberg. His client base not only includes private individuals who commission their own favourite pieces, but also international design companies like Kvadrat. In 2012, he took the plunge, opening his own showroom in Mitte (*see page 211*).

danielheer.com

Photos Max Zerrahn

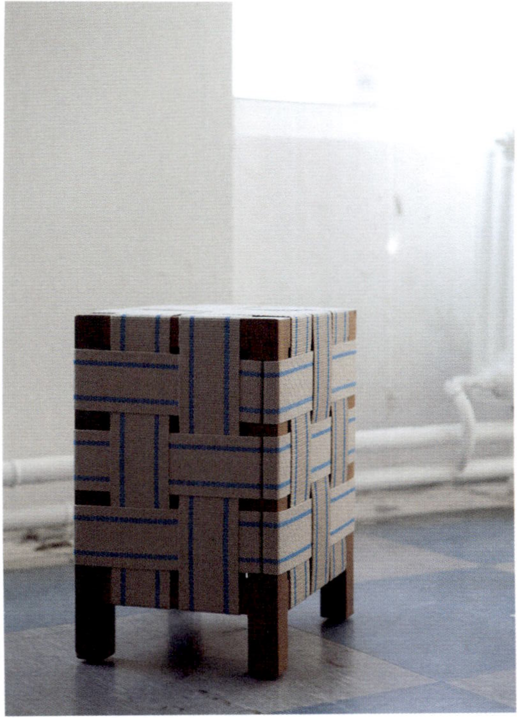

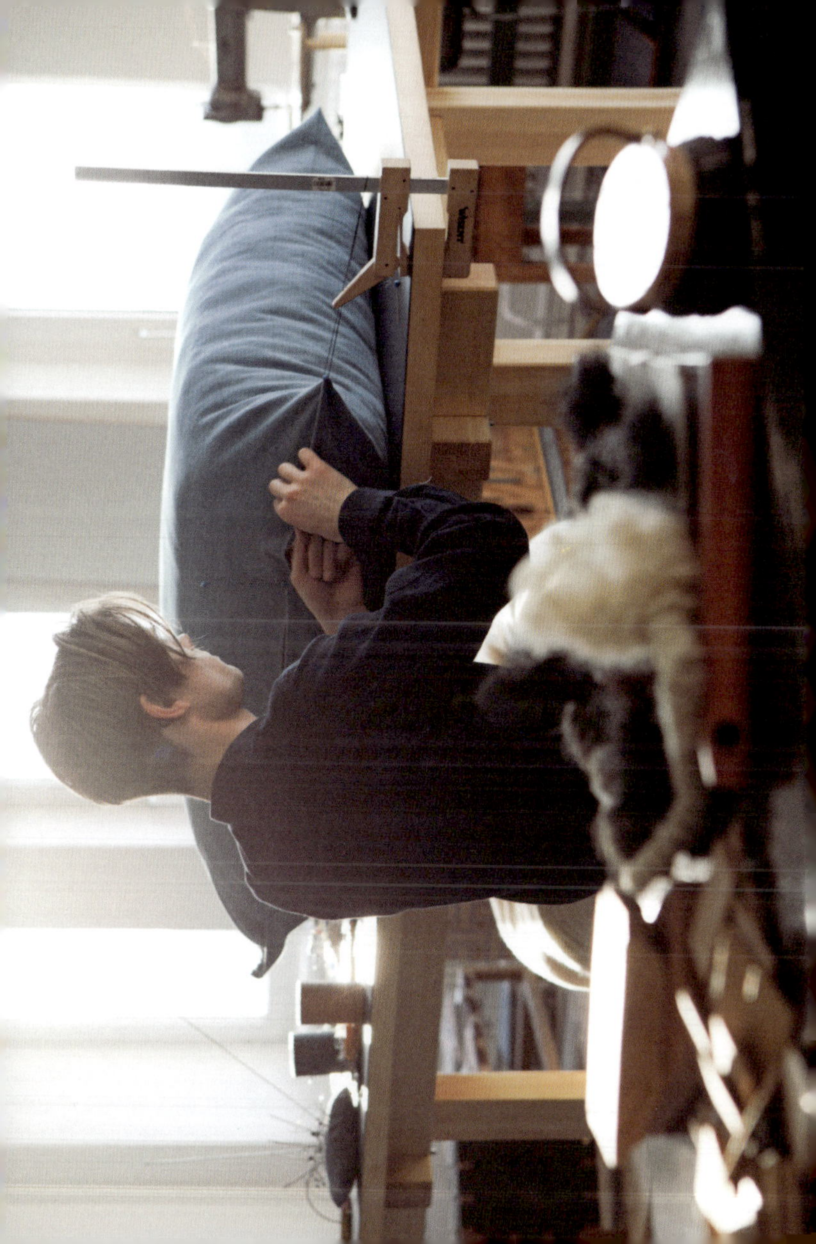

BETWEEN THE PAGES

Print isn't dead, especially not in Berlin. Here, every art, design and architecture devotee will find just the right publication to satisfy their yearning for a tactile reading experience.

Because this cultural metropolis has no shortage of interested buyers – or at least browsers – the city's proliferation of bookstores and magazine stores is not only in healthy condition, but continues to grow with new niche additions.

Motto Distribution

The reputation of this art publication and zine store, housed in a former picture frame factory in Kreuzberg, stretches far beyond the borders of Berlin and the continent. A favoured haunt of zine lovers and indie publishers, its staff don't miss a beat. Motto is the brainchild of Swiss photographer Alexis Zavialoff, who initially started a distribution company for independent publications. Now with a second, smaller space at Markthalle IV, it also appears Motto is aiming for world domination as it lends its good name to temporary and not-so-temporary publication outlets in Basel, Copenhagen, Melbourne, Brussels and Vancouver.

U ***Schlesisches Tor*** | *Skalitzer Str. 68, Kreuzberg* | *Mon to Sat 12–20*
Inside Markthalle IV | *Entries on Eisenbahnstr. 42/43 and Pücklerstr. 34, Kreuzberg* | *Sat 11–17* | *mottodistribution.com*

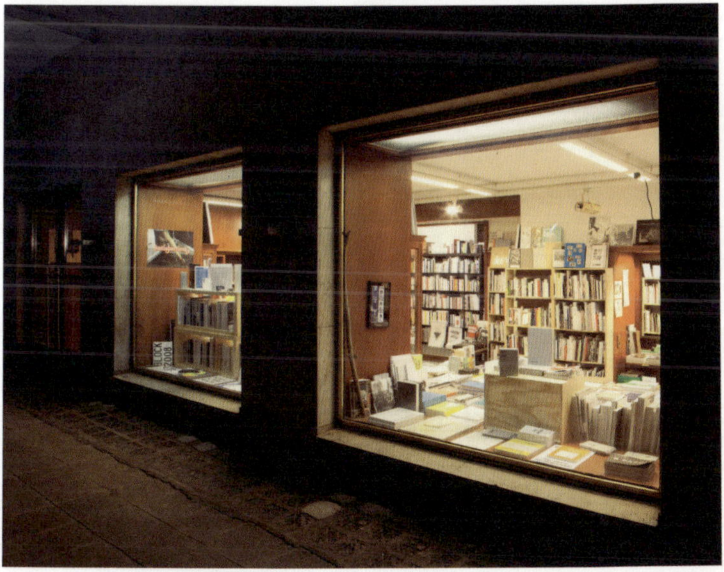

Do you read me?!

Since it opened in 2008, Do you read me?! in Mitte has become the ultimate resource for discovering new contemporary publications and periodicals in the fields of fashion, art and architecture. Designer Mark Kiessling and book trader Jessica Reitz had frequently encountered well stocked, carefully curated magazine stores on their international travels but felt Berlin was lagging behind. While their Mitte store carries over 1,500 publications, predominantly magazines, there is now also a second location on up-and-coming Potsdamer Str. Nestled among the city's most forward-thinking art galleries, the aptly titled Reading Room & Shop features a curated book selection and hosts exhibitions and events.

Tip ... The **Reading Room & Shop** (*see image below*) on Potsdamer Str. is a perfect addition to the art tour 'Adventure Capital', (*see page 84*).

Potsdamer Str. 98, Tiergarten | Thu to Sat 12–18

U ***Weinmeisterstraße*** | *Auguststr. 28, Mitte | Mon to Sat 10–19.30*

JESSICA SAYS...

— ***Do You Read Me?!*** *co-owner Jessica Reitz suggests these three Berlin-based publications:*

032c, *because its design and content set the bar high.*
032c.com

Mono.kultur *is a real niche publication, devoted to a different artist each time.*
mono-kultur.com

I love you, *a beautifully designed fashion magazine, proves that the net and print content can complement one another perfectly.*
iloveyou-magazine.com

Photo Achim Hatzius

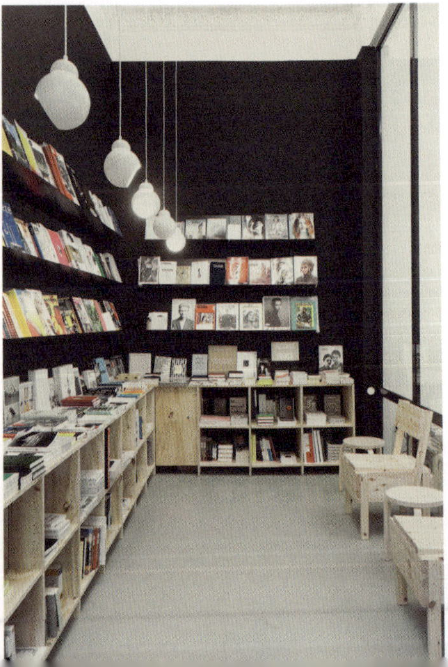

Gestalten Space

In the year 1994, three young designers first ventured into the world of book publishing. Little did they know that a decade and a half later they would be counted among the world's most influential design-oriented publishing companies. Today, Kreuzberg-based Gestalten remains faithful to its original vision of being a truly global company. They publish predominantly in English and sell more books outside Germany than at home. In early 2011, Gestalten's founders decided it was time to show some presence in Berlin. They did so by renting an impressive 1,000sqm retail area in one of Mitte's hidden courtyards, the Sophie-Gips-Höfe, where Gestalten publications share space with their art book brethren and the products and limited edition pieces created by the subjects of Gestalten's work.

Tip ... Keep your ear to the ground for events and book launches here; it's a great opportunity to meet this city's visual designers.

U ***Weinmeisterstraße*** | *Sophie-Gips-Höfe, Sophienstr. 21, Mitte* | *Sun to Fri 12–20, Sat 10–20, closed Tue* | *gestalten.com*

Photo Gestalten 2012

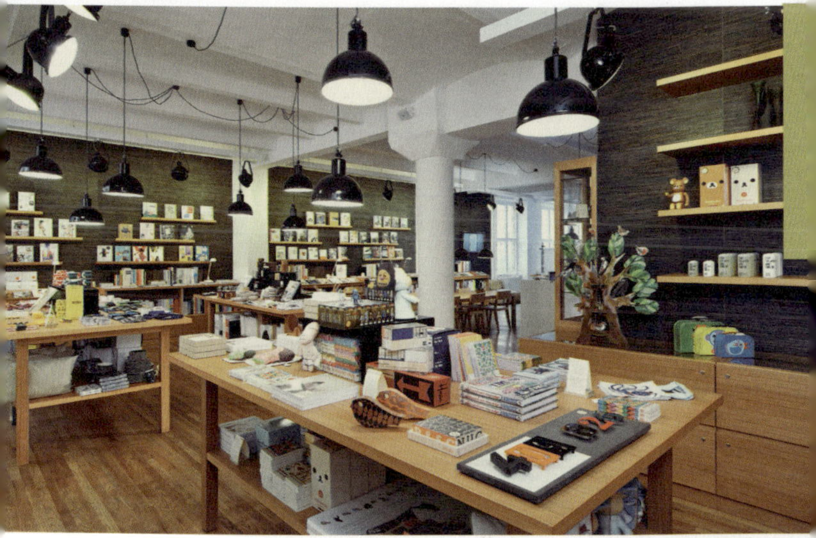

25 Books

This bookstore is the antidote to the crammed-to-the rafters chain outlets that dominate more commercial streetscapes. The shop's name says it all. At 25 Books, just over two dozen books take centre stage, all of which are curated by Hannes Wanderer, who also runs a small but busy publishing venture by the name of Peperoni Books. Both the store and Peperoni books focus on the the photographic monograph, with the exploration of cities and other locations an oft-recurring theme.

U ***Bernauer Straße*** | *Brunnenstr. 152, Mitte* | *Wed, Fri & Sat 14–19*
25books.com

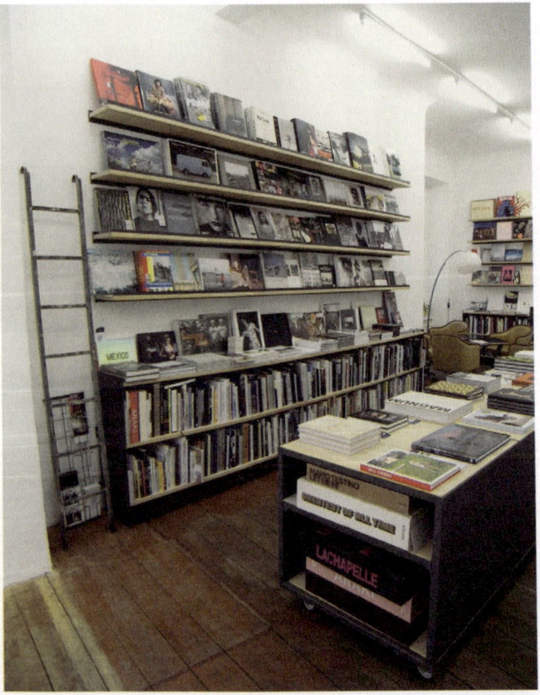

THE PUBLISHER AS SELLER

— *A larger art publishing enterprise that unites both publisher and bookseller is that of Walther König. He started out in Cologne in the late 1960s and also runs a handful of museum bookstores in Berlin, the biggest of which is near Museum Island.*

Burgstraße 27, Mitte
buchhandlung-walther-koenig.de

Pro qm

This bookstore, which largely stocks works on architecture, art and urban issues, has become a stalwart of Berlin's independent bookstore scene. When the store opened in 1999, it was located on Alte Schönhauser Str. and – while signs of gentrification were starting to emerge – the area was a far cry from the shopping destination it is today. Eight years later the shop fell victim to rising rents and relocated just a few hundred metres away into a quieter, though larger location. Pro qm's three proprietors are serious about the subjects they propagate, as shown by the roster of talks and exhibitions they organise alongside their regular activities.

U *Rosa-Luxemburg-Platz | Almstadtstr. 48-50, Mitte | Mon to Sat 11–20 | pro-qm.de*

Bücherbogen

It may lack some of the hip glamour that characterises other shrines to the printed page in Mitte, but the Bücherbogen, located near Charlottenburg's tame Savignyplatz, is a true institution when it comes to books about art, architecture and associated creative pursuits. The store, which opened in a former mechanic's workshop in 1980, is frequented by long-term Berlin artists and creatives, who list it as one of their favourite destinations. Its busy events schedule features appearances by international design world celebrities.

S *Savignyplatz | Stadtbahnbogen 593, Charlottenburg | Mon to Fri 10–20, Sat 10–18 | buecherbogen.com*

DUSSMANN DAS KULTURKAUFHAUS

— *Berlin's largest general bookstore occupies 7,000sqm over several storeys on high-end Friedrichstr. As you can imagine, Dussmann das Kulturkaufhaus offers anything from software to language books, kids' books and stationery, but most notable is its extensive foreign language section, as well as the well-organised department specialising in local history.*

Friedrichstr. 90, Mitte
Mon to Fri 9–24, Sat 9–23.30
kulturkaufhaus.de

INK & PAPER

Paper, bookbinding and model making are the passions of a select few, but in Berlin this minority aggregates to a larger than normal subculture.

Here, where an experimental spirit, affordable rents and serendipitous encounters can be a winning formula to combine success in business with personal satisfaction and at times altruism, a number of unusual enterprises cater to those who can't pass up a beautifully bound book, an unusual material or a piece of paper with a story.

Planet Modulor

It's taken straight from the official press release, but there is probably no description that befits this new institution better than 'creative Eldorado'. Although this venture was only just over a year old at the time this book went to print, the site of a former piano factory at the once-barren Moritzplatz is a destination where anyone fascinated with materials can easily while away a rainy afternoon or three. Taking up most of the space, Modulor is a store that once specialised in materials for architectural model-making but has expanded to stock everything from specialty papers to craft supplies since its move to the enormous three-storey location. However, true to its founders' vision, the refurbished building also incorporated a number of specialty stores and other creative enterprises to become a destination that combines culturally and socially-oriented enterprises with traders and service providers linked to the creative industries. Other tenants of the building include the well-established publisher Aufbau as well as Minimum, one of Berlin's most cherished proprietors of designer furniture.

U ***Moritzplatz*** | *Prinzenstr, 85, Kreuzberg* | *Mon to Fri 9–20, Sat 10–18* | *planetmodulor.de*

Photo Modulor

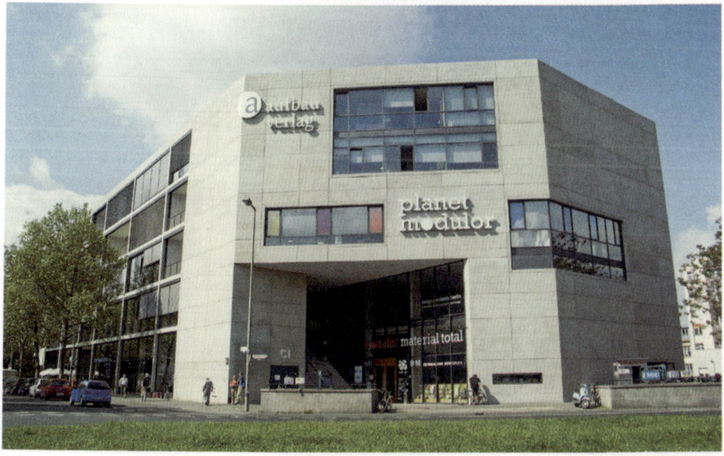

Pleased to Meet – Februardesign

Here's a good example of a passion-driven business which, by virtue of having a storefront, slowly but surely climbed toward success. Partners in business and life Marcel Hornung and Daniela Köhn initially settled in Berlin in 2004 to run their own design studio, Februardesign. Their passion for creating products and printing fine stationery steered them towards the occasional self-initiated project, which eventually lead to the production of their own cards, tags, journals and notebooks. The somewhat retro look is inspired by the occasional childhood memory and a passion for mid-century American design.

U ***Bernauer Straße*** | *Brunnenstr. 42, Mitte* | *Mon to Fri 9.30–18* | *pleasedtomeet.de*

WEDNESDAY PAPERWORKS

— *Not all good businesses have a physical retail outlet, but some are so inspiring that they deserve a mention regardless of whether there's a location where you can surround yourself with their product.* ***Wednesday Paperworks*** *is such a business. Fascinated with the physical qualities of ink and paper, and jaded by the fact that contemporary design is dictated by pixel pushing and the delete button, a graphic designer and a book binder joined forces to create bespoke paper products for private clients. Their hands-on Kreuzberg studio soon began to produce a range of paper products and notebooks that are far from the ordinary and are available in select stores and online.*

wednesday-paper-works.com

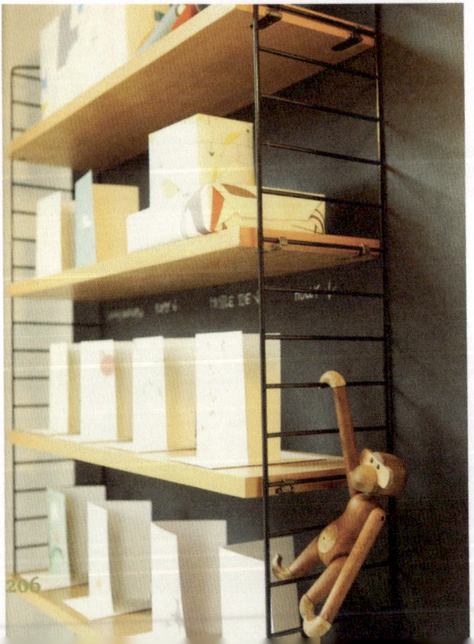

Photo © pleasedtomeet

S.wert design

Anyone who's ever tried to find a Berlin souvenir that doesn't involve a felted miniature television tower or a keyring inspired by former East Berlin's traffic light figures knows the levels of despair the search can arouse. S.wert design operates on the principle that products inspired by the monuments and hallmarks of the city don't necessarily have to be free of imagination. Trained architect Sandra Siewert applies literal and abstracted imagery derived from Berlin's architecture to materials and objects as diverse as curtains and cutlery.

U ***Rosenthaler Platz*** | *Brunnenstr 191. Mitte* | *Mon to Fri 11–19, Sat 11–18*
s-wert-design.de

R.S.V.P. Papier in Mitte

R.S.V.P.'s floor-to-ceiling shelves are not even fully stocked, yet stationery lovers will still find it easy to spend ages browsing the wares. The products on offer include stationery, notebooks, papers and pens from the world's most iconic makers of such items, as well as the occasional limited-edition print or calendar by local designers, and, of course, R.S.V.P.'s own small range of writing materials.

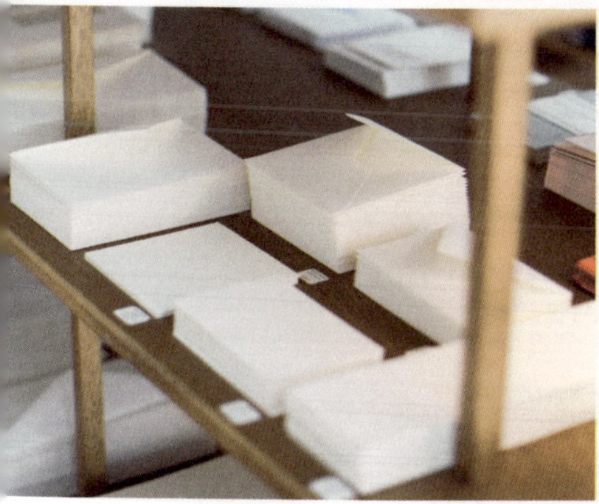

U ***Weinmeisterstr or Rosenthaler Platz***
Mulackstr. 14, Mitte | *Mon to Sat 12–19* | *rsvp-berlin.de*

EXPAND YOUR HORIZONS

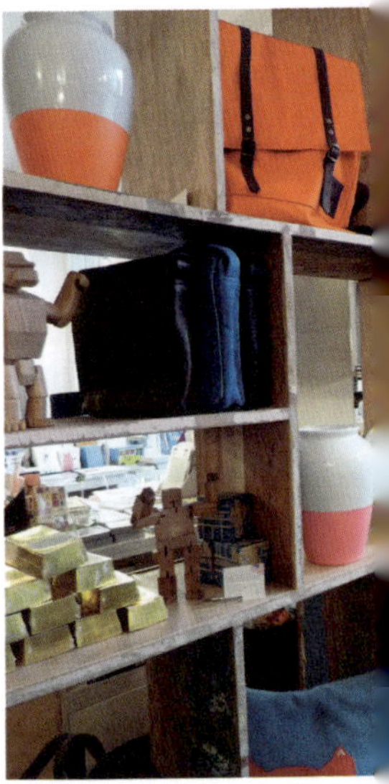

As you may have gathered, Berlin is not the place for chasing your average highly polished designer paraphernalia (although, if that's your bag, it's out there). Rather, prepare yourself for encounters of another kind – unusual ideas sometimes lacking in perfect execution, but abundant in creativity and experimentation, paired with beautiful showrooms that specialise in extraordinarily crafted objects.

Erfinderladen

Berlin wouldn't be Berlin if it didn't have institutions such as the 'inventor's shop', where the authors of new products can test drive their creations. The store began as a sideline to a patent consultancy, but has developed an identity of its own as well as a second arm, the 'Museum of Future Inventions', which hosts temporary exhibitions.
U *Eberswalder Straße*
Lychenerstr. 8, Prenzlauer Berg | Mon to Sat 11–20
erfinderladen-berlin.de

Ok Versand

Household objects maintain similar functions the world over, yet minute differences in form, colour, and decoration are part of establishing a visual sense of place. Ok Versand specialises in importing objects manufactured internationally for regional markets out of local – and often low-cost – materials. Fascinatingly familiar yet completely different, their housewares, accessories and trinkets are a world apart.
U *Weinmeisterstraße* | **Alte Schönhauser Str. 36/37, Mitte | Mon to Fri 12–20, Sat 12–16 | okversand.com**

into art&furniture

Imagine how great it would be if every designer had a public space where you could view their work in its natural habitat. Two design practices are doing just that. Lineal is the studio of two architects who got their start designing shelves and now produce a range of furnishings. Product designer Martin Holzapfel designs streamlined, form-reduced objects for daily use. Their shared showroom also features shows by external curators.
U *Rosenthaler Platz*
Ackerstr. 165, Mitte
Wed to Fri 13–19,
Sat 11–17 | into-berlin.de

Supergrau

The creative roots of this product design label rest in Solingen, a small city in Germany's far west. However, Supergrau's work, combining precious materials with a self-described 'laissez-faire DIY art deco-mashup' aesthetic, couldn't be more Berlin. That's why founders Björn Berger, Denis Cegielski und Tobias Welzel opened their first showroom in the capital in 2012.
U *Rosenthaler Platz* **| Gartenstr. 6, Mitte | Mon to Sat 10–18 | supergrau.de**

Kunstschule

The 'art school' successfully combines a store for interior products with the practice of interior architects and sisters Melanie and Stefanie Nölken. After the pair began custom-designing furniture for their clients, they figured they may as well replicate their most successful pieces and sell them in small quantities, alongside the work by other designers.
U *Senefelderplatz (or Tram on Greifswalder Str.)* **|Hufelandstr. 13, Prenzlauer Berg Mon to Fri 10.30–20, Sat 11.30–18 | kunstschule.net**

Formfalt

The souvenir seemingly occupies a blind spot in the design industry, the only occasional development being the increasing garishness of the bags, T-shirts and trinkets available to travellers. However, changes are afoot in the museum shop thanks to outfits such as Formfalt, who've been operating for eight years and now run a small retail outlet in a Friedrichshain side street. The Formfalt product combines the elements of art education, practice and history in one small object.
U *Samariterstraße* **| Colbestr. 18, Friedrichshain | Mon to Fri 11–19, Sat 11–16 formfalt.com**

Left Pomeranza Design Ranch
Below The into art&furniture showroom in Mitte.

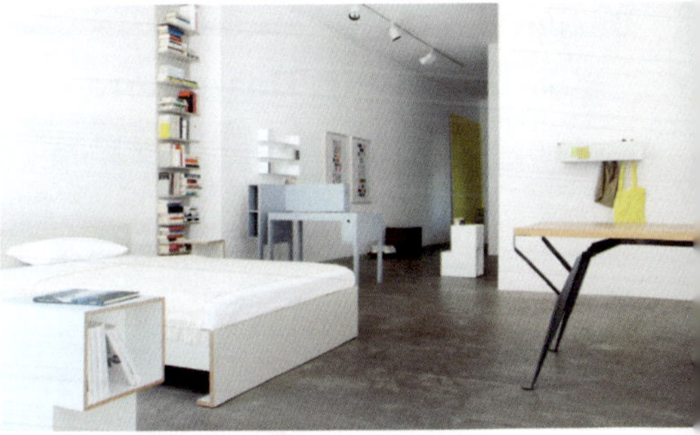

Etsy Labs

Etsy is best-known as an online platform where makers of handmade objects are linked directly to buyers. Their pervasive community spirit has made its way offline: Etsy has opened one of their Labs in Kreuzberg's IMA village where they hold regular workshops on every aspect of DIY culture, from increasing your PR skills to sharpening your craft. Eschewing the traditional start-up path of building capital before producing work, Etsy Labs focuses on equipping people with good products and equally strong business savvy.
U *Moritzplatz* | **Ritterstr. 12-14, Kreuzberg | Workshops by registration**
Etsy.com

Pomeranza Design Ranch

This store sticks out from the sea of Prenzlauer Berg knickknack shops due to its focus on the work of up-and-coming designers and traditionally manufactured goods. The collection is complemented by products that are curated according to a changing theme.
U *Eberswalder Straße* | **Raumerstr. 19, Prenzlauer Berg**
Mon to Fri 10–19, Sat 11–18
pomeranza-shop.com

Minimum

When it comes to high-end design pieces, Minimum is the most notable and commendable store in town. Not only because they hold an exclusive licence to sell Vitra furniture, but because founder Wilfried Lembert espouses the philosophy that design should enhance and simplify daily life, whether at home or at the office, and promotes local and up-and-coming designers.
U *Moritzplatz* | **Minimum im Aufbau Haus | Prinzenstr. 85 C, Kreuzberg | Mon to Fri 10–18 | multiple locations, see minimum.de**

Unser Store

Unser ('Our') Store in Steglitz is a haven for those who can't leave a museum without a trip to the gift shop. Operated by two passionate individuals who work on object and store design for museums, Unser Store is a carefully curated collection of beautiful and practical things from the world over.
U *Bundesplatz* | **Stubenrauchstr. 46, Steglitz | Fri 11–19 and by appointment**
our-store.de

Stilwerk

Stilwerk is an interior design lover's candy shop. Try to contain your glee as you skip through this expansive forum uniting high-end design brands under one roof. The emphasis is on homegrown products from local purveyors of kitchens, couches and so on, so you could call Stilwerk a living commercial monument to Germany's status on the international design scene.
S *Savignyplatz* | **Kantstr. 17, Charlottenburg | Mon to Sat 10–19 | stilwerk.de**

Staub Shop & Studio

Although Berlin is renowned for its collaborative spirit and collective work

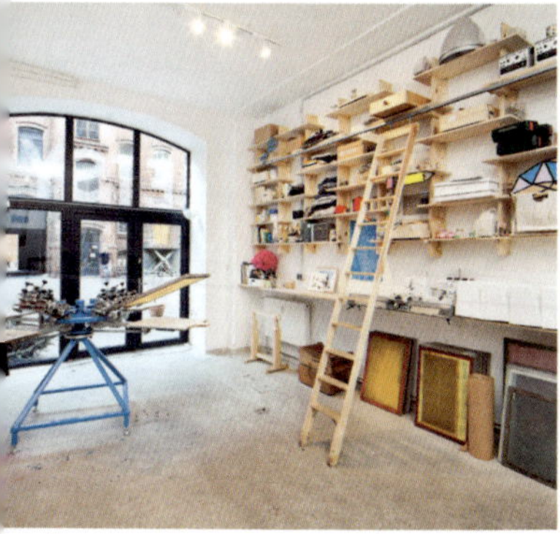

JR Ledermanufaktur

Strongly steeped in the traditions of leather making, Jörn Rischke's Mitte manufactory produces handmade, individualised pieces for sale exclusively in the store or by special order. The store-cum-workshop is a sight in itself, with JR's elegant and refined pieces made using antique tools.
U *Weinmeisterstraße* | **Gipsstr. 7, Mitte**
Tues to Fri 12–18, Sat 12–17
ledermanufaktur-berlin.de

spaces, there are far too few designery types who combine their experimental spirit with a little bit of commercialism. So put your hands together for the five or so creative minds behind the collective Staub, who frequently throw open the doors of their shared studio and store to sell their work alongside that of a few others, with a couple of drinks and laughs along the way.
U *Görlitzer Bahnhof* | **Manteuffelstr. 48, Kreuzberg Wed to Sat 12–19 staubtemporary.com**

Daniel Heer

Daniel Heer is a true craftsman. His horsehair mattresses and leather bags have long established him as a shining example of Berlin-based design. In 2012 he opened a showroom in Mitte, where one can marvel at the beauty and simplicity of his handmade products.
U *Rosa-Luxemburg-Platz*
Rosa-Luxemburg-Str. 26, Mitte | Wed to Sat 11–20
danielheer.com

Jan Kath

The scion of a German carpet-making dynasty, Jan Kath's carpets are the stuff of fantasy. Their rich colours and dreamlike patterns are recognizably inspired by classic carpet design but belie an expressedly modern twist.
U *Rosenthaler Platz* | **Brunnenstr. 3, Mitte | Tues to Sat 11–19 | jan-kath.de**

Königliche Porzellanmanufaktur

Having produced porcelain for the royalty of yore, KPM is by far the most established firm in this guide. More recently, they have been known to break from tradition, working with avant-garde designers.
S *Tiergarten* | **Wegelystr. 1, Charlottenburg | Mon to Sun 10–18 | kpm-berlin.de**

Above Etsy Labs workshop in Kreuzberg

EAT/DRINK/SLEEP

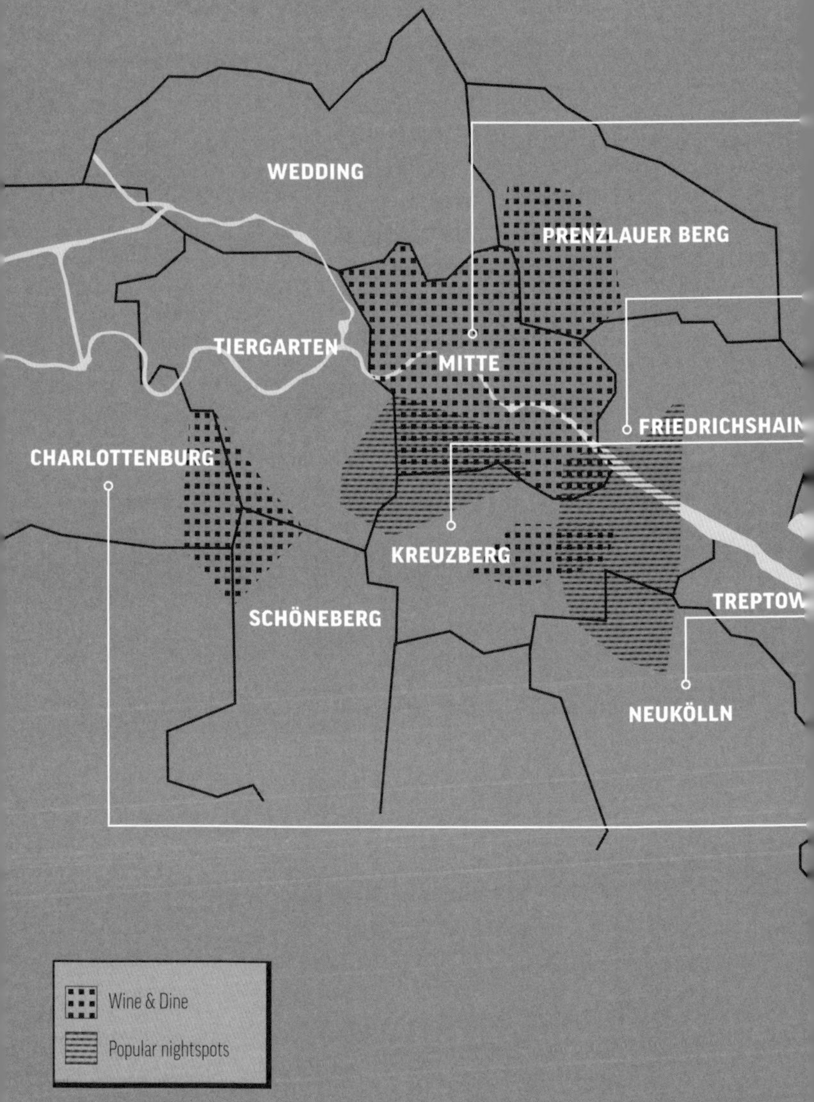
WEDDING
PRENZLAUER BERG
TIERGARTEN
MITTE
FRIEDRICHSHAIN
CHARLOTTENBURG
KREUZBERG
SCHÖNEBERG
TREPTOW
NEUKÖLLN
Wine & Dine
Popular nightspots

THE ESTABLISHMENT

As the city's cultural centrepoint, **Mitte** naturally boasts a plethora of hospitality ventures that are intrinsically linked to the art and fashion world. It's the place for fine dining followed by a cultured drink or twelve.

THE ARTERY

The party never stops along the bustling strip between **Kreuzberg** and **Friedrichshain** and many of the city's famed clubs are situated along the riverside.

THE CONSTANT

Many districts have gone in and out of fashion when it comes to entertainment. But **Kreuzberg**, the heart of alternative culture during the Wall years, continues to be a reliable destination for food and fun.

THE ROOKIE

In line with everything that's been written in this book about **Neukölln**, it shouldn't come as a surprise that this is the place where the nightlife is currently at its most dynamic. Besides many drinking spots, some of the most interesting – and sometimes ephemeral – dining experiences can be had in the neighbourhood.

THE GRAND DAME

The 'Old West' – **Charlottenburg**, **Wilmersdorf** and **Schöneberg** – may not be crowded with the international party scene, but it is the area to go looking for the authentic old-world drinking spots and restaurants that have serviced the cultural community for decades.

THOUGHT FOR FOOD

HOW GREAT FOOD, DRINK AND ENTERTAINMENT MAKE A CREATIVE CITY – AND VICE VERSA

Although good décor is always a good idea, the success or failure of any hospitality venture, whether a bar, restaurant, or hotel, is based on the same principles as any other creative endeavour; the willingness of the proprietors to take a risk and the existence of a clientele eager to experiment.

Atmospheric bars, cutting-edge restaurants and unheard-of hotel concepts may seem a natural part of the landscape in Berlin, but these spaces are new to the scene. While the city is famed for its musical developments, from the alternative and punk culture that took the world by storm from Kreuzberg in the 1970s to the electronic music venues that have lured crowds since the fall of the Wall, Berlin's reputation for refined food and drink culture is an entirely recent development.

“The best recipe for a thriving culture of food and drink includes a healthy dose of international influences.”

Thanks to its increasing internationalisation, Berlin has added an important ingredient to its creative melting pot – a new standard for wining, dining and unwinding. A refined hospitality scene needs cross-pollination and exchange with global trends as well as a healthy dose of competition to reach its true potential. When it comes to this crucial element, Berlin is blooming. In the following chapter, we present a snapshot of the part of Berlin's burgeoning hospitality scene that's intricately connected to this city's creative life, rounded off by a selection of places to rest your head or your laptop.

OUR PARTNER

BERLIN – UP CLOSE & PERSONAL

airbnb.com

Creativity is often born out of dire straits. To make ends meet, three San Francisco friends founded Airbedandbreakfast. For a small fee, they let strangers stay on airbeds in their homes and served them breakfast.

Fast forward four years and this simple idea has helped to revolutionise the way we travel. In almost every country, private individuals provide strangers with a home away from home by renting out their own abodes, a spare room or more exotic locations like tree houses or entire islands.

In Berlin this way of travelling gives visitors an instant connection to the city: by placing them among like-minded people and in authentic spaces found via Airbnb, the anonymity of a hotel is traded for a genuine experience of local life.

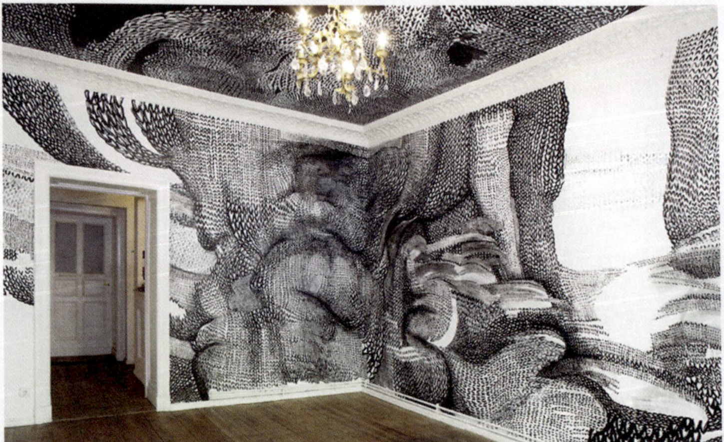

New Friends

There is no better way to discover a new city than with a local guide. Why not join in an extended family dinner or discuss the city's history with a professor of literature? Airbnb lets you choose whether you'd like to stay in a private apartment or – even better – in a guest room while your host is around.

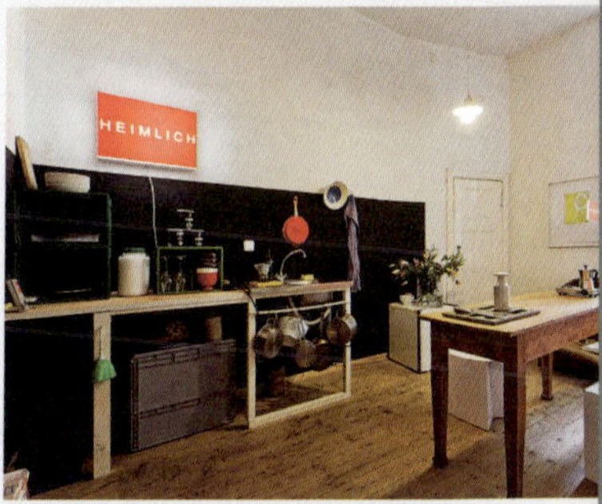

A Focus on Design

The founders of Airbnb were designers, and their passion for the subject continues to attract like-minded individuals to participate in the experience as hosts and guests. Some locations may make you feel like you've entered the pages of an architecture magazine, or that you could be sleeping in the bed of an up-and-coming artist. The creative edge is always in sight.

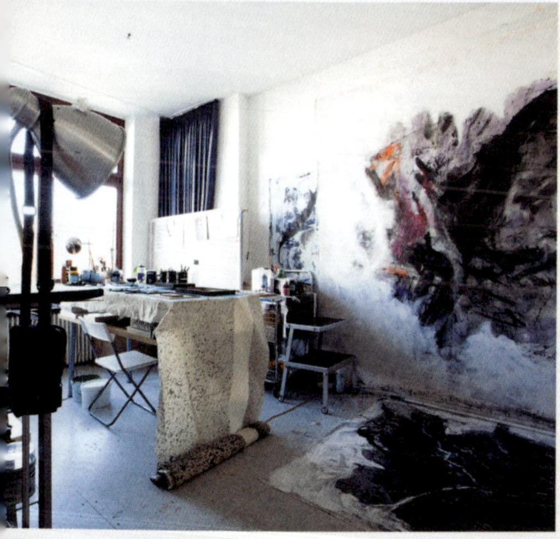

The Wish List

Seasoned travellers know that a good recommendation is worth its weight in gold. That's why Airbnb helps you find the perfect place to stay with the help of kindred souls. Not only does the Airbnb website offer thousands of accommodation options, it also allows every guest or host to curate selections of the most exciting and interesting destinations they encounter.

airbnb.com/wishlists

THE URBAN BAROMETER

Berlin's huge variety of dimly lit drinking houses is as famed as the Brandenburg Gate. As in any city, there are places to hook up, get drunk, or be seen, but Berlin's bars also tell a million tales about the city's social history.

Berlin's bars are essential public spaces, gathering places away from cramped city tenements, hideouts where every local can find their brethren. They also gauge social change, as their presence or absence – and their clientele – point to urban decay, renewal or transition. This journey through some of the institutions of the bar scene paints a picture of the city's colourful Kneipe culture, its past, present and perhaps its future. Who says you can't delve into a city's history with a drink in hand?

Attitude: SO36

Nearby... **Trinkteufel**, (Naunynstr. 60) the drink devil, is SO36's smaller sibling around the corner, a grungy, avowedly late opener that blares punk, metal and thrash deep into the night. Legendary **Bei Schlawinchen** (Schönleinstr. 34) never closes – at 8am it's often still packed with a motley assortment of the city's most committed drinkers.

In today's Berlin, traces of the radical 1970s and 80s are rare. Because young West Germans living in Berlin were spared from mandatory military service, an alternative culture thrived, creating a milieu of DIY bars and squats. The great symbol of this scene still stands. SO36, referring to the area's former postcode, is a punk and hard rock music bar and club in the heart of once-crumbling Kreuzberg. David Bowie and Iggy Pop, then Berlin locals, famously attended the opening in 1978. Apart from punk bands, the tolerant venue soon attracted the LGBT (lesbian, gay, bisexual and transgender) scene. Today, the pan-Arab and Turkish LGBT community lets loose to oriental beats at the club's regular Gayhane parties.

Photo Matthias Zickrow

U *Kottbusser Tor* | *Oranienstr. 190, Kreuzberg* | *so36.de*

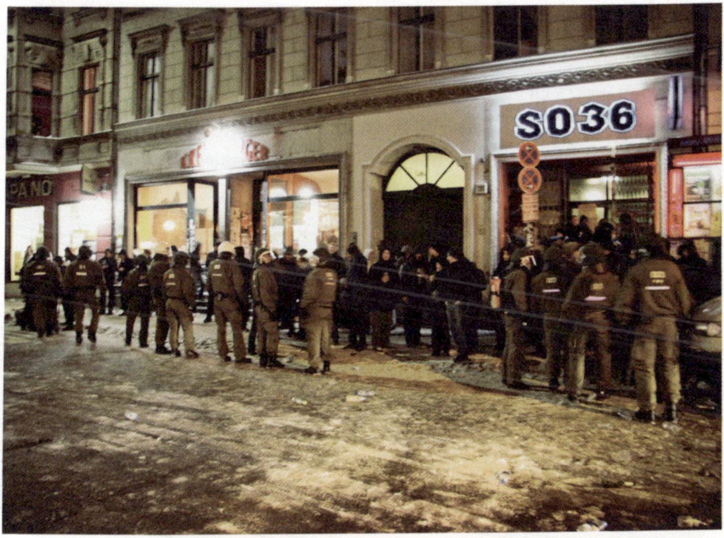

Tradition: E. and M. Leydicke

Before the rise of the retro-furnished DJ bar, the traditional Berlin *Kneipe* was a second living room for many locals, defining the city's distinctive bar culture. Although some fear its demise, a few classic bars of yore have miraculously survived. Schöneberg's E. and M. Leydicke first opened in 1877. Featuring pre-war art deco signage and an original 19th century interior, the rustic bar is famed for producing a concoction of flavoured spirits. Leydicke became a haunt of students and leftists in the 1960s and 70s and today hosts a crowd as mixed as Berlin.

Other places ... **Max and Moritz** (Oranienstr. 162, Kreuzberg) is a more upmarket "Altberliner Wirtshaus" that has changed little since opening in 1902. In the east of the city, tradition reigns in bars like **Alt Berlin** (Münzstr. 23, Mitte), a beautifully dim, dark and smoky relic in Mitte. The nearby **Clärchens Ballhaus** (Augustr. 24, Mitte) is a wonderfully preserved 1920s dance hall, restaurant and pub where punters drink champagne and dance the tango in a grand ballroom.

U *Yorckstraße | Mansteinstr. 4, Kreuzberg | leydicke.com*

Anything goes: Kumpelnest 3000

Whereas punk may have ruled Kreuzberg before the Wall fell, further west - near the gay district of Schöneberg - bars were more likely to play disco music. The infamous Kumpelnest 3000, located in a former brothel off Potsdamer Str., has been a haven for Berlin's early morning allsorts for over 25 years. Decaying chandeliers illuminate gaudy carpet and tinsel-lined walls, colourful cocktails are served and a sexually ambiguous crowd lets go on the crammed dance floor as the sun rises. Lurid, kitsch and transgressive, Kumpelnest might only be a bar, but it remains an enduring statement of Berlin's diversity - allegedly even Karl Lagerfeld once dropped in to check out a drag show.

U *Kurfürstenstraße | Lützowstr. 23, Tiergarten | kumpelnest3000.com*

Diversity and Leisure: Ankerklause

Tip ... On the other side of the canal, **Das Hotel** (Mariannenstr. 26a) is representative of Berlin's more contemporary bar scene and also has two apartments available for rent by the night.

While beach bars and clubs line the Spree River, Ankerklause is a marine-themed beacon on the bridge that spans the more humble Landwehr Canal. It is one of the best places to observe the diverse cross-section of residents that now populate the German capital. In another city, this exotic locale might have become a drinking hole for the elite, but like most Kreuzberg bars, the vibe remains modest and slightly dishevelled. It's a well-worn hangout in which the locals, with the help of some tourists, while away the hours as the hordes trip by the markets lining nearby Maybachufer.

U *Schönleinstraße* | *Kottbusser Damm 104, Kreuzberg* | *ankerklause.de*

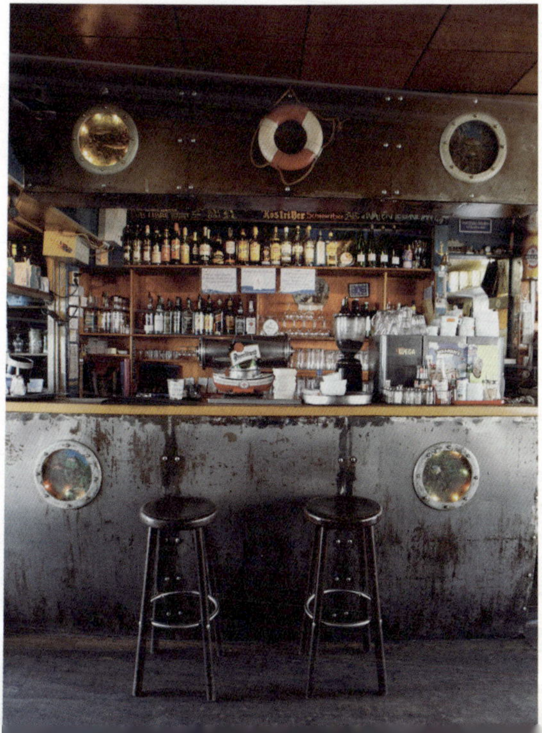

Photo Wolfgang Borrs

Urban Pioneers: Freies Neukölln

It's no secret that the hipster tribes cramming into DIY revamps of the traditional corner *Kneipe* are the ultimate indicators of gentrification. Not long ago, Neukölln was a no-go zone, Berlin's – indeed Germany's – poorest and most broken district. Now it is the city's artistic frontier, and a thriving bar and gallery scene has evolved around Weserstr., one that is rapidly spreading through the neighbourhood. Freies Neukölln was one of the first "Szene" pubs in the area, and remains the hub of the Weserstr. strip. Understated and casual, with strong local patronage and simple meals on offer, its owners are also committed to maintaining the old *Kiez* (neighbourhood) spirit.

Other places ... **Ä Bar** down the road (Weserstr. 40) is a lively bohemian den where quality live music happens weekly in the back room. Across the road, **Späti International** (Weserstr. 190) looks like one of the myriad late night convenience/liquor stores but doubles as a bar and gallery space.

U ***Hermannplatz*** | *Pannierstr. 54, Neukölln*

New Dimensions: Minibar

Next stop: *Graefekiez*, Kreuzberg, where discreet late night bars are community institutions. Minibar befits its name. The truly miniscule bar stands testament to the fact that Berliners can convert each and every locale into an atmospheric watering hole. Squeeze onto a counter stool and conversation with the rugged regulars can carry on till 8am, inevitably touching upon this town's relaxed licensing regulations that allow places like this to exist.

U ***Schönleinstraße*** | *Graefestr. 77, Kreuzberg*

Other places ... To be really accurate, the opening of **Bar Tausend** in 2007 probably marked the transition mentioned on the next page. Located in a vault beneath the train tracks at Schiffbauerdamm 11, only a hop, skip and a jump from King Size Bar, this rather elegant space is characterised by a strict door policy, yet offers a relaxed atmosphere and, again, an excellent cocktail list.

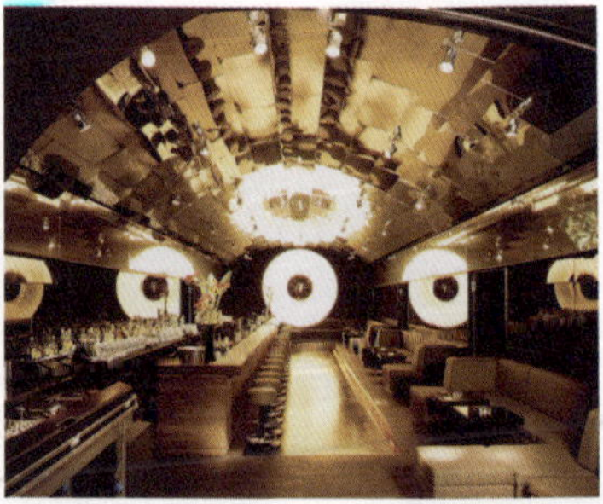

International Jet Set: King Size Bar

At some point in the first decade of the new millennium, Berlin officially graduated from underground rookie metropolis to a true international destination. The nightlife manifestation of this development was first visible when the DIY drinking holes and semi-legal nightclubs - which sprouted up and disappeared just as quickly - were joined by a third type of bar: the drinking destination for the grown-up global artist. Opened in 2010, the ironically named King Size Bar (which is tiny) is an easily overlooked destination on the northern end of Friedrichstr. Run by a triumvirate of local celebrities (a party veteran, a restauranteur and an art collector), King Size successfully marries a laid back, art-inspired interior (although the Jonathan Meese portrait of Hitler has been removed by request of offended patrons) to a superb cocktail list. Despite the lack of a designated dance floor, the venue's many patrons, among them many art and literary types over 30, like to let loose.

U ***Oranienburger Tor*** | *Friedrichstr. 112b, Mitte*

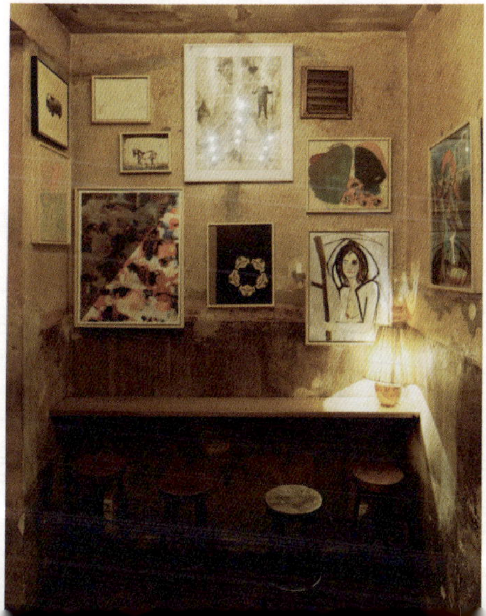

Far left Bar Tausend
Photo Martin Eberle

Left King Size Bar
Photo Stefan Korte

MY CITY WITH

CORY ANDREEN

Coffee Specialist

The Professional

To the untrained eye, Berlin's inner city neighbourhoods seem like an endless string of cafés. The quality of the coffee they're serving, though, can differ wildly from one place to the next. Few people know this as well as Cory Andreen. A native of Washington, D.C., Cory first came to Berlin as an exchange student, returning a few years later armed with the desire to teach Berliners about good coffee. Cory and his business partner Kerstin Winkelbaum opened Café CK in the heart of Prenzlauer Berg in early 2009. They now run a second location, CK pour Voo, in the Voo store on Oranienstr. So where does a man with such a well-developed radar for international food trends spend his spare time?

Addresses see page 230

1 **"Chez Gino is the best place for German food in the city, leaving kitschy brass band style behind in favour of simple, humble fare, like Flammkuchen and Spätzle, along with a changing daily menu.**

It has the feel of a farmhouse in the countryside, complete with 'farmer's daughter'-type waitresses with whom you could imagine living a simple, wholesome kind of life if only you could settle down with one. It's housed in a former Italian restaurant that still says 'Ristorante Gino', but they changed the name to Chez Gino for a French twist. I've never had anything there that I didn't like."

U ***Schlesisches Tor | Sorauerstr. 31, Kreuzberg***
Daily from 18

2 **"The Botanical Gardens are one of my absolute favourite places in the city.**
It's the perfect summer place to sneak in a bottle of wine and some charcuterie for a picnic. I highly recommend going during

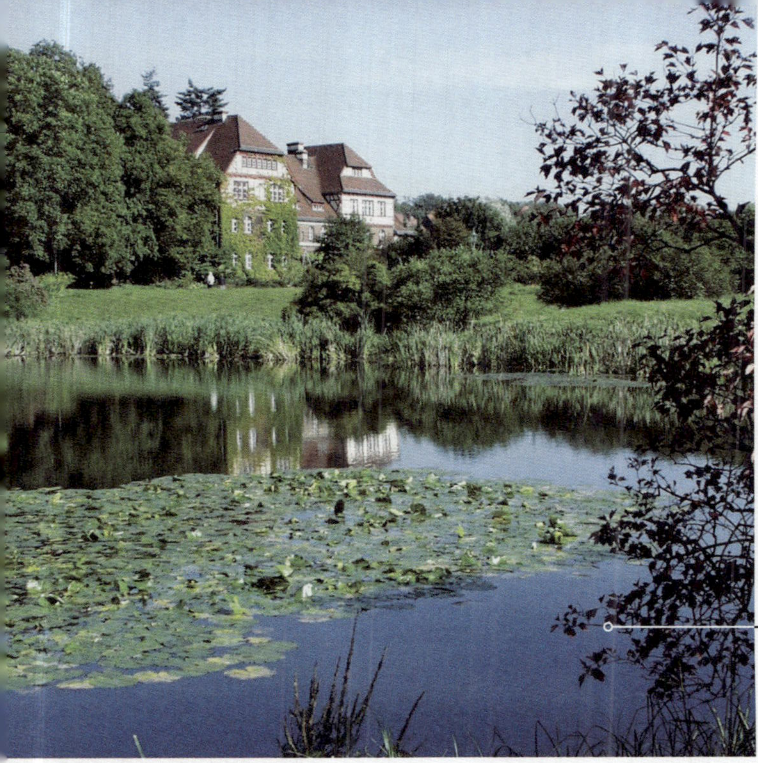

the annual wine festival when you can meander through the seemingly endless gardens with a glass of Riesling. The pavilion is very special. It is elegant and enormous and, even though it's over 100 years old, is still the largest glass house in the world."

U *Rathaus Steglitz | Königin-Luise-Str. 6-8, Steglitz | Open daily, seasonal hours | bgbm.org*

3 **"Tier on Weserstr. in Neukölln is one of the best places in the city to get a drink.** Comfortable and beautifully designed, it offers good drinks and fantastic service, and serves flawless versions of standard cocktails. The music is played off vinyl and the crowd is there to relax and enjoy the atmosphere."

U *Rathaus Neukölln | Weserstr. 42, Neukölln Open daily from 19*

Left The 'Amerikasee' at Botanical Gardens *Photo* © I. Haas, Botanischer Garten und Botanisches Museum Berlin-Dahlem

THE THIRD WAVE ROLLS IN

With an ever-expanding retinue of internationally renowned, world champion roasters, baristas and tasters, this is a city that takes coffee seriously.

While Berlin's café scene abounds with fluorescent-lit *Stehcafés* and retro-furnished rooms full of laptops, some cafés set themselves apart. A development of the so-called 'third wave' of coffee, these cafés move one step beyond the coffee-as-urban-consumption phenomenon that characterized the 1990s and early 2000s. Whereas this period was marked by the frothy, machine-made 'latte macchiato', today's coffee aficionados are returning to the very base – the quality of the coffee itself. Choosing direct trade with farmers and often roasting their own beans, these venues use a variety of techniques to reveal the myriad flavours of the beloved bean while teaching their customers to approach coffee consumption from a new angle. These cafés are the place to witness the international face of cosmopolitan Berlin, as native and adopted Berliners mingle over roasts and brews imported from the world over and perfected on home turf.

DoubleEye

Few Berlin cafés are as busy as Schöneberg's DoubleEye. By owner Arno Schmeil's estimate, he and his team make somewhere between eight hundred to one thousand coffees a day - yet the baristas remember customers by name. Like his fellow Berlin coffee makers, Arno is keenly interested in the cycle of coffee production. He worked for years as a building engineer before opening the café – which he designed himself – in 2001 and became European Barista Champion at the Tea and Coffee World Cup in 2005. The mission is simple: good coffee shouldn't be exclusive, and DoubleEye aims at creating a positive cycle between coffee growers, makers and consumers while offering all the trappings of a neighbourhood café.

U ***Eisenacher Straße*** | *Akazienstr. 22, Schöneberg | Mon to Fri 9.31–18.29, Sat 10.05–15.29 | doubleeye.de*

Godshot

This "Future Urban Coffee Klub" is a laid-back location with comfy seating and a relaxed vibe. Don't let the pervading sense of ease fool you, though. At Godshot, the perfect espresso is an ever-evolving science and each shot perfectly pressed and weighed. Kai-Uwe Beyer, a native Berliner trained as a social worker, was inspired to open the café in 2008 after realising that the coffee made in his kitchen was better than most available in the city's cafés. Using three different kinds of beans, Godshot crafts divine lattes and hosts monthly classes on coffee and latte art for baristas and the uninitiated alike.

Tip ... No coffee ramble through the corner of Prenzlauer Berg known as the Kaffeeviertel would be complete without a stop at **No Fire No Glory** (Rykestr. 45). Their filter brew bar offers an assortment of coffees from some of Europe's best roasters.

U ***Senefelder Platz*** | *Immanuelkirchstr. 32, Prenzlauer Berg | Mon to Fri 8–18, Sat 9–18, Sun 13–18 | godshot.de*

Café CK/CK pour Voo

To 2012 World Cup Tasters Champion Cory Andreen, a barista is more like a DJ or a gallerist than a waiter; the work of art is in your hands, but it's up to you how to present it. Cory and his partner Kerstin Winkelbaum are using their two cafés, Café CK in Prenzlauer Berg and CK pour Voo inside the Kreuzberg concept store of the same name, as testing grounds for a new form of coffee consumption. Though they still take pride in producing the perfect made-to-order brew, CK aims to alter the way this drink is typically served and enjoyed. Their coffees are served in whisky tumblers and other barware to distinguish taste from the traditional coffee ritual.

U ***Senefelderplatz*** | *CK* | *Marienburgerstr. 49, Prenzlauer Berg* | *Mon to Fri 8–19, Sat & Sun 9–19*
U ***Kottbusser Tor*** | *CK pour Voo* | *Oranienstr. 24, Kreuzberg* | *Mon to Sat 11–18*
cafeckberlin.com

Five Elephant

This is perhaps the most well-rounded of all Berlin cafés. Kris Shackman and Sophie Weigensamer combined his love of coffee with her passion for baking in the former working-class stretches of Kreuzberg. While the creation of a specialty café in the neighbourhood angered some longtime residents (to many Berliners, nice cafés herald uncontrolled gentrification), the pair quickly put them at ease, keeping prices low and integrating themselves into the community – rumour has it that local residents have a secret signal which gives them a discount on their drinks.

U ***Görlitzer Bahnhof*** | *Reichenberger Str. 101, Kreuzberg*
Mon to Fri 8.30–19, Sat to Sun 10–19 | *fiveelephant.com*

Below Kris and Sophie are heavily involved in direct trade, and some of the farmers they work with have even travelled to Berlin.
Photo Five Elephant

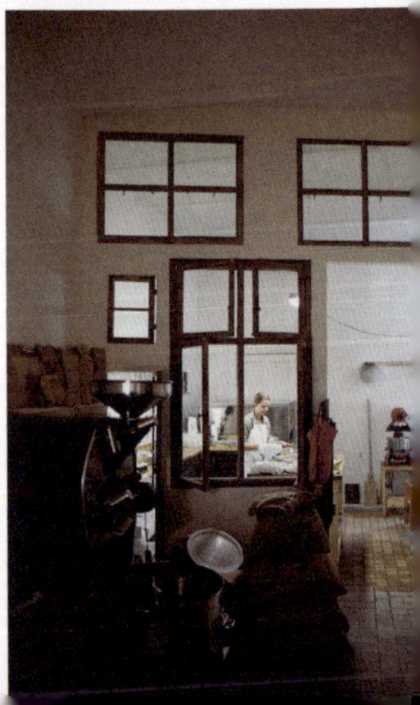

The Barn

Despite its Mitte location, The Barn is not just another specialty café. The owner, Ralf Rüller, is what you could call fanatic about ensuring that your coffee experience is of the highest absolute quality. Rüller and his team of baristas evaluate which of their roasts is best suited to the variety of brewing methods on offer, while very strongly suggesting that customers appreciate the flavour by abstaining from milk and sugar. Although music and laptops are notably absent, The Barn maintains some of the trappings of a traditional café, serving snacks produced from Rüller family recipes. A second, newer location, the Barn Roastery, is designed as a manufacturing space with front brew bars.

U ***Torstraße*** | *The Barn* | *Auguststr. 58, Mitte* | *Mon to Fri 8–18, Sat & Sun 10–18*

U ***Rosa-Luxemburg-Platz*** | *The Barn Roastery* | *Schönhauser Allee 8 Prenzlauer Berg* | *Mon to Fri 8–18, Sat and Sun 10–18* | *thebarn.de*

Tip ... For a coffee experience that wouldn't seem out of place along the Mediterranean coast, slip out of the crowds around Hackescher Markt to **Buscaglione** (Rochstr. 3), a tiny café serving up flavourful espressos and cappuccinos. This neighbourhood joint sees customers crowd around the counter to talk football with owner Steffen Riemann, while a large poster by the bar pays homage to its silver-tongued namesake.

Photo **Ralf Rüller**

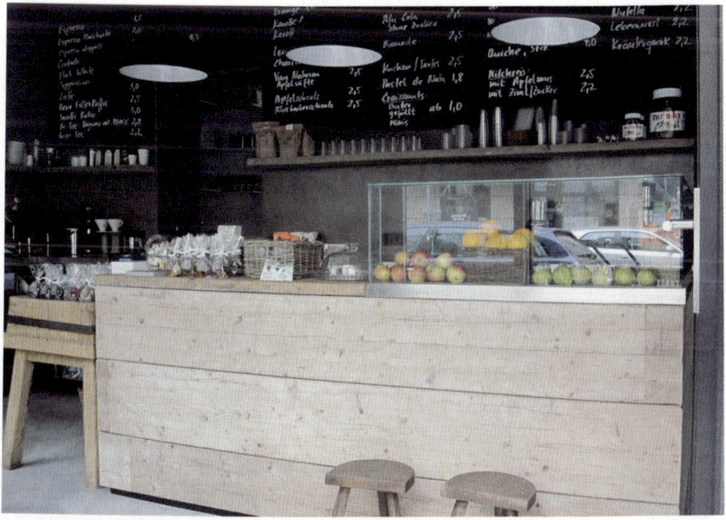

Katie's Blue Cat

The owners of this new-ish and incredibly loved locale, Olivia Wood and Ngoc Duong, met in a prenatal class and laboured over the concept for their café for almost ten years. Unsurprisingly, their easygoing business, built around the idea of Anglo-American style baking, seems exceedingly refined, giving traditional German *Kaffee und Kuchen* culture an international edge that perfectly reflects the changes happening in multicultural and multilingual Kreuzkölln. With a cosy interior and sweet baked goods made with as many locally sourced and organic ingredients as possible, the pair's thoughtfulness spills over into their coffee. The cakes may draw you in, but rest assured that every aspect of the accompanying brew has been carefully considered.

U ***Schönleinstraße*** | *Friedelstr. 31, Neukölln* | *Tue to Fri 8.30–18.30, Sat & Sun 10–19*
katiesbluecat.de

Chapter One

The oldest café on this list is indirectly responsible for the newest. Nora Šmalehová and Björn Köpke met while working at DoubleEye, forging a friendship that lead to the opening of Chapter One in Kreuzberg's *Bergmannkiez* in 2011. The café exudes a cozy Old Berlin feel with its tiled floors and high ceilings but doesn't invite hours of loitering over a milky cup – process and taste rule the day. While Björn is a herbalist by trade and Nora an industrial designer, coffee is their prevailing passion. Chapter One often hosts coffee talks, competitions and training.

U ***Gneisenaustraße*** | *Mittenwalder Str. 30, Kreuzberg* | *Tue to Sat 9–18, Sun 11–18* | *chapter-one-coffee.com*

Photo Dipl.-Des. Nora Šmahelová, Chapter One Coffee Berlin 2012

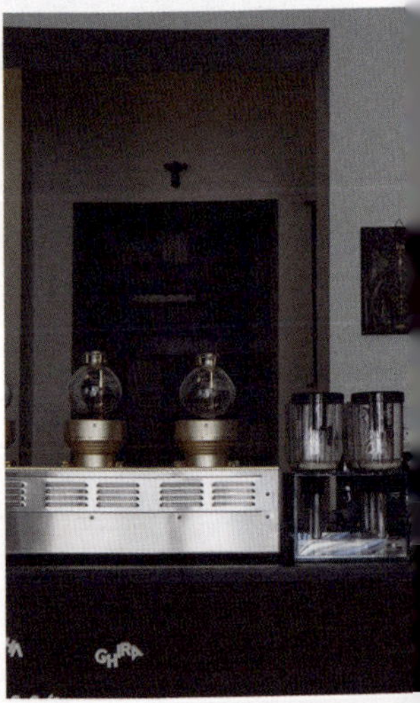

Bonanza Coffee Heroes

Ask anyone where to get a decent coffee in Berlin, and they're likely to point you towards Bonanza Coffee Heroes. Initially, native Berliners Kiduk Reus and Yumi Choi planned to open a boutique, but a chance coffee encounter lead to the purchase of a professional espresso machine for Yumi's apartment and a desire to know everything possible on the subject. Since 2007, Bonanza has been a landmark on the international coffee map, with their small space near Mauerpark packed with tourists and locals alike. The Heroes have always considered roasting their own coffee as an essential part of the task of knowing their product, and like many of their Berlin brothers-in-arms, they aim to open a more egalitarian dialogue between coffee producers and consumers.

U ***Eberswalder Straße*** | *Oderberger Str. 35 , Prenzlauer Berg | Mon to Fri 8.30–19, Sat & Sun 10–19 | bonanzacoffee.de*

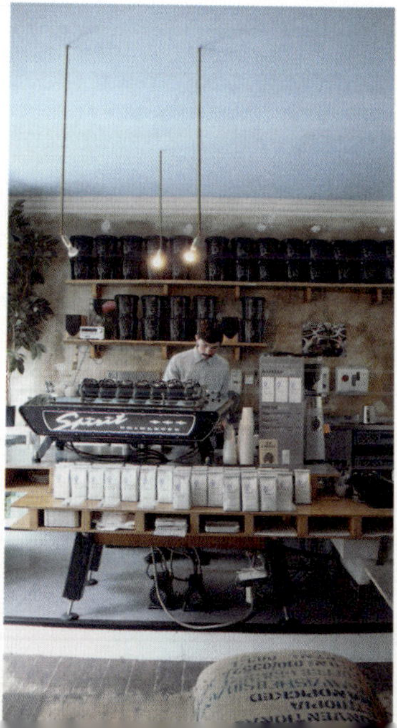

THE BERLIN COFFEE SOCIETY

— *After* ***Bonanza Coffee Heroes'*** *Yumi Choi gave a speech in 2011 about the coffee shop rivalries that were impeding the development of high-end coffee in Berlin and the rest of Germany, several independent Berlin cafés banded together to form the* ***Berlin Coffee Society****. The Society, while in its infancy, has the goal of bolstering Berlin's barista community and promoting higher standards and quality in coffee beyond the walls of their individual establishments. To this end, it frequently organises lectures and tastings to celebrate coffee and spread the word about their achievements.*

facebook.com/BerlinCoffeeSociety

Photo Yumi Choi

CULTURAL COOKS

To the untrained eye, Berlin may resemble a vast expanse of döner shops and currywurst stands. Times are changing, though. With a growing international community obsessed by good food and a collection of creative entrepreneurs working to meld flavour, art and their personal culinary experiences, restaurant culture in Berlin is experiencing a surge that is slowly trickling down to the neighbourhood snack stop. Here is a rundown of some of the city's tastiest movers and shakers.

Grill Royal

Every city boasts an 'it' restaurant, and Berlin is no exception. Grill Royal's opening in early 2007 marked the occasion when Berlin's post-Wall generation of artists, art collectors, media types and their influential brethren had reached the age and the level of success which called for a decadent, exclusive place to get together. Loved by some, loathed by others, it is nevertheless the one place where the city's network of well-heeled creatives love to combine business with carnivorous pleasures. That's if they're admitted entry into this space, run by a powerful trifecta of Berlin art and cultural players – gallerist Thilo Wermke, party king Boris Radczun, and art collector Stefan Landwehr.

U *Friedrichstraße* | *Friedrichstr 105b, Mitte* | *daily from 18*
grillroyal.com

Bebe Rebozo ... Hidden behind drawn curtains deep in the Moabit district, this restaurant bearing the name of a notorious Cuban mafia fixer stays true to the spirit of his era in its American stylings. Its chic black and white décor is livened by a colourful abstract mural, while the three classic menu offerings, steak, oysters, and ceviche, are immaculately prepared to the diner's desires.

Heidestr. 54, Mitte | *Wed to Sat 18–1*

Photo Lepkowski Studio Berlin

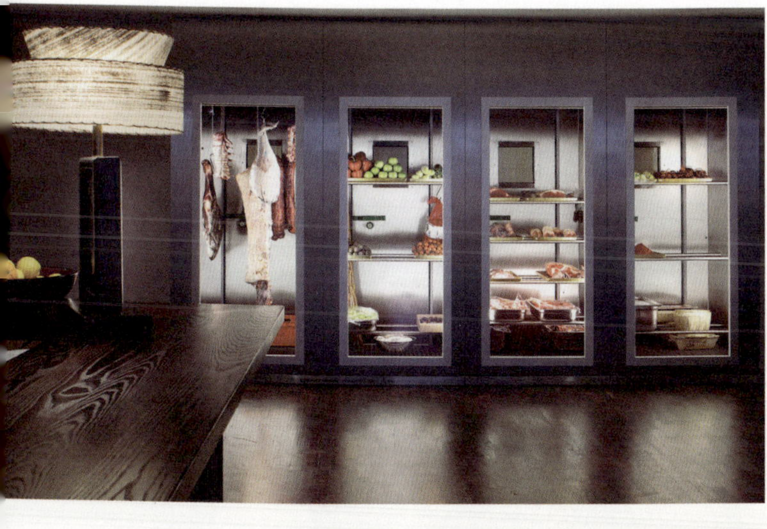

Cookies Cream

Cookies Cream is a must for all discerning vegetarians. Renowned for its creative, regional and seasonally inspired vegetable kitchen, this culinary extension of the Cookies night club is a stylish destination for both veggie gourmets and night cats. Owner Heinz Gindullis, better known as Cookie, laid the cornerstone for his Berlin empire in 1994 with a small meeting spot in Auguststr. that was popular with squatters and artists. Today, Cookie is one of Berlin's most renowned hospitality entrepreneurs, running Cookies Club, Cookies Cream, Drayton Bar and the easygoing restaurant Chipps, tucked away behind the German Foreign Office, which is also open for breakfast.

U ***Französische Straße*** | *Cookies Cream, Cookies Club & Drayton Bar* | *Behrenstr. 55, Mitte* | *Tue to Sat from 19* | *cookiescream.com*
U ***Hausvogteiplatz*** | *Chipps* | *Jägerstr 35, Mitte* | *Mon to Fri from 8* | *Sat & Sun from 9*

Goldneun

Although located smack in the middle of touristy Berlin, Goldneun (previously .hbc) in the former Hungarian Club at Alexanderplatz, is anything but easy to find. The socialist building with its raw walls and open ceilings oozes stereotypical 'Berlin.' The restaurant perfectly melds a starched-tablecloth affair with casual dining, lit by custom designed concrete lights by architects Unit Berlin.

Photo unit-berlin

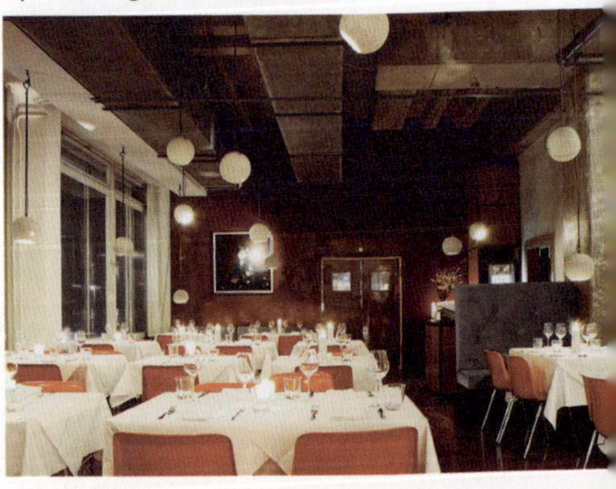

U S ***Alexanderplatz*** | *Upstairs, Karl-Liebknecht-Str 9, Mitte* | *Tue to Sat from 19* | *goldneun.de*

Katz Orange

A recent addition to Berlin's hospitality landscape, Katz Orange is yet another manifestation of ideas collected elsewhere and realised in Berlin. Founder Ludwig Klett-Cramer realised the project as the culmination of his longstanding interest in food and community, conceived in his travels around the world. The restaurant isn't a meditation temple, but reflects these interests with a relaxed atmosphere and interior punctuated by personal mementos and art pieces. The food is eclectic and inspired by various food cultures.

U ***Rosenthaler Platz*** | *Bergstr 22, Mitte | Tue to Fri 11.30 to 2.30, Tue to Sat from 18 | katzorange.com*

Themroc ... Located along busy Torstr., it's easy to overlook this tiny restaurant. Named after a 1970s French film, its moniker reflects the program. Depending on which of the two owners is in charge, the daily menu is either French or Moroccan-inspired and comes at prices that are, even for Berlin, incredibly affordable. Unpretentious though carefully furnished, with a clear passion for food, Themroc has established a dedicated following.

Torstr. 183, Mitte | Tue to Fri 12–15, Mon to Sun 19–2
themroc-berlin.de

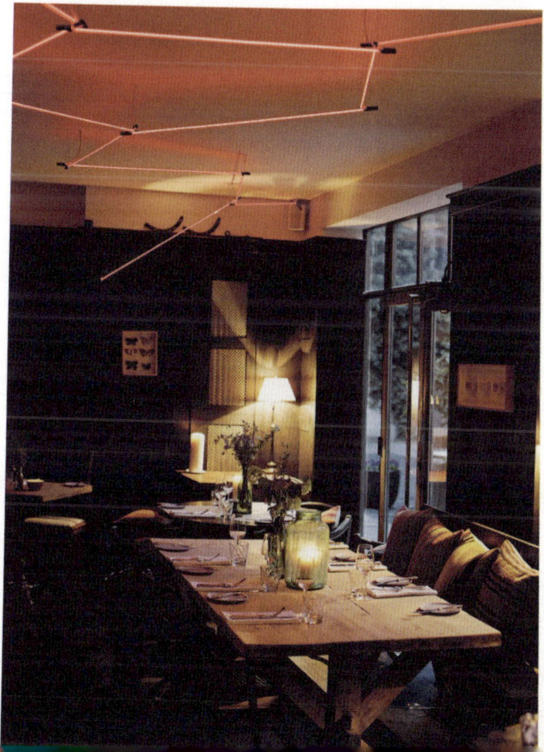

Left Katz Orange
Photo Juliane Spaete

Kimchi Princess

Kreuzberg is swiftly advancing as the area for new and hip multicultural cuisine. The neon-lit, canteen-style Korean restaurant, designed by Büro Pulver Interieur, also features graphics by Paul Snowden, a creative multi-activist who lends his style to projects like his own beer brand and young fashion labels. The Kimchi Princess team also runs the popular, pitch-dark Soju Bar around the corner and snack bar Angry Chicken to handle pre or post-party hunger.

U ***Görlitzer Bahnhof*** | *Skalitzer Str. 36, Kreuzberg | Daily 18–23*
kimchiprincess.com | soju-bar.com | angry-chicken.com

Long March Canteen ... The Long March Canteen serves up humble Dim Sum in all varieties – cold, warm, steamed, grilled and baked – and despite its contemporary touch, the offerings are authentic, going so far as to include pig stomach or chicken claws. The interior, designed by product designer Ett La Benn and graphic designer Darius Ghanai of Lichtrausch, conjures up street style Asian kitchen.

Wrangelstr. 20, Kreuzberg | Daily 18–24 | longmarchcanteen.de

La Raclette

A tiny piece of the French Alps in the heart of Kreuzberg, La Raclette's specialty is, as the name implies, raclette – a close cousin to fondue, where a sizeable portion of ingredients are mixed with a selection of cheeses and grilled or baked on a tabletop set. The restaurant's brick walls and roaring fireplace exude a feeling of warmth, transporting diners from the grey Berlin winter to a cosy, convivial mountainside cabin. To ensure that their offerings convey the full French dining experience, its owners also run La Provence, a mobile restaurant that caters summertime open-air meals in any number of locations.

U ***Görlitzer Bahnhof*** | *Lausitzer Str. 34, Kreuzberg | Mon to Sun from 18*
la-raclette.de

Photo Sabine Münch

Café Jacques ... In the relaxed atmosphere of Maybachufer, Café Jacques is a true neighbourhood institution, an extension of many a Kreuzbergian's living room. Generally packed, this restaurant sits on the same street as the twice-weekly Turkish market (Tue and Fri 11–18.30), and stays true to the international spirit of the neighbourhood, serving up Moroccan and French-inspired grill and grain dishes perfectly conceived to satisfy any carnivorous appetite.

Maybachufer 8, Kreuzberg | Mon to Sat 18–2, Sun 18–24

Lavanderia Veccia

The darling of local artists and creatives, Lavanderia Veccia is as loved for its food as it is for the story behind it. Husband and wife Renate and Andreas Hoffmann were so enamoured with Italian cuisine that they decided to share their passion with the rest of the world. Lovingly decorated to replicate a homey Italian streetscape within an unassuming residential building, Lavanderia Veccia opens its doors at 19.30 on the dot to let in a crowd of diners eager to indulge in the set menu that can involve up to ten courses. Reservations for dinner are essential, as the love isn't going to stop anytime soon.

U ***Boddinstraße*** | *Flughafenstr. 46, Neukölln | Tue to Fri 12 –14, Tue to Sat from 19.30 | lavanderiavecchia.de*

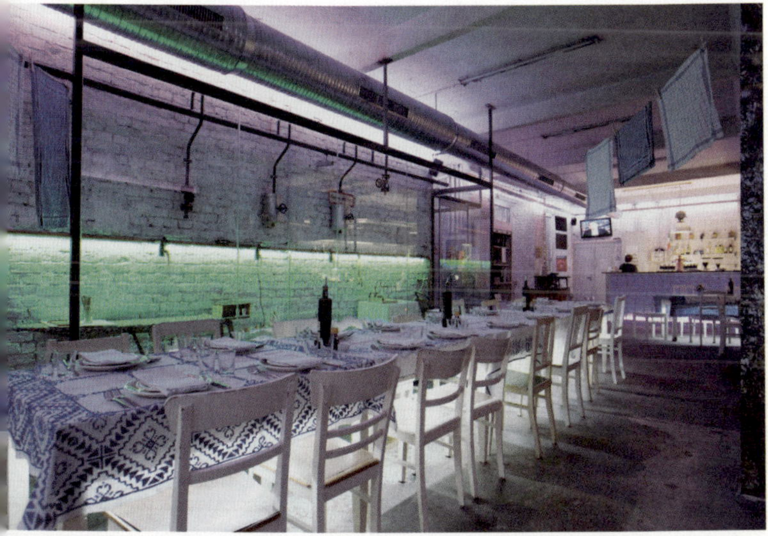

Mogg & Melzer Delicatessen

Located in the same building as Pauly Saal, Oskar Melzer's restaurant transports New York food culture to Berlin through its perfect pastrami sandwich. From early in the morning to late at night, punters can indulge in the delights of Jewish deli-inspired snacks such as barbecued brisket or matzo ball soup. The interior was inspired by 1930s era American delis, coupled with European design classics.

S ***Oranienburger Straße*** | *Auguststr. 11-13, Mitte* | *Mon to Fri from 8, Sat & Sun from 10* | *moggandmelzer.com*

Right Lokal
Photo CeeCee.cc

Below right photo
Stefan Korte

Below photo
Steve Herud

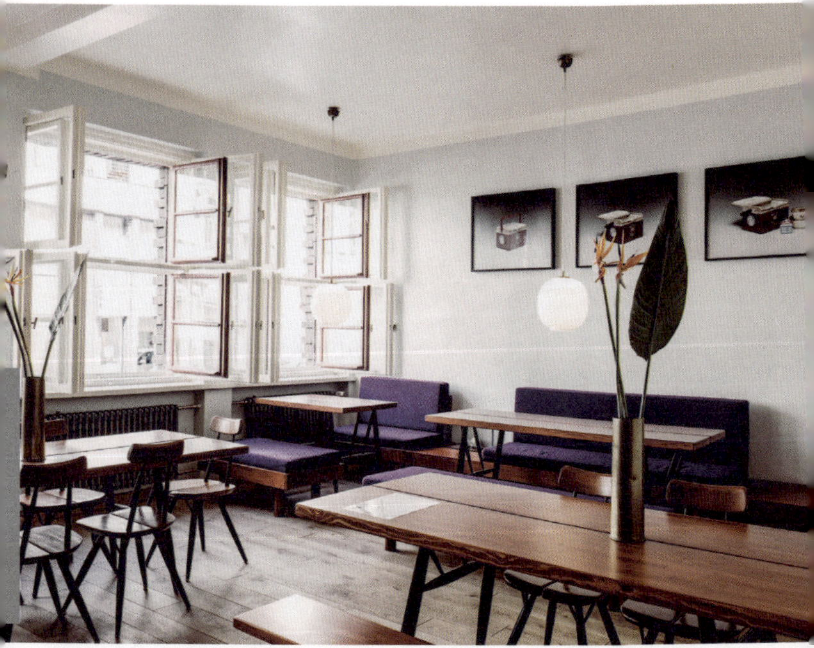

Lokal

German food often comes with a seemingly irredeemable reputation. Thankfully a few alternatives exist in Berlin, serving up traditionally inspired meals with a contemporary, much lighter twist, prepared with seasonal and regional ingredients and served in a breezy atmosphere. Lokal is such a place. A colloquial term for 'restaurant', the plain name personifies its uncomplicated, white-walled interior, furnished with simple wooden tables and chairs. During the day, Lokal is a popular lunch spot, while at night the Mitte crowd congregates for a contemporary take on the pig on a spit.

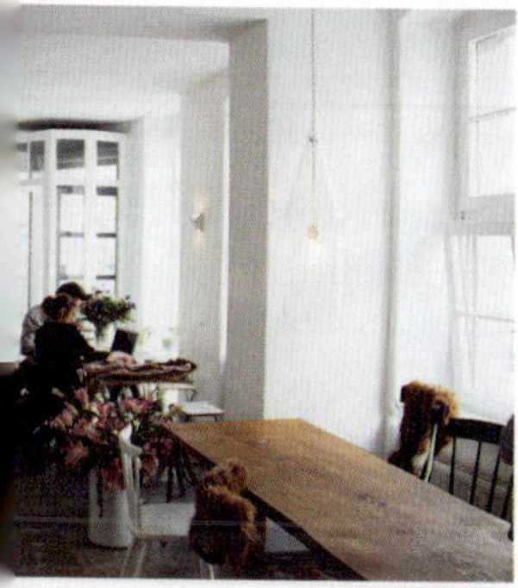

U ***Rosenthaler Platz*** | *Linienstr. 160, Mitte | Sat to Mon from 17, Tue to Fri from 12 | lokal-berlin.blogspot.de*

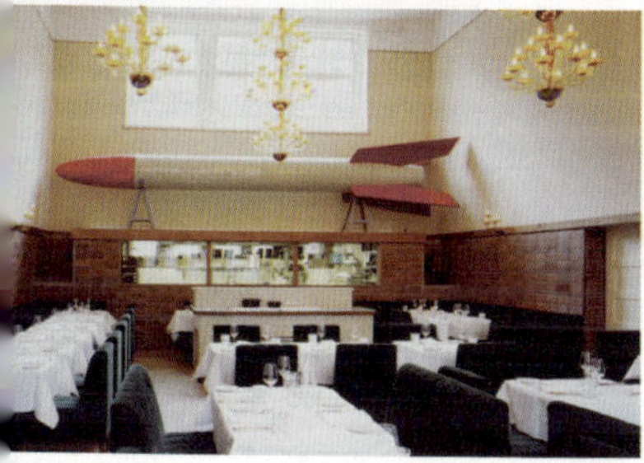

Pauly Saal

This latest addition to Berlin's upmarket restaurant scene caused a big splash when it opened in early 2012. Run by the people behind Grill Royal and King Size Bar, it is located in the Former Jewish Girls' School in Mitte, a new cultural destination featuring branches of a number of prestigious galleries. Inspired by the golden 1920s, the former school gym has been turned into an elegant, chandeliered dining room where 'new German cuisine' is served at its very best. Besides being a popular dining spot, Pauly Saal is a good lunch stop during an extended tour of the area's galleries.

S ***Oranienburger Straße*** | *Auguststr.11-13, Mitte | Open daily from 12 | paulysaal.com*

DOWN BY THE RIVER

Long before parts of the river that runs through Berlin became a natural fortification of the East/West border, industrialisation had turned the Spree into little more than a contaminated sewage pipeline. Now, after a century of turning its back on its central waterway, Berlin has rediscovered the riverbank.

Both sides of the river are lined with celebrated party and recreational venues run by an industrious crowd of activists. Ironically, Berlin's rising international appeal also endangers these spaces – several enterprises have begun erecting office buildings along the river and the fate of many sites is still unknown. This little excursion – down the river on one side, up on the other – will have you exploring this phenomenon with a drink in hand and a beat in the background.

Yaam

Wedged between Ostbahnhof and the Spree in an area formerly occupied by the 'death strip' of the Wall, the longest-running cultural venue by the river occupies a 10,000sqm parcel of land. The initiative, which was originally conceived as a youth centre with a focus on African culture (the acronym stands for 'Young African Arts Market') started in the compound now known as Arena (*see page 76*). The space has always focused on music and relaxation by the river, with varied intercultural and food-based events. When Arena was sold to an investor, Yaam moved to a vacant lot just down the road on Cuvrystr., only to be forced to relocate again two years later. At the time of writing, Yaam was endangered once more, this time because increased real estate sales activity in the area might affect their land.

Ⓢ ***Ostbahnhof*** | *Stralauer Platz 35, Friedrichshain* | *yaam.de*

RAW

— *Just down the road and across the train tracks towards Friedrichshain, another cultural compound awaits. Though not on the river,* **RAW** *illustrates the appeal of Berlin's deserted industrial areas, not only for parties, but for the recreation of residents. Here, 'beach bars' complete with artificial sand exist side by side with neighbourhood gardens, youth projects, artist studios, a regular flea market and a dancing school.*

Below Don't be fooled. This image doesn't show Yaam's current location. It's a nod to its short-lived stay on Cuvrystr., which lasted about two years.
Photo Yaam

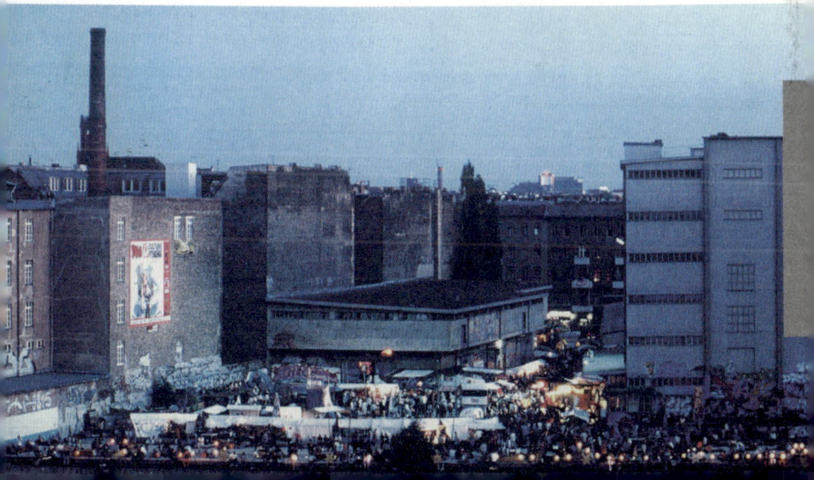

Club der Visionäre & Freischwimmer

After crossing the river and heading towards the large compound which houses Arena (*see page 76*), keep an eye out for two venues in the mouth of the canal that branches off toward Kreuzberg. The first, Club der Visionäre, bears the typical ramshackle Berlin charm that exports so well via colourful magazine spreads. It is one of the longest-running river bars in Berlin, and used to include swimming pontoons next to its boathouse. With a musical lineup featuring big names in the DJ world, the relaxed, willow-treed atmosphere can sometimes turn into a three-day party. Across the canal, bar and restaurant Freischwimmer, located in a former boat rental shack, is a little more tame.

Tip ... On the way to the canal and Arena, you will pass what's probably Berlin's most contested empty lot, on the corner of Schlesische Str. and Cuvrystr., watched over by three giant figures painted on the adjacent building's walls (*see page 107*). The second location of Yaam, the space was slated to become a shopping mall ten years ago, but civic activism has played no small part in preventing the project. In 2012, the site was earmarked to host the BMW-sponsored Guggenheim Lab, a travelling urbanism think tank, but local protest prompted the organisers to find another location.

U ***Schlesisches Tor*** | *Am Flutgraben, Alt-Treptow / Kreuzberg*
clubdervisionaere.com | *freischwimmer-berlin.de*

Right photo **Carolin Saage**
luciundcoma.de

Below photo © **joachimwagner.net**

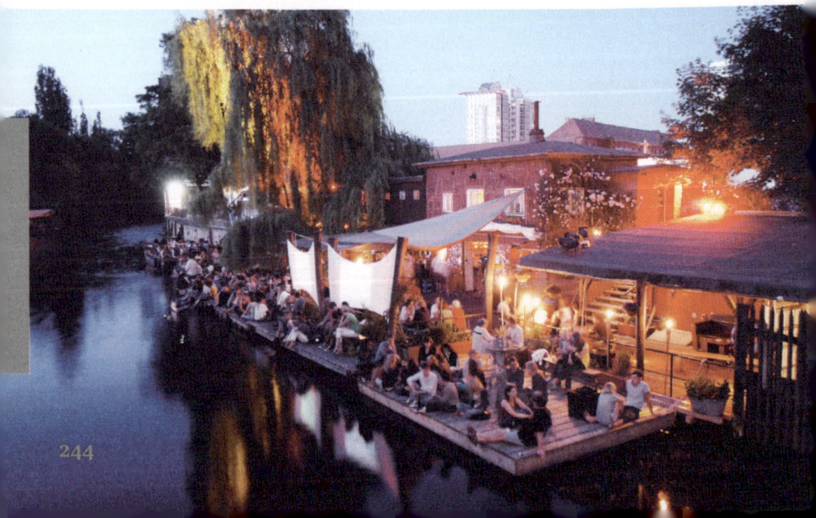

Kater Holzig

The space between the row of houses on Köpenicker Str. and the riverbank has seen many venues come and go, but the latest and busiest is Kater Holzig. The site, whose entrance is just before the bridge, comes with an impressive pedigree. Its predecessor on the other side of the river, Bar 25, was the stuff of legend. With a club, restaurant, bar, hostel and circus, Bar 25 was a true adventure playground for party-hungry twenty-somethings. After seven years of promoting a lifestyle where anything seemed to be possible, this pulsating, self-contained universe shuttered its gate in 2010, but Kater Holzig threw open its doors just a year later. Located in and around a former soap factory, this venue is a cultural paradise complete with a cinema, an excellent restaurant, theatre and bar and, of course, multiple dance floors. Its days may be numbered, since the party here happens on borrowed time in the shape of a restricted lease agreement, but a new coup is in the making – a utopian village complete with living, working, and yes, partying facilities.

U *Heinrich-Heine-Str.* | *Michaelkirchstr. 23, Mitte* | *katerholzig.de*

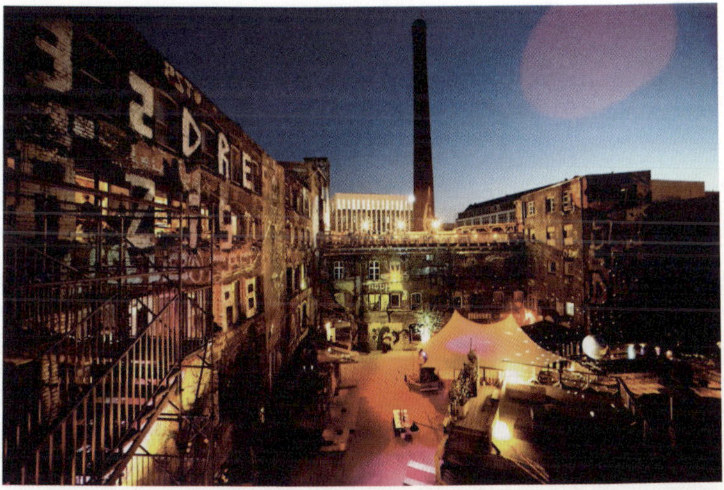

DESIGNED DREAMING

With an ever-increasing influx of visitors each year, accommodation options in Berlin are as wide and varied as the colourful city itself. A decade ago, visitors had to choose between a limited offering of youth hostels, solemn Pensionen *and five star hotels, but today 500-bed hostels and design hotels cater to each and every budget. With so much on offer, finding a place to sleep is easy. We've unearthed some temporary abodes that promise to satisfy the needs of every design-conscious visitor, and by design, we mean originality and ingenuity just as much as nice chairs and tables.*

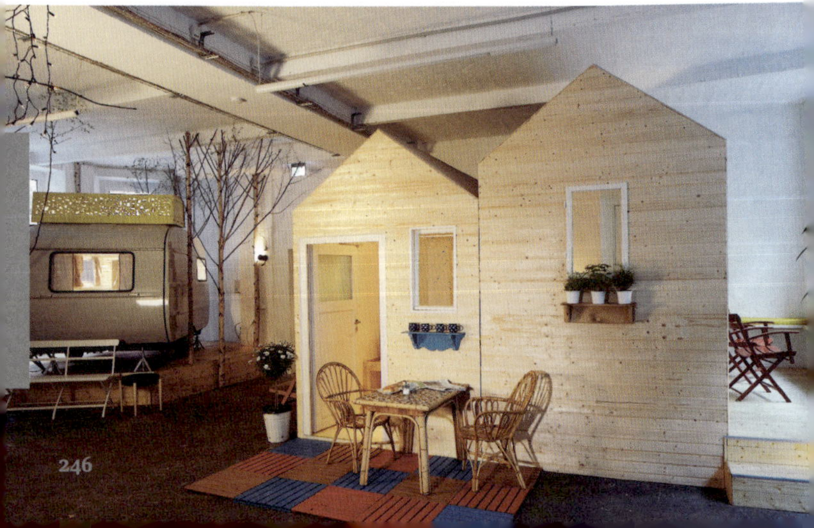

Michelberger Hotel

The WG (short for *Wohngemeinschaft*, 'living community') is a rite of passage for many young, creative residents of the city – most spend years sharing rundown *Altbau* apartments. Michelberger Hotel melds this archetypal Berlin living arrangement with an international atmosphere, including a quirky interior designed by Werner Aisslinger, the city's most famous design export. Located in a former industrial loft building on the ugly but lively party artery between Kreuzberg and Friedrichshain, each of the 119 rooms features re-purposed objects and flea market finds. The restaurant and bar is still a meeting place for hip young things from all around the world and shows no signs of fading into mainstream dullness.

U S *Warschauer Straße*
Warschauer Str. 39/40, Friedrichshain
michelbergerhotel.com

Right Remise
Photo Felix Oberhage

Left Hüttenpalast
Photo Jan Brockhaus

Hüttenpalast

True to the DIY spirit that's prominent in the newly hip party area of Kreuzkölln, Hüttenpalast is equal parts experiment and tribute to Germany's love affair with camping. Set in a 200sqm factory space, Hüttenpalast's guests stay in East German camper vans that have been lovingly restored, as well as some purpose-built huts and – for those who appreciate more privacy – actual hotel rooms. With its bustling café and relaxed garden, Hüttenpalast preserves some of the experimental spirit that has transformed the entire city into a giant adventure playground.

U *Hermannplatz* | **Hobrechtstr. 66, Neukölln | huettenpalast.de**

Remise

Many visitors wonder what's at the end of the seemingly endless rows of houses and courtyards beyond the entrance of an *Altbau*. Traditionally, the representative 'front house' is followed by less generous buildings until the ensemble is concluded by squat buildings once used as small workshops or stables. Due to destruction and dilapidation, functioning examples of these structures are rare, but not extinct. To hold on to a piece of Berlin's past, two local architects saved a couple of heritage-listed backyard stables (known as 'Remise'), to turn them into neat, self-contained guesthouses to rent by the night, week or month.

U *Rosenthaler Platz (& Tram on Kastanienallee)* | **Kastanienallee 21, Prenzlauer Berg | remise-berlin.de**

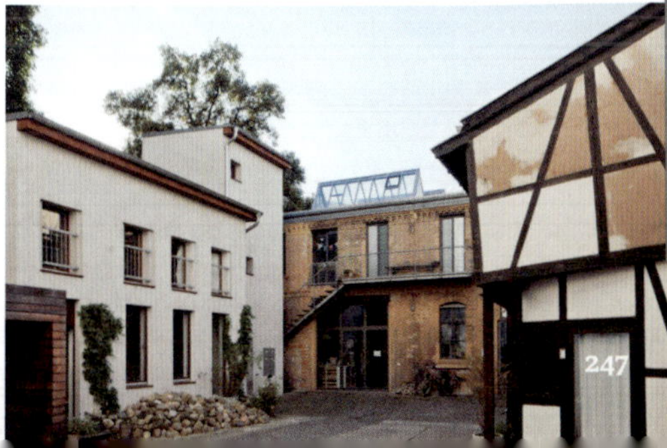

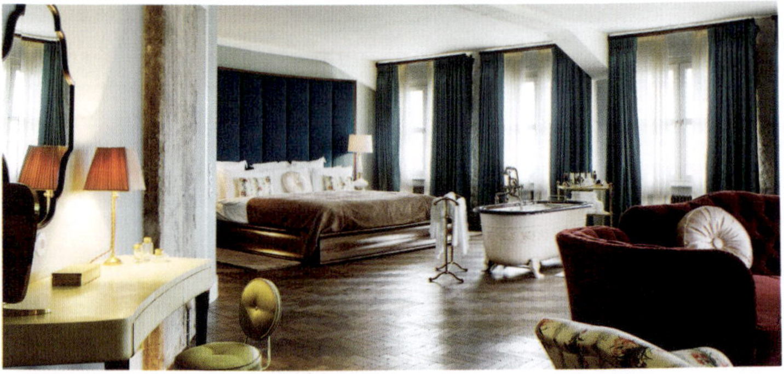

Soho House

Berlin has been home to branches of international luxury hotels for eons, but the arrival of international private members' club Soho House still caused a splash in the creative scene. Although comparisons between Berlin and New York fly thick, no one had really dared to place the German metropolis on par with the capital of cool when it came to a certain level of luxury – until now. The club is usually bustling with the international creatives and start-up types who work, socialise and have themselves pampered here, and for the price of a hotel room you can get in on the action in this building with a more than turbulent past, overlooking Torstr. toward Alexanderplatz.

U *Rosa-Luxemburg-Platz*
Torstr. 1, Mitte
sohohouse.com

IMA Design Village

Staying at one of IMA's 22 loft apartments provides a glimpse into Berlin's art and culture scene. The apartments are located in a former factory, which is also home to a completely incorporated creative network of dance schools, artist lofts, design firms and workshops.

U *Moritzplatz* | **Ritterstr. 12-14, Kreuzberg**
imalofts.com

Tautes Heim

Not only is Berlin a great place to explore classical modernism in residential architecture, it also offers the opportunity to experience it firsthand. Thanks to the passion of Ben Buschfeld and Katrin Lesser, design aficionados and residents of the Bruno Taut designed Hufeisensiedlung (*see page 60*) in Britz (just south of Neukölln), visitors can reside in a small two-bedroom townhouse lovingly restored to Taut's specifications – down to the exact wall colour and bedside clock.

U *Parchimer Allee*
Gielower Str. 43, Britz

Casa Camper

If you like the style of Camper shoes, you'll love Casa Camper. The sleek boutique hotel is a manifestation of the strength of the hip young Spanish community in the city. On top of being super stylish, it is located smack in the middle of everything.

U *Weinmeisterstraße*
Weinmeisterstr. 1, Mitte | casacamper.com

Miniloft

For those interested in 21st century architectural practice, Miniloft is the ideal place to stay. It's a perfect case study of a run-down stock-standard residential building transformed into a rather unusual piece of contemporary architecture. Its location in an up-and-coming part of Mitte is a stone's throw from many of the city's museums and galleries.

U *Naturkundemuseum*
Hessische Str. 5, Mitte
miniloft.com

11 Himmel

For many, especially architects, Berlin's ubiquitous *Plattenbau* buildings are as fascinating as they are grim. However, during the GDR years, living in such an abode was the ultimate luxury, as it provided access to otherwise scarcely available services such as heating and indoor sanitary facilities. Many residents still cherish this form of living, with its great views, a sense of community and access to parklands. For those willing to experiment, a guesthouse run by youths from a *Plattenbau* community in the Eastern district of Marzahn may be just the right way to experience life in former East Berlin on a budget.

S *Ahrensfelde*
Wittenberger Str. 65, Marzahn-Hellersdorf
pension-11himmel.de

Top left photo Soho House Berlin
Below True to Taut's original plans: Tautes Heim.
Photo © Tautes Heim

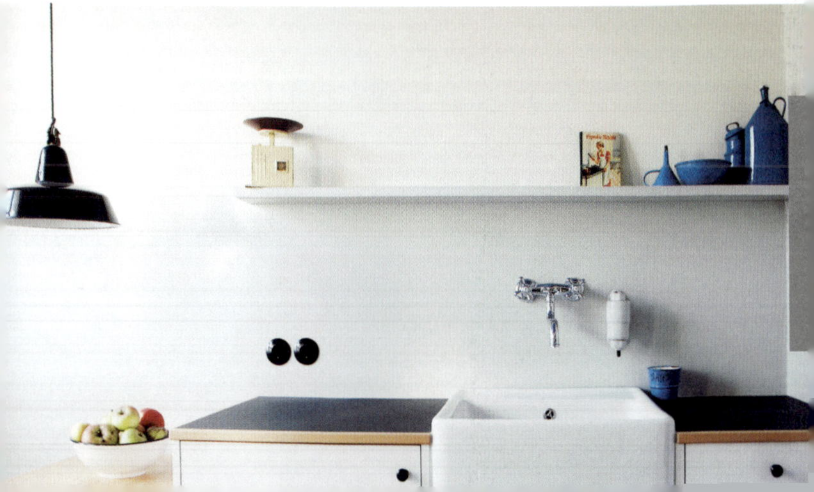

TEAMWORK

While Berlin's buzzing creative industry boasts some large agencies and design studios, most of this city's creative output is produced by freelancers. Because the very nature of their work can change from project to project, renting a space in a traditional office or shared studio can be too restrictive.

The solution: 'co-working spaces', a type of communal office-cum-studio available to freelancers as needed. The idea has taken off in Berlin. At the time this book went to print, we counted about 40 such spaces, most of them in Kreuzberg and Neukölln. Here's a quick insight into the evolution of a way of working that has become synonymous with the city.

Betahaus

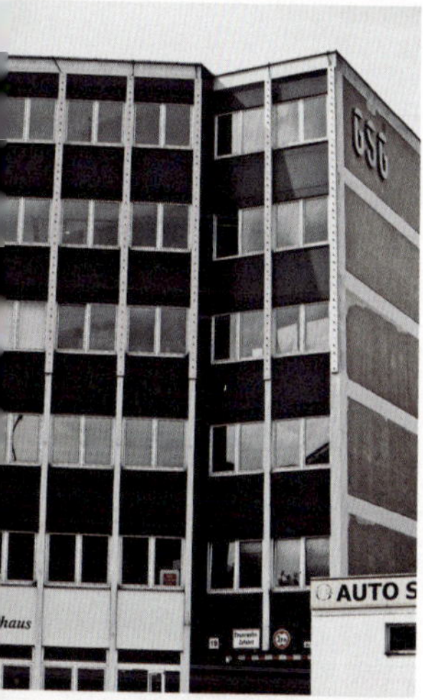

Its opening in 2009 was the big bang that heralded the evolution of the Berlin co-working scene. Under the watchful eyes of its founders, the 'Beta Six', the 2,000sqm space near Moritzplatz has become an institution. Its expansive loft offers silent areas, team spaces, meeting rooms and a busy café, and often hosts workshops to help members navigate the complexities of freelancing. The enterprise has now grown beyond Berlin, with locations in Hamburg, Cologne and Sophia; more cities are in the works.

U ***Moritzplatz*** | *Prinzessinnenstr. 19-20, Kreuzberg*
betahaus.de

Wostel

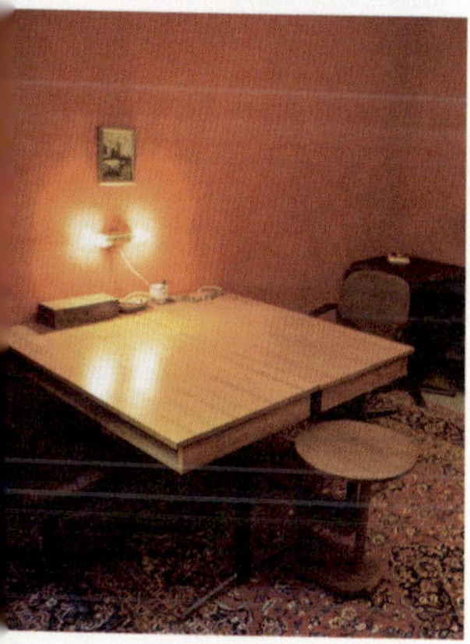

Above photo Marc Stephan

Top photo Maximilian Knop Konsole Labs GmbH

True to its Neukölln location, Wostel is the most social and experimental space in the co-working scene. There's much to discover in this former storefront in the *Reuterkiez*. Furnished with secondhand tables and chairs – some of them acquired from Berlin theatres and institutions – the Wostel pulses with the neighborhood's easygoing, DIY spirit. The space was opened in December 2010 by friends Marie Jacobi and Chouente Noufena, who believe that the creation and communication of ideas can only thrive in a comfortable, welcoming atmosphere.

U ***Hermannplatz*** | *Hobrechtstr. 66, Neukölln* | *wostel.de*

Weserland

The true Berliner's natural habitat is their *Kiez*, the village-like parcel of their larger neighbourhood that offers comfort in the anonymity of the big city. Weserland in Neukölln, while smaller than other spaces, seems to attract creative locals with 20 flexible workplaces over two rooms in a former corner tavern.

U ***Hermannplatz*** | *Weserstr. 21, Neukölln* | *weserland.net*

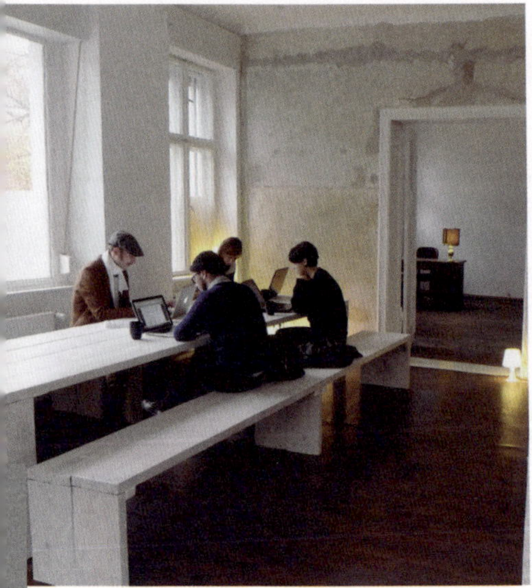

Above Weserland
Photo Georg Gajewski

Right The Wye
Photo Courtesy The Wye, 2012

Tip ... If you only need a few hours behind your laptop, head over to where the co-working craze got started, **Café St. Oberholz** on Rosenthaler Platz. The hip locale and free Wi-Fi ensured that creative jetsetters could hang out with their own as far back as 2005. To keep up with its younger brethren, Oberholz now also boasts 'proper' co-working spaces.

Rosenthaler Str. 72a, Mitte
sanktoberholz.de

Tip ... Anyone looking for a longer-term arrangement in one of Berlin's former industrial lofts might find the best company at **IMA Design Village**, a 2009 addition to the scene run by an Israeli designer and a Russian-born brand specialist. The village's light-filled lofts are home to a number of creative enterprises including some – like the Etsy Labs (*see page 210*) – that are open to the public. IMA has built a true community with events that foster creative exchange amongst its members.

Ritterstr. 12-14, Kreuzberg
imavillage.com

The Wye

One of the latest reclaimed industrial buildings in the city is the enormous former postal building on Kreuzberg's Skalitzer Strasse, now home to The Wye. Opened by three friends in September 2012, this 2000sqm working playground is a dream come true for artists and creatives from all walks of life. The space boasts an array of studios and offices for short or long-term projects, an apartment for visiting co-workers, and an enormous event hall for when projects are ready for the world.

U ***Görlitzer Bahnhof*** | *Skalitzer Str. 86, Kreuzberg* | *thewye.de*

Tip ... The beautiful brick warehouse that encapsulates **Agora Collective** is certainly worth the trip to the heart of Neukölln. The usual co-working spaces are complemented by the can-do buzz of the start-up scene that gathers here, and sustenance for those long hours is delivered courtesy of an excellent café.

Kopfstr. 48 (enter via Mittelweg 50), Neukölln | *agoracollective.org*

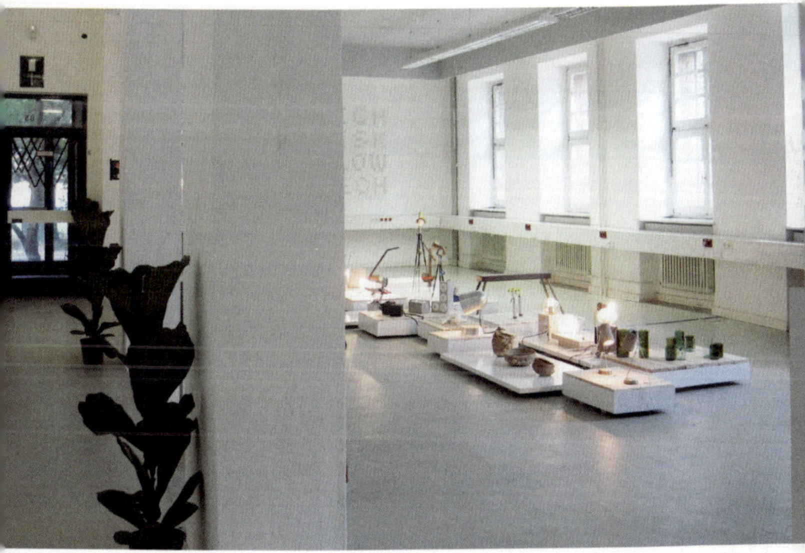

CORE TEAM

Kristina Leipold – A tried-and-tested cultural manager with a passion for new cultures and cities, Kristina has lent her managerial skill to large undertakings such as the German Federal Foreign Office's Germany Year in China. In 2010, she moved to Berlin to work on several intercultural projects. Driven by her curiosity about Berlin and about design in general, she tirelessly worked on partnerships, sponsors and project management to bring this book to fruition.

Viviane Stappmanns – With a degree in journalism and another in design, Viviane has clocked up a decade editing and writing for design magazines and books, as well as teaching at university. She also co-initiated and edited Design Guides for Sydney and Melbourne. Passionate about discovering the connections between creative places and creative people, she's looking to expand the Design Guide series to other metropoles.

Shona Stark & Lily Tidhar – Graphic designers Lily and Shona have been working together since 2008, when they launched their award-winning letterpress-printed 'Cookbook' series in their then hometown Melbourne. Now based in New York and Berlin respectively, Lily and Shona continue to collaborate both on self-initiated and client-driven design projects.
wolfgangshlomoandmax.com

CONTRIBUTORS

Nina Altschiller – A talented writer with a knack for quirky prose, Nina completed a degree in Film, Media and Theatre Studies and dipped her toes into the film, advertising and publishing businesses before becoming Berlin's most eloquent Cantienica instructor. For this book, Nina has acquainted herself with the city's prolific jewellers.

Dan Borden – A native Texan, Dan spent 20 years working as an architect in New York before escaping to Berlin in 2006 to write and make films. He has contributed to books on the history of film and architecture, and writes the monthly urban planning column in Berlin's English-language magazine, Exberliner.

Stuart Braun –Originally from Australia and based in Berlin since 2009, Stuart writes and produces radio documentaries - covering arts, culture and politics – for newspapers and radio stations the world over. He is currently working on a non-fiction book on Berlin that traces the appeal of the city for artist-exiles over the last century.

Becky Crook – Having moved to Berlin from Seattle in 2008, Becky is the founder of SAND, Berlin's English literary journal as well as an editor and translator for semikolon.com. She has also published her own writing, and is currently working on finishing her first novel.

Tara Dominguez – Born and raised in Ottawa, Canada, Tara arrived in Berlin via Montreal and Paris in 2009. As an editor, writer and translator, she has lent her voice to a number of international fashion and culture publications.

Megan Gannon – An intrepid writer and editor, Megan Gannon has completed a degree in writing and editing after being introduced to journalism at a young age because her parents owned her hometown's newspaper. Uniting her passion for writing with that for design, Megan, who was also part of the Melbourne Design Guide team, researched and questioned Berlin's designers for this book.

Leonie Pfennig – Leonie Pfennig arrived in Berlin in 2004 and completed an MA in Art History at Humboldt University. Her passion for the local art scene lead her to work with one of Germany's major galleries for contemporary art in Berlin, Eigen + Art, while also practising as a photography editor for various magazines and newspapers and as a freelance writer for artists and galleries.

Celina Plag – A Berliner since 2009, Celina completed a degree in studied fashion journalism and is currently studying art history. She writes for a number of international fashion publications.

Niche Art & Architecture Tours – Art historians Nele Heinevetter and Stefanie Gerke, and architect Katharina Beckmann have turned their infatuation with Berlin into a thriving business. They conduct tailored tours into the art and architecture niches of this city according to their clients wishes, interests and constraints. *nicheberlin.de*

Nina Trippel – With a degree in integrated design focusing on fashion, and a lifelong passion for travel, Nina works as a freelance writer in the areas of fashion, design, lifestyle and travel for a number of German and international clients. She's also the editor in chief of Derzeit, a daily fashion journal that appears during Fashion Week Berlin, and is co-founder of the hugely popular weekly newsletter Cee Cee. *ceecee.cc*

Max Zerrahn – Our photographer Max Zerrahn, who visited Berlin's designers in their studios for this book, is a photo editor for Berlin-based agency fstop and Opak Magazine. Over the past decade, he has been busy with a large variety of projects; he operated a small record label, worked for a film-production company, co-initiated an Internet startup and tried to survive as a graphic designer. *maxzerrahn.com*

INDEX

A

B

C

D

Special thanks to Paul Charlwood and Ewan McEoin, who were part of the founding Design Guide team in Melbourne.

THANK YOU

The book you are holding in your hands is a collaborative project. Thank you for your creativity, inspiration, support, advice, trust, energy and hard work.

André Gstettenhofer
Andres Schabelmann
Anna-Zöe Schmidt
Arne Eberle
Brigitte Stappmanns
Buerau N
Cameron Stevens
Caroline Drucker
Christian von der Heyden
Claudia Assmann
Cornelia Horsch
Emily Pelich
Frank Schirrmeister
Gesa Schenk
Gesche Joost
Giuseppe Fiordispina
Helmut Gossmann
Joachim Wagner
Jörg Suermann
Julian Sorge
Julian von Klier
Jürgen Siebert
Jürgen Schwämmle
Katharina Beckmann
Lina Kunimoto
Margit Kleibaum
Mateo Kries
Matthias Zickrow
Max Zerrahn
Nadine Jüdes
Nele Heinevetter
Nina Mehr-Aine
Oliver Helbig
Onlab
Philip Meuser
Raban Ruddigkeit
Raukia Abrantes
Richard Bosley
Samiha Bayoumi
Sarah Tietze
Seiji McCarthy
Sharmila Sandrasegar
Sonja Flöckemeyer
Stefanie Gerke
Susanne Hauser
Susanne Ullerich
Thomas Egle
Tobias Kohlhaas
Ulrich Umlauf
Uwe Gralapp
Valeska Schmidt-Thomsen
Wolfgang Leipold